AN INTRODUCTION TO PROPERTY THEORY

This book surveys the leading modern theories of property – Lockean, libertarian, utilitarian/law-and-economics, personhood, Kantian, and human flourishing – and then applies those theories to concrete contexts in which property issues have been especially controversial. These include redistribution, the right to exclude, regulatory takings, eminent domain, and intellectual property. The book highlights the Aristotelian human flourishing theory of property, providing the most comprehensive and accessible introduction to that theory to date. The book's goal is neither to cover every conceivable theory nor to discuss every possible facet of the theories covered. Instead, it aims to make the major property theories comprehensible to beginners, without sacrificing accuracy or sophistication. The book will be of particular interest to students seeking an accessible introduction to contemporary theories of property, but even specialists will benefit from the book's lucid descriptions of contemporary debates.

Gregory S. Alexander is a nationally renowned expert in property and trusts and estates and the A. Robert Noll Professor of Law at Cornell University. Following his graduation from Northwestern University School of Law, he clerked for the Honorable George Edwards of the U.S. Court of Appeals for the Sixth Circuit. Alexander is the winner of the American Publishers Association's 1997 Best Book of the Year in Law award for his work *Commodity and Propriety*. More recent books include *The Global Debate over Constitutional Property: Lessons for American Takings Jurisprudence* and *Property and Community* (with Eduardo M. Peñalver). He is co-author of the most widely used property casebook in the United States (with James Krier and Michael Schill). His articles have appeared in such journals as the *Columbia Law Review*, the *Stanford Law Review*, the *Michigan Law Review*, and the *Cornell Law Review*.

Eduardo M. Peñalver is a professor of law at Cornell University. Upon graduating from Yale Law School, he clerked for the Honorable Guido Calabresi of the U.S. Court of Appeals for the Second Circuit and for Justice John Paul Stevens of the U.S. Supreme Court. His research interests focus on property and land use, as well as law and religion. He is the author of numerous books and articles on property and land use law, and his work has appeared in several leading law journals. His book *Property Outlaws* (co-authored with Sonia Katyal) explores the role of disobedience in the evolution of property law.

CAMBRIDGE INTRODUCTIONS TO PHILOSOPHY AND LAW

Brian H. Bix
University of Minnesota

William A. Edmundson
Georgia State University

This introductory series of books provides concise studies of the philosophical foundations of law, of perennial topics in the philosophy of law, and of important and opposing schools of thought. The series is aimed principally at students in philosophy, law, and political science.

Normative Jurisprudence: An Introduction, by Robin West

Objectivity and the Rule of Law, by Matthew Kramer

An Introduction to Rights, Second Edition, by William A. Edmundson

Demystifying Legal Reasoning, by Larry Alexander and Emily Sherwin

Crime and Culpability: A Theory of Criminal Law, by Larry Alexander, Kimberly Kessler Ferzan, and Stephen J. Morse

Contract Law, by Brian H. Bix

An Introduction to Property Theory

GREGORY S. ALEXANDER

Cornell University, School of Law

EDUARDO M. PEÑALVER

Cornell University, School of Law

CAMBRIDGE
UNIVERSITY PRESS

CAMBRIDGE UNIVERSITY PRESS
Cambridge, New York, Melbourne, Madrid, Cape Town,
Singapore, São Paulo, Delhi, Mexico City

Cambridge University Press
32 Avenue of the Americas, New York, NY 10013-2473, USA

www.cambridge.org
Information on this title: www.cambridge.org/9780521130608

First published 2012

Printed in the United States of America

A catalog record for this publication is available from the British Library.

Library of Congress Cataloging in Publication data
Alexander, Gregory S., 1948–
    An Introduction to Property Theory / Gregory S. Alexander, Eduardo M. Peñalver.
        pages   cm. – (Cambridge introductions to philosophy and law)
    Includes bibliographical references and index.
    ISBN 978-0-521-11365-6 (hardback) – ISBN 978-0-521-13060-8 (paperback)
    1. Property.   2. Property–Philosophy.   3. Right of property.
    I. Peñalver, Eduardo Moisés, 1973–   II. Title.
    K720.A44   2012
    346.04–dc23   2011049203

ISBN 978-0-521-11365-6 Hardback
ISBN 978-0-521-13060-8 Paperback

G.S.A. – *To the memory of Robert D. Evans, Esq., mentor, confidant, friend.*
E.M.P. – *To Mami.*

Contents

Preface

Property theory has undergone something of a renaissance of interest within the legal academy over the past several years. The field has become the site of major disputes concerning both the conceptual nature of ownership and its normative underpinnings. In part, this revival of interest reflects broader social, political, and economic developments. These include controversies surrounding the government's use of its eminent domain power, debates over the state's power to regulate and tax owners, and the dramatic increase in the economic importance of intellectual property assets. Within these arguments, people have (at times implicitly) relied upon divergent understandings of the normative foundations and meanings of ownership.

Property theory can be a daunting topic. For students encountering the subject for the first time, the classic texts in the field are often incomprehensible and the arguments inaccessibly abstract. A common reaction when students are introduced to these sources during the first-year property course is, why bother? There is very good reason to bother. Theory matters. At the base of every single property debate are competing theories of property – different understandings of what private property is, why we have it, and what its proper limitations are. In these disputes, theory as such may not be explicitly articulated, but it is always near the foundation of the disagreement.

Our aim in this book is to survey the leading theories of private property in Western (primarily Anglo American) legal thought. Our goal in this respect is neither to cover every conceivable theory nor to discuss every facet of the theories we do include. Instead, we hope to make the major property theories comprehensible, without sacrificing accuracy or sophistication.

The book's second goal is normative. Among the theories we survey is the human flourishing theory, commonly associated with Aristotle. We believe that this theory, whose counterpart in moral philosophy is enjoying a revival of interest, offers an attractive alternative to the currently dominant legal property theory, utilitarianism, and its cognate, law-and-economics. Our treatment of that theory in both Parts I and II reflects this commitment. However, we have tried to avoid placing too heavy a thumb on the scale, in the hope that readers who are not attracted to the human flourishing theory but who wish to know something about it will find our treatment of it appealing.

This book is a collaboration in more than one way. Not only is it a collaboration between the two of us, but also with a number of individuals who have helped us in various ways. First, our colleagues at Cornell Law School, where we first aired several of these chapters, helped us in more than one way. To them we are immensely grateful for their support and constructive criticism. We count ourselves extremely fortunate to be members of a faculty that is at once intellectually demanding of its members and genuinely collegial. We are particularly grateful to Oskar Liivak for helpful comments on Chapter 9. Second, colleagues at other institutions where we presented various chapters have improved our efforts, whatever the merits of the final product. These institutions include the Fordham Law School, where we discussed themes developed in the book at a conference on "The Social Function of Property" (thanks to Professors Sheila Foster and Daniel Bonilla, the co-organizers). We also presented chapters of the manuscript at the University of Cape Town (particular thanks to Professor Hanri Mostert for inviting us), the UCLA Law School, the University of Michigan Law School, the University of Chicago Law School, and finally, at the University of Stellenbosch in South Africa, where we spent two weeks teaching a group of graduate law students in Professor Andre van der Walt's seminar on property theory. We are deeply grateful to Professor van der Walt for his kind invitation and invaluable comments and to his wonderful students and colleagues, particularly Sue-Mari Maass. We also owe a debt of gratitude to Stewart Schwab, the Allan R. Tessler Dean of Cornell Law School. His support has come in multiple forms, including generous financial support and intellectual encouragement. Finally, we happily acknowledge as collaborators our respective administrative assistants, Lyndsey Clark and Allen Czelusniak, and the superb staff at Cornell Law Library. We thank them all.

Introduction

Disputes over rights of private ownership of property constitute some of the most contentious political issues of our day. Can the government legitimately take property from those with more solely in order to give it to those with less? Can it take someone's land in order to help a private developer build a large shopping center that will bring badly needed jobs and tax revenue to a decaying downtown? To what extent can a business owner control who can come onto her property? Should neighbors have a say in how an owner uses property? Should an owner be allowed, without anyone's input, to tear down an important historic building in order to build a more profitable modern office tower? Should she have the right to fill sensitive wetlands in order to build a home?

Property disputes raise passions, at both personal and political levels, like few other topics can. It is not surprising, then, that some of the most important thinkers in history have focused sustained attention on the nature of and justifications for ownership. In this book, we will provide an introduction to the answers these theorists have proposed.

WHAT IS PROPERTY?

Before we turn to the various theories of property on which this book will focus, it is important to address a few preliminary definitional questions. Most fundamentally, we need to define the boundaries of the category at the heart of those theories: property. Defining *property* turns out to be a very challenging task. Indeed, as Jeremy Waldron has observed, some commentators have argued that the concept of property defies definition.[1] As Thomas Grey put it in an influential 1980 essay:

> How do property rights differ from rights generally – from human rights or personal rights or rights to life or liberty, say? Our specialists and theoreticians have

---

[1]   See Jeremy Waldron, *The Right to Private Property* (1988), 26.

1

no answer; or rather, they have a multiplicity of widely different answers, related only in that they bear some association or analogy, more or less remote, to the common notion of property as ownership of things.... It seems fair to conclude from a glance at the range of current usages that the specialists who design and manipulate the legal structures of the advanced capitalist economies could easily do without using the term "property" at all.[2]

Grey's repeated references to "specialists" suggests that at least part of the difficulty in defining property results from the arguably different ways that lay people and lawyers approach the question.[3] Lay people tend to think of property as a relatively uncomplicated relationship between a person (the owner) and a thing (the owned property). Because of the specific context in which they interact with property law questions, however, lawyers have a tendency to think of property differently.[4] They usually view it as the collection of the individual rights people have as against one another with respect to owned resources, a point of view that makes a great deal of sense when considering conflicts between litigants over what the specific content of property law is with regard to some narrow question.

The lawyer's view of property, commonly referred to as the "bundle of sticks" conception, captures a valuable insight about the substantial flexibility in the design of property institutions. But it can also get in the way of efforts to step back and think about property more broadly as a legal institution or concept. As numerous theorists have observed, the layperson's conception of property as "things" latches onto an equally important truth about the institution.[5] One of the distinctive features of property rights is their in rem quality. Property rights, unlike (say) contractual rights, are good against the entire world. They impose duties on everyone else to respect those rights. As a result, the creation of property rights has an impact on people who did not take part in the transaction concerning the property in question. Because the boundaries of the "thing" play a vital role in defining the scope of people's in rem duties to owners, the layperson is right to think that the "thing" that is the subject of the property forms a crucial component of a workable definition

---

[2]   Thomas C. Grey, "The Disintegration of Property," in *Nomos XXII: Property*, ed. J. Roland Pennock and John W. Chapman (1980), 69, 71–3.

[3]   See ibid; see also Waldron, *Private Property*, 26; Bruce A. Ackerman, *Private Property and the Constitution* (1977); Stephen R. Munzer, *A Theory of Property* (1990), 16. For a different view about the lay person's and lawyer's conceptions of ownership and property, see Gregory S. Alexander, "The Concept of Property in Private and Constitutional Law: The Ideology of the Scientific Turn in Legal Analysis," *Colum. L. Rev.* 82 (1982): 1545 (doubting that the lay person's and lawyer's conceptions are very different from each other).

[4]   But see Alexander, "The Concept of Property in Private and Constitutional Law."

[5]   See Munzer, *Theory of Property*, 72; Thomas W. Merrill and Henry E. Smith, "What Happened to Property in Law and Economics?" *Yale L.J.* 111 (2001): 357, 360–83; Michael A. Heller, "The Boundaries of Private Property," *Yale L.J.* 108 (1999): 1163, 1193.

of property.[6] Taking the lawyer's conception too far risks turning property into a disaggregated collection of narrowly defined rights, causing us to lose sight of the connection of those rights to things. Michael Heller is therefore correct when he says that:

> [W]hile the modern bundle-of-legal-relations metaphor reflects well the possibility of complex relational fragmentation, it gives a weak sense of the "thingness" of private property. Conflating the economic language of entitlements with the language of property rights causes theorists to collapse inadvertently the boundaries of private property. As long as theorists and the Court rely on the bundle-of-legal-relations metaphor, they need some analytical tool to distinguish things from fragments, bundles from rights, and private from nonprivate property.[7]

If we focus too narrowly on any given right with respect to a thing, and conceive of that right independently from other rights in the thing, our conception of property as a distinctive institution begins to fall apart, replaced by disaggregated strands of rights and duties among particular people. As James Penner has observed, "on the 'bundle of rights' picture, 'property' is not really a useful concept of any kind. It doesn't help judges understand what they're doing when they decide cases, because it doesn't effectively characterize any particular sort of legal relation."[8]

To combat the centrifugal tendency of the bundle of sticks metaphor, some contemporary property scholars have attempted to discern a single essential feature of ownership that distinguishes it from other legal concepts. They have, in effect, seized on specific sticks in the bundle, singling them out as uniquely important. The most commonly nominated candidate to serve this property defining role is the right to exclude.[9] Thomas Merrill puts the point very starkly:

> [T]he right to exclude others is more than just "one of the most essential" constituents of property – it is the sine qua non. Give someone the right to exclude others from a valued resource, i.e., a resource that is scarce relative to the human demand for it, and you give them property. Deny someone the exclusion right and they do not have property.[10]

---

[6] See Munzer, *Theory of Property*, 72; Waldron, *Private Property*, 33–4; Abraham Bell and Gideon Parchomovsky, "A Theory of Property," CORNELL L. REV. 90 (2005): 531, 576–7.

[7] Heller, "Boundaries of Private Property," 1193.

[8] J. E. Penner, *The Idea of Property in Law* (1997), 1.

[9] See ibid., 71; Merrill and Smith, "What Happened to Property?"; Thomas W. Merrill, "Property and the Right to Exclude," NEB. L. REV. 77 (1998): 730; Adam Mossoff, "What is Property? Putting the Pieces Back Together," ARIZ. L. REV. 45 (2003): 371. Arguably, Richard Epstein might fall into this category as well, though he would treat all the rights associated with ownership at common law – and not just the right to exclude – as all in some sense essential to our legal concept of private property. See Richard A. Epstein, *Takings* (1985), 35–6.

[10] Merrill, "Right to Exclude," 730.

The problem with privileging one strand in the bundle in this way is that it is a relatively easy task to come up with examples of private property systems in which the right is almost entirely absent or, at best, subordinated to other rights. In Sweden, for example, landowners do not enjoy any overriding right to exclude others from their property. Nonowners enjoy the right to roam where they wish provided they do not interfere with the use the landowner has chosen to make of her land. The Swedish right to roam, known as the *allemansrätt*, is deeply embedded in Swedish culture and is mirrored to varying degrees in other Scandinavian countries. Thus, in Sweden, the owner's privileged position is not created through recognition of a right to exclude in the first instance, but rather by a privileged right to determine the use of the land she owns, to make decisions around which others must navigate when exercising their own rights of access. A similar norm of access has prevailed as a matter of custom in Scotland for centuries, and was recently recognized formally in the Land Reform (Scotland) Act 2003.[11] And yet Scotland and Sweden's systems of ownership are nonetheless easily recognizable as private property.[12]

There are alternatives to treating property as, on the one hand, merely an endlessly complex bundle of discrete rights between people with respect to things and, on the other, searching for one single, essential stick in the bundle of rights that is definitive of the concept of property. Tony Honoré, for example, has identified a limited menu of rights (or incidents, as he puts it) of ownership that are characteristic of most, though not all, systems of property. These include the right to possess (which includes the right to exclude), the right to use, the right to manage, the right to the income a thing generates, the right to the capital (i.e., the thing itself), the right to security, the right to transmissibility and the absence of term (potentially infinite duration), the duty to prevent harm, the liability to execution (e.g., to satisfy a debt), and the incident of *residuarity* (the idea that, when lesser interests come to an end, the full interest in the property reverts to the owner).[13] Collectively, Honoré says, these incidents are essential features of the full concept of property. But "the listed incidents," Honoré says, "though they may together be sufficient, are not individually necessary conditions for the person of inherence to be designated the owner of a particular thing."[14] On this approach, systems of property are something like one of Ludwig Wittgenstein's "family resemblance concepts."[15] They all

---

[11] See John A. Lovett, "Progressive Property in Action: The Land Reform (Scotland) Act 2003," NEB. L. REV. 89 (2011): 301. A similar, though less ambitious, legal recognition of the right to roam was codified in England and Wales in the Countryside and Rights of Way Act of 2000.

[12] See Larissa Katz, "Exclusion and Exclusivity in Property Law," U. TORONTO L.J. 58 (2008): 275.

[13] A. M. Honoré, "Ownership," in *Readings in the Philosophy of Law*, ed. Jules L. Coleman (1999), 557, 563–74.

[14] Ibid., 562–3.

[15] See Ludwig Wittgenstein, *Philosophical Investigations*, trans. G. E. M. Anscombe (1953), § 198, at 80. ("[W]hat has the expression of a rule – say a sign-post – got to do with my actions? What sort of

share a great deal with one another, but there is no definitive set of characteristics that they invariably have. Nevertheless, someone familiar with the concept will still be able to recognize systems of property with sufficient accuracy that the concept is not devoid of meaning.[16]

A somewhat different definitional approach would look not just to the various features or rights within systems of property, trying to determine which ones are essential. Instead, it might start by looking for an interest served by the body of law going under the label "property." James Penner, for example, adopts this kind of definitional strategy (at least in part) when he defines property as the area of law that is descriptively characterized by exclusion rights and normatively grounded in "the interest we have in the use of things, an interest that he in turn grounds largely in the value of individual autonomy."[17] In a sense, though, attempting to shift the focus toward the interest served by property risks producing the bundle versus essence debate. The question simply becomes whether the institution of property serves one interest or several. Penner stakes out the position that property is the area of law narrowly "grounded by the interest we have in the use of things."[18] In contrast to the position advocated by Penner, Hanoch Dagan and others have argued that property simultaneously serves a variety of human values. Dagan "perceives the values of property in an antifoundationalist spirit, as 'pluralistic and multiple, dynamic and changing, hypothetical and not self-evident, problematic rather than determinative.'"[19] Although this disagreement about the interests or values served by property is an important and fruitful one, as a definitional matter it ought to be possible (and it is arguably necessary) to understand what property is in the first instance without taking a position on this normative question.

Perhaps the way out of this definitional muddle is to attempt to define property neither in terms of essential substantive rights that a property system must include nor in terms of the human interests it serves. Instead, we might look to a specific *function* that property performs. Jeremy Waldron takes this approach when he defines the law of property as that area of law concerned with the function of *allocating* material resources.[20] Allocation is the process of "determining peacefully and reasonably predictably who is to have access to which resources for what purposes and when." More specifically, a system of *private* property (as opposed to

---

connexion is there here? – Well, perhaps this one: I have been trained to react to this sign in a particular way, and now I do so react to it.")

[16] See ibid.

[17] Penner, *Idea of Property in Law*, 71.

[18] Ibid.

[19] Hanoch Dagan, "The Craft of Property," CAL. L. REV. 91 (2003): 1517, 1561–2 (quoting Hessel E. Yntema, "Jurisprudence on Parade," MICH. L. REV. 39 (1941): 1154, 1169); see also Gregory S. Alexander, "Pluralism and Property," FORDHAM L. REV. 90 (2011): 101.

[20] See Waldron, *Private Property*, 34–5.

communal or collective property) provides a set of "rules governing access to and control of material resources" that are "organized around the idea that resources are on the whole separate objects each assigned and therefore belonging to some particular individual."[21] But such a system of private ownership is simply one possible specification of the broader concept of a system for allocating material resources. Such a functional definition of property helps to differentiate a domain of legal or social institutions as "property," but it is neutral as to exactly how rights are allocated (in customized bundles or standard blocks with essential features) and as to the normative foundations for structuring the institution in one way rather than another.

From within this view of property as an institution for allocating rights to material things, not all legal doctrines addressing what people can do with material things would count as "property." Waldron gives the example of laws against using knives to stab people, which he classifies as the kind of law that we should not count as "property." Rather, he views these sorts of laws as side constraints that incidentally affect property but that are rooted in broader norms about – for example – respect for bodily integrity.[22] On the other hand, a doctrine like nuisance, which aims to define the boundary between owners' rights to quiet enjoyment and other owners' rights to do what they want with their land, has an allocative function that allows us to correctly treat it as part of the law of property. Closer to the boundary, but arguably still "property," are doctrines that define (and allocate) rights of access and exclusion between owners and nonowners. On this view, then, civil rights statutes prohibiting exclusion from certain categories of property on certain restricted grounds would arguably constitute "property laws."

WHAT IS A THEORY OF PROPERTY?

If we define property as the category of legal doctrines concerned with allocating rights to material resources, we can understand a theory of property as an attempt to provide a normative justification for allocating those rights in a particular way. At the most basic level, a theory of property would answer the question of which human interests are relevant to the project of allocating property rights. Those interests might be human autonomy, self-realization, aggregate well-being, or some combination of these (and perhaps others).

Armed with a conception of the interests served by a system of property, a theory of property would then aim to provide reasons for allocating rights in a particular way. By extension, such a theory would also seek to supply those affected by the property allocation with reasons for respecting it, even when refusing to do so might

---

[21] See ibid., 38.
[22] See ibid.

in some sense make them better off. Depending on the content of the theory, the primary bearer of property rights might be individual human beings or institutions of various sorts, such as families, states, or corporations, among others.

In addition, a theory of property would attempt to specify the content of property rights at various levels of generality – for example, the contours of the owner's right to exclude others from various kinds of property. Related to this process of specification, a theory of property would likely have something to say about whether the law should treat those rights as disaggregated sticks in a bundle of rights that can be individually parceled out among different stakeholders or whether, instead, they should go together in standardized clusters. After all, at first glance, it seems likely that the bundle-of-sticks conception of property might serve various interests – such as individual autonomy or aggregate well-being – differently than, say, a conception that views property as coming in rigid standard-issue clusters.

Our goal in this book is to provide readers with an introduction to the theories of property that have had the most influence on discussions of American property law. In Part I, we provide broad overviews of the contours of these theories. We begin with the two theories that have arguably dominated academic property thought in recent years: utilitarianism (Chapter 1), which is closely aligned – though not identical – with the movement known as "law and economics," and the property theory developed by John Locke (Chapter 2), which has been extremely influential on those who identify themselves as property rights libertarians. In Chapter 3, we describe the elaborate property theory developed by German philosopher Georg W. F. Hegel, as well as the work of more recent theorists who have built on Hegel's *Philosophy of Right*. In Chapter 4, we discuss the property theory articulated by Hegel's fellow countryman, Immanuel Kant. Although less influential in contemporary property circles, Kantian property theory has begun to gain adherents in recent years, particularly among a group of scholars at the University of Toronto. Finally, in Chapter 5, we explore a theory of property rooted in Aristotle's conception of human flourishing. We will discuss the strengths of each of these theories, as well as some of the most trenchant criticisms that have been leveled against them. Our goal is not to provide comprehensive arguments on behalf of (or against) any of these theories, but rather to introduce readers to their broad outlines and, hopefully, to foster a deeper interest in property theory that will spark the reader to pursue these questions in greater depth than a book of this length permits.

Having introduced readers to the principal contending theories, we shift focus in Part II to a series of contemporary debates over issues relating to the nature of property ownership. In Chapter 6, we discuss the problem of redistribution. When, if ever, is the state permitted to take property from one person in order to give it to another? When it does so, should it redistribute property "in kind" by tinkering with the system of property law or should it define property without regard to distributive goals and rely on other mechanisms (e.g., a system of progressive taxation and transfer payments) to pursue distributive justice?

In Chapter 7, we explore the nature of the right to exclude and rights of access as they relate to private property. Should owners enjoy an unqualified right to exclude others from their land or should they be required to permit access under certain circumstances? What if owners choose to open up their property to others in order to do business? Does that change the nature of their rights to exclude or do they retain nearly absolute discretion to control access to their property? Are civil rights statutes that prohibit discrimination in "places of public accommodation" merely a codification of owners' limited rights to exclude or are they a violation of those rights?

In Chapter 8, we discuss the related problems of eminent domain and so-called regulatory takings. Under what circumstances can the state rightfully exercise the awesome power of eminent domain? Can the state legitimately condemn an owner's property to encourage economic development? And when does the state's restriction of an owner's use of property amount to a taking of property that triggers an obligation to compensate the owner for her losses?

Finally, in Chapter 9, we explore the extension of ownership to the domain of ideas, or *intellectual property*. What are the various possible theoretical justifications for giving creators and inventors (and, perhaps, their employers) ownership rights over ideas? Can the theories of property that justify private ownership of tangible property extend unproblematically to a new antibiotic or a musical composition? How robust should rights of intellectual property be in light of the dependence of new creations on prior intellectual achievements?

Our aim in these chapters is not to provide definitive answers to, or comprehensive discussions of, any of these fascinating and important questions. Indeed, each of them could sustain (and have sustained) their own book-length treatments. Instead, our goal in Part II is to deepen readers' understandings of the theories of property by exploring how the theories we have introduced in Part I might approach the various topics.

PART I

1

Utilitarian Property Theories

As a leading property law casebook puts it, "[u]tilitarian theory is, without doubt, the dominant view of property today, at least among lawyers."[1] This is certainly true, but the story is also significantly more complicated. Although utilitarian analysis provides tremendous insight into the institution of property, it raises a number of important questions when treated as a comprehensive theory of property. Moreover, the term *utilitarian* masks a great deal of intellectual and methodological diversity. Rather than a single utilitarian theory, it is more appropriate to speak of a number of utilitarian (or even utilitarian-influenced) property *theories*. For our purposes, these utilitarian-influenced theories include many contemporary theories that refer to themselves as *economic* or *welfarist*.[2] In this chapter, we will explore the broad outlines of these theories, focusing on their points of overlap and also on key areas of disagreement.

A BRIEF INTRODUCTION TO UTILITARIANISM

Utilitarianism is a consequentialist moral philosophy, that is, one that judges the rightness and wrongness of actions or rules or institutions by the goodness and badness of the consequences they bring about.[3] Utilitarianism assesses the goodness or badness of consequences in terms of their tendency to maximize utility or welfare.[4]

---

[1] Jesse Dukeminier et al., *Property*, 7th ed. (2010), 50.
[2] We understand *welfarism* to mean the capacious view that social choices should be evaluated on the basis of their impacts on human well-being, with well-being understood as some singular value. Welfarism and utilitarianism obviously share a great deal. Indeed, the two terms are sometimes used almost interchangeably. Nevertheless, classical utilitarianism is properly understood as a *species* of welfarism, the broader category. See Louis Kaplow and Steven Shavell, *Fairness versus Welfare* (2002), 5 n. 8. Our focus in this chapter is on utilitarianism, but much of what we say will apply to welfarist theory as well.
[3] See J. J. C. Smart and Bernard Williams, *Utilitarianism: For and Against* (1973), 12.
[4] Amartya Sen and Bernard Williams, introduction to *Utilitarianism and Beyond*, ed. Amartya Sen and Bernard Williams (1982), 1, 4.

Bernard Williams has observed that "[t]he fathers of utilitarianism thought of it principally as a system of social and political decision," as opposed to "a system of personal morality."[5] As Williams correctly notes, it is sometimes hard to keep these two domains apart. Nevertheless, it is plainly as a theory of social choice that utilitarianism has been deployed in the context of property theory.

How does utilitarianism judge the goodness or badness of property institutions and laws? The utilitarian evaluation can be broken down into two related questions: (1) how to define the good (or utility) at which social decision makers are to aim and (2) how to aggregate individual experiences of that utility in order to evaluate the overall consequences of social choices. The classic utilitarian theory of social choice, exemplified by the thought of Jeremy Bentham, equates goodness with the sum total of pleasure (minus the pain) that people (*all* people) experience as a result of making one decision over the possible alternatives. It enjoins decision makers to act so as to maximize total net pleasure.[6] But subsequent utilitarians (broadly speaking) have expressed a wide range of views on these points. We will briefly consider each of these questions in turn. We will then turn to the important problem of how utilitarians actually go about collecting the information they need to evaluate a particular social choice. Once we have introduced the general contours of – and challenges faced by – utilitarian theory, we will turn to its application within the specific domain of property.

The Nature of Utility

On the classical Benthamite view, the good we are to pursue in our social choices is pleasure, and individually experienced pleasures differ from one another only in some quantitative respect (such as intensity or duration or some combination of the two). Thus, as Bentham famously put it, "[p]rejudice apart, the game of push-pin is of equal value with the arts and sciences of music and poetry. If the game of push-pin furnish more pleasure, it is more valuable than either."[7] The simple pursuit of pleasure has proven problematic to utilitarians and nonutilitarians alike for at least two reasons. First, by ignoring the source of pleasure, Bentham's hedonistic version of utilitarianism raises the possibility that, were certain morally perverse pleasures (e.g., sadism) sufficiently widely shared, the actions that generate them might be deemed good. A typical response to this objection has been to complicate the notion of pleasure, for example, by arguing that there are a variety of types, some of which should count more than others. John Stuart Mill famously

---

[5]   Smart and Williams, *Utilitarianism: For and Against*, 135.
[6]   See generally Jeremy Bentham, *An Introduction to the Principles of Morals and Legislation* (1789).
[7]   Jeremy Bentham, *The Rationale of Reward*, Bk. 3 (1825), ch. 1.

distinguished between "higher" and "lower" pleasures, with intellectual pleasures holding pride of place.[8]

Rather than follow Mill's attempt to refine the conception of pleasure, however, contemporary successors of classical utilitarianism have abandoned pleasure altogether in favor of thinner conceptions of goodness, such as preference satisfaction. This focus has yielded a conception of utility (or, more properly, welfare) that is all-encompassing, including "everything that an individual might value."[9] Modern theorists have thereby avoided the difficulty of justifying the normative significance of pleasure, or of particular types of pleasure. But such thin conceptions of utility leave contemporary welfarist theories even more exposed to the objection that some preferences are unworthy and ought not be satisfied. A common response to this problem has been to run actual preferences through some sort of filter such that only worthy or reasonable preferences count in the utilitarian calculus.[10] It is not clear, however, whether such scrubbing is consistent with the consequentialist commitments of utilitarian theory, since the satisfaction of hypothetical preferences (rather than actual ones) is not an actual consequence of the decision being evaluated.[11] The problem of how to deal with apparently mistaken or immoral preferences remains a challenge for utilitarian (and many welfarist) theories.

Although they differ among themselves in their precise answers to the definitional question, utilitarian theorists of all stripes have generally been in agreement that the sort of goodness that counts in their moral calculation is rooted in the subjective experiences of individual human beings.[12] Whether they define the relevant quality as pleasure (of a higher or lower sort) or something else, such as the satisfaction of preferences, goodness for utilitarians is something experienced by people as individuals. In this sense, utilitarian theory is individualistic. But defining goodness is just the first step in the utilitarian moral calculus.

Aggregating Utility

Insofar as the goodness or badness of a set of consequences depends on its impact on more than one individual, utilitarian theories require some means of aggregating those different experiences along a single dimension in order to generate a bottom-line moral judgment. Bentham's solution to the problem of aggregation was merely to add up the total net pleasure of all the people affected by a decision. His simple

[8] John Stuart Mill, *Utilitarianism* (1863), 14.
[9] Kaplow and Shavell, *Fairness versus Welfare*, 18.
[10] See, for example, John C. Harsanyi, *Rational Behavior and Bargaining Equilibrium in Games and Social Sciences* (1977).
[11] See Amartya Sen, "Utilitarianism and Welfarism," *J. Phil.* 76 (1979): 463, 474–6.
[12] See ibid., 463–4.

additive approach, sometimes referred to as *sum ranking*, generates another common objection to classical utilitarianism: its insensitivity to distribution.[13] Bentham's simple formula means that a state of affairs in which there is more total pleasure, but where a small elite enjoys all the pleasure, must be preferred over a state of affairs in which there is slightly less total pleasure, but where everyone enjoys it equally.

In welfare economics, the closest modern analog of Bentham's additive sum ranking principle of aggregation is known as the Kaldor-Hicks criterion of efficiency. In practice, it is perhaps the most common aggregative principle among contemporary welfarists. The Kaldor-Hicks definition holds that a social decision is superior to available alternatives if the people who benefit from the choice gain enough that they could, hypothetically, fully compensate those individuals who lose out from it such that the losers consider themselves no worse off than they were before.[14] But there is no requirement that the compensation actually occur. In practice, Kaldor-Hicks amounts to the view that a social decision is an improvement if it increases total well-being, however distributed.

Defenders of utilitarianism have responded to the problem of distributive insensitivity by measuring utility in ways that can take distributive considerations into account and by developing more sophisticated methods of aggregating overall utility. Mill combined his distinction between higher and lower pleasures with an argument that a quantum of higher pleasures should count for more in the utilitarian calculus than an equivalent quantum of lower sorts of pleasures. "It is better to be a human dissatisfied than a pig satisfied," he said. "Better Socrates dissatisfied than a fool satisfied."[15] One way to read this is as claiming that, while the fool's pleasure and Socrates' pleasure both count in the utilitarian calculus, Socrates' pleasure counts for more of the total goodness of a state of affairs. Alternatively, a utilitarian concerned about inequality can aggregate utility (however defined) so as to count the well-being of the least well off more heavily than those who have more.[16] The math becomes more difficult, but the basic evaluative structure remains intact and distributive concerns are brought into the picture.

Gathering Data on Utility

Theoretically speaking, once we have defined utility and developed a formula for weighing the consequences of different decisions, we have created a complete theory

---

[13] See ibid., 468.

[14] Jeremy Waldron, "Nozick and Locke: Filling the Space of Rights," Soc. Phil. & Pol'y 22 (2005): 81, 101.

[15] Mill, *Utilitarianism*, 260.

[16] Prioritarians, for example, aggregate utility in a way that gives more weight to increases in the well-being of the least well off. See, for example, Matthew D. Adler, "Future Generations: A Prioritarian View," G.W. L. Rev. 77 (2008–9): 1478, 1478–9.

of social choice. But, while utilitarianism offers a simple and powerful evaluative method, it is a method that, as Williams has observed, "make[s] enormous demands on supposed empirical information."[17] Depending on the principle of aggregation being employed, the information demanded by utilitarian theories can vary quite dramatically. Bentham's principle of aggregation is simple addition of the net pleasure of the affected individuals. The possibility of such additive aggregation requires two things to be true about utility. First, it must be quantifiable as a *cardinal* value, that is, as a value along a single scale that provides information about both the absolute ranking of a particular state of affairs relative to alternatives and about the distance between them. For example, if we are discussing Borges's preferences among different flavors of ice cream, Bentham's principle requires information demonstrating not only that Borges prefers chocolate ice cream to strawberry and strawberry to vanilla, but *how much more* he prefers each to the others. That is, it must be able to communicate that Borges likes chocolate a great deal more than strawberry, but strawberry only slightly more than vanilla.

Second, Bentham's additive principle of aggregation requires that utility (however defined) be susceptible to interpersonal comparison. This means that, for Bentham, a unit of pleasure experienced by one person must be the same as an equivalent unit of pleasure experienced by another. If Borges has a friend, Neruda, who is indifferent between particular flavors but likes all ice cream equally and very intensely, Bentham's measure of utility must be able to indicate how Neruda's desire for ice cream (or the pleasure he derives from it) compares with Borges's. Even more ambitiously, it must be capable of comparing the pleasure Borges derives from chocolate ice cream with the pleasure Neruda gets from reading a poem.

Among contemporary theorists, the most common means of expressing information about the intensity of preferences is in terms of how much a person would be willing to pay for a particular preference to be satisfied.[18] The more a person is willing to pay, the more intense the underlying preference is assumed to be. We would represent the intensity of Borges's ice cream preferences, for example, in terms of his willingness to pay \$3 to have chocolate ice cream, \$2 to have strawberry, and \$1.75 to have vanilla. Using this common metric of willingness to pay, distinct preferences held by two different people but backed by equal willingness to pay are assumed to be equivalently intense.

How do decision makers employing this approach actually go about collecting the information necessary to determine the net utility gain or loss generated by a particular social choice? One strategy is to look to the choices individuals make in the marketplace. When Borges actually pays \$3 for a scoop of chocolate ice

---

[17] Smart and Williams, *Utilitarianism: For and Against*, 137.
[18] See Matthew D. Adler and Eric A. Posner, *New Foundations of Cost-Benefit Analysis* (2006), 18.

cream when strawberry and vanilla ice cream are available at the same price, he has revealed something about the nature and intensity of his preferences. Another way is simply to ask people what they would be willing to pay to satisfy various preferences. Of course, the information gathered in these ways is susceptible to numerous questions.

When Borges pays $3 for chocolate ice cream, how do we know he wouldn't have paid more if the price had been higher? Suppose Neruda is so poor that he cannot afford ice cream that costs more than $1. If he refuses to buy the chocolate ice cream for $3, even though he wants it badly, is it accurate to conclude that he desires chocolate ice cream less intensely than Borges, who is rich and merely likes to buy ice cream to watch the patterns it makes when it melts? Similar concerns about so-called wealth effects – the distorting impact of wealth differences on individual people's willingness to pay to satisfy their preferences – make it difficult to place too much weight on preference data gathered through surveys.[19] Nevertheless, market data and surveys may provide a rough approximation of the content and intensities of people's preferences.

The difficulty of actually collecting information about preferences has led many theorists to search for less informationally demanding principles of aggregation. According to one approach, a social choice is good if it makes at least one person better off without decreasing the utility of anyone else. This demanding maxim – known as the Pareto Principle – does not require a metric of individual well-being that is capable of cardinal ranking or that supports interpersonal comparison.[20] It merely requires that decision makers gather data about each person's preferences in the form of a rank ordering of possible states of affairs. If a decision generates a state of affairs that is higher (than the alternatives) on at least one person's ordinal rankings and not lower than the current state of affairs on anyone else's, the decision is said to be Pareto superior to alternatives in which no one's situation is made better or someone is made worse off. For Paretian analysis, the size of the gaps between the rankings on any one person's list is irrelevant. Even this principle, however, places significant informational demands on decision makers, who must somehow assemble the information necessary to ascertain each person's ranking of consequences and determine how a particular social choice will interact with each such list.

The informational challenges of carrying out utilitarian calculations are not decisive arguments against the possibility of utilitarian theories. They simply highlight

[19] See ibid., 17–18. There are other problems with these methods as well. For a thorough discussion, see Frank Ackerman and Lisa Heinzerling, *Priceless: On Knowing the Price of Everything and the Value of Nothing* (2004); Mark Sagoff, *The Economy of the Earth* (1988), ch. 4.

[20] The Pareto criterion is not really utilitarian in the classical sense. It would be more accurate to describe it as welfarist. Nevertheless, Paretianism originated in an attempt to overcome problems associated with classical utilitarian theory, and shares many of the theory's normative assumptions.

the fact that, even if one fully accepts the moral intuitions behind utilitarian analysis in the domain of social choice, the value of any particular utilitarian prescription will only be as good as the empirical information on which it is based. As we will see, that informational challenge will greatly complicate the predictions and prescriptions of utilitarian property theory.

UTILITARIANISM WITHIN PROPERTY THEORY

The utilitarian theory of property, in its most basic form, asserts that property institutions should be shaped so as to maximize net utility. Because of the widespread tendency among property theorists to use wealth as a proxy for utility (or welfare), this often amounts, in effect, to an assertion that property institutions should be shaped so as to maximize society's net wealth. Although we will go into more detail shortly, at the outset it is important to note a significant feature of this theory: It treats property, and property rights, as instrumental to a more basic good – utility or welfare. As we will see in later chapters, the instrumentalism of utilitarian theory stands in contrast to rights-based theories of property, such as the entitlement theory of property proposed by Robert Nozick.[21] Unlike utilitarian theories, rights-based property theories do not treat the system of property as a mere means to some further end but rather as directly mandated by (or reflecting) underlying moral entitlements. Property rights are, on the utilitarian view, valuable because of the results they generate. In contrast, a rights-based theorist, like Nozick, argues that we award property rights to those who labor on an unowned piece of land because such labor generates a moral claim over the improved land, irrespective of the consequences of recognizing such claims. Indeed, on some rights-based views, we should award private property to the laborer even if it turns out that doing so would create vastly more costs (overall) than benefits.

Considered broadly, instrumental accounts of property, of which utilitarian analysis is but one example, go back as far as Aristotle. As we discuss in Chapter 5, Aristotle argued that private property rights are important because, among other things, "[w]hen everyone has his own separate sphere of interest, there will not be the same ground for quarrels; and the amount of interest will increase, because each man will feel that he is applying himself to what is his own."[22] Although not ultimately grounded in strictly utilitarian moral philosophy, this brief passage from Aristotle shares important features with most utilitarian accounts of property. Discussions of private property centered on instrumental concerns, such as incentives and coordination costs, also appear in Thomas Aquinas's discussion

---

[21]   See infra Chapter 2.
[22]   *The Politics of Aristotle*, trans. Ernest Barker, Bk. 2, (1958), chap. 5, § 6.

of property[23] and among eighteenth-century thinkers such as David Hume.[24] For all of these theorists, however, discussions of property as instrumentally valuable are embedded within broader moral frameworks that are not themselves strictly utilitarian.

Thoroughgoing and systematic *utilitarian* analyses of property are largely a product of the twentieth-century movement known as Law and Economics. The relationship between Law and Economics and utilitarianism is not completely uncontroversial. For example, Richard Posner, a founding figure in Law and Economics, has at times claimed that he is not in fact a utilitarian.[25] But it is hard to deny that Law and Economics owes a great deal to utilitarian moral theory.[26] Like utilitarian moral theory, economic analysis generally employs a single metric of value, which is itself defined in terms of individual experience (e.g., preference satisfaction). And it attempts to assess social choices in terms of consequences of those choices on some aggregative measure of that single value.

Proponents of Law and Economics use the tools of economic analysis to shed light on how the law operates and how to improve it. Law and Economics has both a positive (descriptive or predictive) dimension and a normative (prescriptive) one. In its positive mode, Law and Economics aims primarily to employ economic tools, such as the rational actor model of individual human behavior (about which we will have more to say shortly) and game theory, to explain or make predictions about the various consequences of different legal regimes. Operating in this positive mode, Posner is clearly right in insisting that there is no *necessary* connection between economic analysis and utilitarian moral theory.

Legal economists, however, often move beyond description and prediction to prescription. It is not uncommon for legal economists to argue that, to the extent that the law already fosters efficiency, it should (at least as a prima facie matter) be preserved, and where it fails to do so, it should be reformed. In this normative mode, Law and Economics espouses something that looks very much like a broadly utilitarian moral theory. Indeed, as Posner admits, a great deal of contemporary economic analysis amounts to a form of "applied utilitarianism."[27] Thus, while their precise terminology varies, legal economists generally argue that a social choice is efficient to

---

[23] St. Thomas Aquinas, *Summa Theologica*, trans. Fathers of the English Dominican Province, 5 vols. Christian Classics (1981), IIa, IIae Q. 66, art. 2.

[24] See David Hume, *A Treatise of Human Nature*, Bk. 3, (Clarendon 1967) (1739), pt. 2, § 3.

[25] See Richard A. Posner, "Utilitarianism, Economics, and Legal Theory," J. LEGAL STUD. 8 (1979): 103, 119. But see Richard A. Posner, "The Ethical and Political Basis of the Efficiency Norm in Common Law Adjudication," HOFSTRA L. REV. 8 (1980): 487, 497, 506 (describing his position as one of "constrained utilitarianism").

[26] Cf. Posner, "Ethical and Political Basis of the Efficiency Norm," 506 (noting that the results of utilitarian and economic analysis of law usually coincide).

[27] See Posner, "Utilitarianism, Economics, and Legal Theory," 119.

the extent that it maximizes net utility or welfare, and that a social choice is good or better when it is more efficient than its alternatives. In this chapter, then, we will treat Law and Economics as a version (or at least a close cousin) of utilitarian theory.

The Tragedy of the Commons: Rational Actors, Externalities, and Transaction Costs

The starting point for virtually all contemporary utilitarian accounts of property is the so-called Tragedy of the Commons. The Tragedy of the Commons refers to the socially wasteful overuse that can occur when individuals enjoy open access to valuable resources. Credit for formalizing the concept of the Tragedy of the Commons usually goes to Garrett Hardin, an ecologist who in 1968 published an influential article of that name in the journal *Science*.[28] As Aristotle's observations about private ownership make clear, however, the challenges of managing common resources have been understood in general terms for millennia.[29] More recently, the tragedy was extensively explored in both biological and economic scholarship decades before Hardin's influential article appeared.[30] In one particularly important early article, Indiana University economist H. Scott Gordon outlined the problem for fisheries but went on to generalize about other open access resources. In words that echoed Aristotle he concluded that "[t]here appears...to be some truth in the conservative dictum that everybody's property is nobody's property. Wealth that is free for all is valued by none because he who is foolhardy enough to wait for its proper time of use will only find that it has been taken by another."[31]

Despite these earlier discussions, Hardin's article became the classic statement of the problem, probably because of its memorable title and because it presented the issue in a uniquely clear and accessible manner. Hardin described the tragedy as follows:

> Picture a pasture open to all. It is to be expected that each herdsman will try to keep as many cattle as possible on the commons.... As a rational being, each herdsman seeks to maximize his gain. Explicitly or implicitly, more or less consciously, he

---

[28] See Garrett Hardin, "Tragedy of the Commons," SCIENCE 162 (1968): 1243.

[29] See James E. Krier, "Evolutionary Theory and the Origin of Property Rights," CORNELL LAW REVIEW 95 (2009): 139, 142–3.

[30] Henry Smith shows that the problem was "systematically studied" in the early years of the twentieth century. See Henry E. Smith, "Exclusion Versus Governance: Two Strategies for Delineating Property Rights," JOURNAL OF LEGAL STUDIES 31 (2002): S453, S457 n. 9 ; see also H. Scott Gordon, "The Economic Theory of a Common-Property Resource: The Fishery," JOURNAL OF POLITICAL ECONOMY 62 (1954) cited in Robert Dorfman and Nancy S. Dorfman, eds, *Economics of the Environment: Selected Readings* (1972), 88; R. J. H. Beverton, "Some Observations on the Principles of Fisheries Regulation," JOURNAL DU CONSEIL PERMANENT INTERNATIONAL POUR L'EXPLORATION DE LA MER 19 (1953): 56.

[31] Gordon, "The Fishery," 99.

asks, "What is the utility *to me* of adding one more animal to my herd?" This utility has one negative and one positive component.

1. The positive component is a function of the increment of one animal. Since the herdsman receives all the proceeds from the sale of the additional animal, the positive utility is nearly + 1.
2. The negative component is a function of the additional overgrazing created by one more animal. Since, however, the effects of overgrazing are shared by all the herdsmen, the negative utility for any particular decision-making herdsman is only a fraction of –1.

Adding together the component partial utilities, the rational herdsman concludes that the only sensible course for him to pursue is to add another animal to his herd. And another.... But this is the conclusion reached by each and every rational herdsman sharing a commons. Therein is the tragedy. Each man is locked into a system that compels him to increase his herd without limit – in a world that is limited. Ruin is the destination toward which all men rush, each pursuing his own best interest in a society that believes in the freedom of the commons. Freedom in a commons brings ruin to all.[32]

Building on the assumptions that human beings are both capable of discerning the course of action that is most advantageous to them and narrowly motivated to maximize their own private gain (i.e., are rational actors), what powers Hardin's model is the mismatch between the benefits of consuming the commons, which are enjoyed exclusively by those self-interested individuals, and the costs of its consumption, which are shared with all other users. Individual rational actors maximize their private gains by consuming the commons even when that consumption generates more costs than benefits overall.

Economists use the term *externality* to refer to the consequences of an actor's choices that are not included in (i.e., that are external to) the actor's private cost-benefit analysis. Externalities provide another lens through which to view the commons tragedy. In a classic article written a year before Hardin's,[33] Harold Demsetz identifies the same dynamic of overconsumption of commons resources, but uses the externality as his central analytic tool:

Suppose that land is communally owned. Every person has the right to hunt, till, or mine the land. This form of ownership fails to concentrate the cost associated with any person's exercise of his communal rights on that person. If a person seeks to maximize the value of his communal rights, he will tend to overhunt and over-work the land because some of the costs of his doing so are borne by others. The stock of game and the richness of the soil will be diminished too quickly.... If a

---

[32] Hardin, "Tragedy of the Commons," 1244.
[33] Harold Demsetz, "Toward a Theory of Property Rights," Am. Econ. Rev. 57 (1967): 347, 354–8.

single person owns the land, he will attempt to maximize its present value by taking into account alternative future time streams of benefits and costs and selecting that one which he believes will maximize the present value of his privately-owned land rights…. The land ownership example confronts us immediately with a great disadvantage of communal property. The effects of a person's activities on his neighbors and on subsequent generations will not be taken into account fully. Communal property results in great externalities. The full costs of the activities of an owner of a communal property right are not borne directly by him, nor can they be called to his attention easily by the willingness of others to pay him an appropriate sum…. [34]

Like Hardin, Demsetz identifies the division of the commons into private property as a key tool for overcoming the inefficiencies generated by pervasive externalities. "[P]rivate ownership of land," he says, "will internalize many of the external costs associated with communal ownership." This is because the private owner "can generally count on realizing the rewards associated with husbanding game and increasing the fertility of his land." Because the owner's wealth is now tied to the skill with which she cares for her property, she has the incentive to use the resources on that property as efficiently as possible. [35]

Private property directly internalizes many of the externalities caused by overuse. Of course, some mismatch between the benefits of individual ownership and the consequences of individual choice will remain. But even as to these surviving externalities, Demsetz argues, private ownership may constitute an improvement. This is because reducing the number of decision makers reduces the transaction costs that stand in the way of the affected parties coming together to reach a successful bargain over who should bear the burdens generated by a particular activity. [36] As Demsetz notes, the creation of a system of private ownership is not free. But when externalities are expensive enough, establishing a system of private ownership becomes cost-effective.

According to Hardin, the only two options for realigning an individual's calculation of private gain with the collective costs and benefits of commons consumption are either to parcel the commons into private shares so that the individual bears more of the costs of his consumption or to enact coercive regulations that prohibit overexploitation. From a utilitarian perspective, in choosing between these two options (regulation and privatization), society should opt for the least costly. The costs of regulation include the costs of generating and enforcing rules, as well as inefficiencies that result when the rules fail to mandate the most efficient conduct. The costs of privatization include the costs of establishing and enforcing property

---

[34] Ibid.
[35] See ibid., 356.
[36] See ibid., 356–7.

rules as well as inefficiencies that result when owners' incentives are not aligned with aggregate utility. We will discuss how such a misalignment might occur in connection with our discussion of redistribution in Chapter 6. For our present purposes, however, it is sufficient to observe that determining which of Hardin's two strategies is more cost-effective will be an incredibly complex and controversial undertaking.

The Free Rider

Overcoming wasteful overconsumption of common resources is only half of the utilitarian account of property. The other half revolves around the story of the free rider. The free rider is someone who sits back and lets others do the work so he can enjoy the benefits. Of course, if everyone is a free rider, even the free riders lose. Nevertheless, the threat of free riding may discourage anyone from doing his fair share.

Go back to the hypothetical open access commons field. But this time, instead of a field for grazing, assume it would most productively be used to cultivate corn for home consumption. Before they can consume the corn, users of the field must contribute labor – tilling, sowing, weeding, harvesting – in order to produce a good crop. Absent the power to exclude those who have not contributed labor from coming in at the last moment and enjoying the ripe ears of corn, rational actors are confronted with a cost-benefit analysis in which it may not be cost-effective (from an individual standpoint) for them to contribute their labor to the field's cultivation. Even if laboring collectively on the field to raise corn would enhance overall utility, it is in no individual's interest to contribute her own labor. Rational individuals will instead prefer to simply stand by (that is, take a free ride) while others do the work. They can then step in at the final moment to enjoy benefits.

Thus, armed with most of the same assumptions at work in the Tragedy of the Commons, utilitarian property theory argues that, in an open access regime, externalized benefits result in their own sort of Tragedy of the Free Rider. Instead of *over*consumption, this tragedy generates pervasive *under*production because of the failure in an open access regime to provide adequate incentives for rational actors to engage in unpleasant, utility-enhancing labor. This analysis of positive externalities yields the same prescription as the first tragedy story: the creation of private property rights that allow individuals to keep for themselves more of the positive consequences their efforts generate, thereby better aligning their private cost-benefit analysis with that of the community as a whole.

Exploring the Assumptions behind the Tragedy of the Commons

Both Demsetz's and Hardin's accounts depend on four elements that contribute to the genesis of a commons tragedy: (1) a community made up of rational actors who unfailingly aim to maximize their own individual material gain; (2) a resource whose consumption is "rivalrous," that is, one whose use progressively diminishes or degrades the remaining supply of the resource; (3) users of the resource who are able to keep for themselves the full benefits of their use while the costs of their use are shared by all others; and (4) use of the resource that is unregulated (either formally or informally) and open to all. When all four of these factors are present, individuals will continue to use a resource even when the overall costs of such use (which are shared) exceed the overall benefits (which are retained by the individual as private gains). On the other hand, the absence of any one of these factors makes it less likely that the commons tragedy will arise.

The free rider is really a version of the same story. The crucial difference is that the free rider story does not depend on the rivalrousness of consumption. As long as the creation of benefits, whether rivalrously consumed or not, depend on labor and can be enjoyed by someone other than the laborer, utilitarian theory (when coupled with a rational actor model) predicts that individuals will fail to maximize utility because they will have an incentive to free ride on the hard work of others. Insofar as it is based on many of the same assumptions of the Tragedy of the Commons, the free rider story is subject to the same limitations as the overconsumption story. If actors are not narrowly rational or if a community can restrict access to a commons and monitor the conduct of its members, it is perfectly possible that productive labor will occur even in the absence of a regime of private ownership to capture positive externalities for the owner.

In order to better understand the limitations these assumptions impose on the reach of traditional utilitarian arguments for private property, we will consider each assumption in turn.

Rational Actors

Utilitarian analysis within property theory has traditionally – although by no means exclusively – relied very heavily on a rational actor model of individual motivation. According to the version of this model that, until recently, was most commonly employed within property scholarship, human beings base their decisions on a private cost-benefit analysis in which they invariably opt for the course of action that will yield them, as individuals, the greatest net wealth.[37] Any significant deviation of private owners' actual preferences from self-interested wealth maximization undermines the likelihood of a commons tragedy developing. If, for example, people in a particular community turn out not to be self-interested (e.g., if they are altruistic or

---

[37] The classic rational actor model actually goes beyond providing a self-interested theory of human motivation and posits, at least implicitly, that human beings also have unlimited cognitive abilities, perfect information, and unlimited willpower. See, for example, Gary S. Becker, *The Economic Approach to Human Behavior* (1976), 14.

masochistic), they would voluntarily refrain from trying to use commons resources as intensively as possible in order to allow others to do so.[38] Conversely, if people are self-interested, but seek to amass for themselves some value other than wealth (say, immediate gratification of hedonistic desires or ascetic purity or communion with God or with other human beings), they may not be very interested in seeking out economically valuable open access resources to overexploit.[39]

Although the wealth maximizing rational actor has played a particularly influential role in utilitarian property theories, one can be a utilitarian or engage in economic analysis without adopting the rational actor model or identifying wealth as the precise good the rational actor seeks to acquire. Recent efforts to introduce more complex behavioral models into economic analysis of individual and communal conduct depart in significant ways from the rational actor model.[40] Experimental economists studying human behavior in the laboratory, for example, routinely observe that people cooperate even in settings where incentives are structured to reward them for free riding. According to one report based on extensive cross-cultural studies of experimental economic behavior, "there is no society in which experimental behavior is consistent with the canonical model [of the rational actor] from economic textbooks."[41]

In public good games, for instance, individuals are given an initial endowment (say, five dollars). They are then told that any money (secretly) contributed to a common pool will be doubled by the researcher and then redivided equally among all the participants. The overall income maximizing strategy is for everyone to contribute their entire endowment to the common pool (yielding an income of ten dollars for each participant). But an individual could make even more money by being the only person to contribute nothing while everyone else contributes their entire endowments. If there were five participants, this would lead to thirteen dollars for the defector and eight dollars each for the cooperators. A rational actor would therefore

---

[38] Carol Rose's memorable characters, "Mom" and "Hit Me," are good examples of this mindset. See Carol M. Rose, "Property as Storytelling: Perspectives from Game Theory, Narrative Theory, and Feminist Theory," YALE J.L. & HUMAN. 2 (1990): 37, 44–8. If we asked, "Hit Me" would probably say she would rather not be hit with her neighbor's externality, but if she is hit, she might not object and instead simply assume that she somehow deserved it. Martha Nussbaum makes a similar point in her discussions of adaptive preferences. See Martha C. Nussbaum, Women and Human Development (2000), 126.

[39] See, for example, Carl J. Dahlman, The Open Field System and Beyond (1980), 40.

[40] See, for example, ibid.; Robert Ellickson, "Bringing Culture and Human Frailty to Rational Actors: A Critique of Classical Law and Economics," CHI.-KENT L. REV. 65 (1989): 23, 25–6; Elinor Ostrom, Governing the Commons (1990).

[41] Lynn Stout, Cultivating Conscience (2010), 82 (quoting Joseph Henrich et al., Foundations in Human Sociality: Economic Experiments and Ethnographic Evidence from Fifteen Small-Scale Societies (2004), 10.); see also Herbert Gintis, "Strong Reciprocity and Human Sociality," J. THEOR. BIOL. 206 (2000): 169, 177 ("[P]eople tend to behave prosocially and punish antisocial behavior, at a cost to themselves, even when the probability of future interactions is extremely low, or zero.").

contribute nothing to the common pool. In a group made up exclusively of rational actors, no one would contribute anything, and everyone would lose. Contrary to this prediction, however, public goods experiments routinely find that people contribute something on the order of forty to sixty percent of their endowment to the common pool. In other words, free riding is a problem, but not nearly to the degree predicted by the rational actor model.[42]

Similarly, experimental economists find sharing behavior where the rational actor model would not expect to find it. In ultimatum games, for example, one player is empowered to divide up a pool of money subject to a veto by the second player (which, if exercised, results in both players getting nothing). The traditional rational actor model robustly predicts that the first player will give the second player almost nothing and that the second player will accept it (since almost nothing is more than nothing). But in the experiments, the first player usually offers to divide the sum fairly evenly and, when this does not occur, the second player routinely exercises her veto, making substantial sacrifices in order to punish what she interprets to be unfair behavior by her counterpart.[43]

Finally, the rational actor model predicts that mere communication between subjects in these sorts of experiments would have absolutely no impact on subjects' tendencies to cooperate. Game theorists refer to such communication without any power to enforce promises or sanction misconduct as "cheap talk." It turns out, however, that providing participants with the opportunity to communicate prior to making a decision typically yields significantly higher levels of cooperation.[44]

These observed propensities toward cooperation are not without their limits. As Nobel Prize-winning economist Elinor Ostrom has pointed out, commons tragedies actually do occur – as the collapse of high seas fisheries demonstrates – but these experiments suggest that context is crucial. Where anonymity makes it difficult to punish those who refuse to play by agreed rules, a few uncooperative people can reap large rewards by taking advantage of those prone to forego private gains in the interest of cooperation. Experiments suggest that, when this happens, participants' behavior over time converges on the predictions of the rational actor model.[45] Interestingly, however, providing participants with robust opportunities to

---

[42] See John O. Ledyard, "Public Goods," in *The Handbook of Experimental Economics*, ed. John H. Kagel and Alvin E. Roth (1995), 111, 113, 121–2.

[43] See Ernst Fehr et al., "Strong Reciprocity, Human Cooperation, and the Enforcement of Social Norms," HUMAN NATURE 13 (2002): 1, 10–11 (summarizing studies of ultimatum game behavior); see also Alvin E. Roth, "Bargaining Experiments," in *The Handbook of Experimental Economics*, ed. John H. Kagel and Alvin E. Roth (1995), 253.

[44] See Elinor Ostrom, "A Behavioral Approach to the Rational Choice Theory of Collective Action," AMERICAN POLITICAL SCIENCE REVIEW 92 (1998): 1, 6–7; Ledyard, "Public Goods," 156–8.

[45] See Ostrom, "A Behavioral Approach," 5; Elinor Ostrom et al., "Covenants with and without a Sword: Self-Governance Is Possible," AM. POL. SCI. REV. 86 (1992): 404.

communicate can significantly impede the observed deterioration of cooperative behavior.[46]

In response to these sorts of observations, some economists have embraced a more complex model of human motivation characterized by assumptions of "bounded self-interest."[47] Commons tragedies can and do arise, even employing these more sophisticated theories of human behavior. But shifting to these kinds of empirically grounded models leads us toward two important qualifications of the tragedy story. First, tragedies are neither as inexorable nor as pervasive as Hardin and Demsetz assume. Second, overreliance on the assumptions of the rational actor model will blind us to the possibility of different strategies for solving the problems of overconsumption and free riding, strategies that go beyond Hardin's short menu of private property and centrally planned coercive regulation.

Rivalrous Consumption

If consumption of a resource does not in any way degrade the remaining supply, that is, if use of the resource is what economists call "nonrivalrous," then there is no risk of overuse and the Tragedy of the Commons does not arise. This is the case, for example, with the consumption of information. One person's consumption of information does not leave any less for others to consume. As we will see in Chapter 9, this nonrivalrousness means that the utilitarian case for property in information (intellectual property) will look very different from the utilitarian case for private property in tangible resources. It will focus almost exclusively on the problem of free riding for the production and maintenance of information.

Open Access

The Tragedies of the Commons and of the Free Rider are most likely to arise with resources from which no one can be excluded, so-called open access resources. If some functioning entity (a local community or a government) can limit access to the resource or monitor and control the behavior of those who use it, that entity can, in theory, leverage its power to prevent overuse of the resource, even in the absence of private ownership. Thus, the name "Tragedy of the Commons" is actually a misnomer since, traditionally, medieval grazing commons of the sort that Hardin uses as his principal example were not open access lands. Those lands could only be used by lawful village residents. Use of the commons by nonresidents was a trespass, and

---

[46] See Ledyard, "Public Goods," 156.

[47] See, for example, Christine Jolls, Cass Sunstein, and Richard Thaler, "A Behavioral Approach to Law and Economics," *STAN. L. REV.* 50 (1997): 1471, 1479. In addition to limited self-interest, behavioralist approaches also conclude that people have limited cognitive abilities when it comes to discerning what the costs or benefits to them of a particular course of action will be. Scholars refer to this limitation as "bounded rationality." Ibid., 1477.

the ability to become a new village resident was largely under the control of current residents.[48] Even for residents, as Gordon accurately noted in his important paper on fisheries, use of the commons was governed by "elaborate rules regarding the use of the common pasture, or 'stinting' the common: limitations on the number of animals, hours of pasturing, etc., designed to prevent the abuses of excessive individualistic competition."[49] Ironically then, the actual common grazing pastures from which Hardin took the name of his article did not in fact suffer from the Tragedy of the Commons. They were, instead, a relatively well-managed "common pool resource," to use Ostrom's terminology.

Another example of a sustainably managed commons, mentioned in passing in Gordon's 1954 paper but subsequently studied and described in more detail by others, is the Maine lobster fishery. As Gordon observed at the time, while fisheries are generally prime examples of open access resources subject to overexploitation, "[i]n a few places the [lobster] fishermen have banded together into a local monopoly, preventing entry and controlling their own operations."[50] Three decades after the publication of Gordon's paper, James Acheson conducted a groundbreaking study, *The Lobster Gangs of Maine,* in which he detailed how groups of local fishermen regulate access to the lobster fishing grounds, preventing overconsumption and managing to maintain remarkably steady harvests over an extended period of time.[51] The lobster fishermen are aided in this effort by the fact that lobsters live primarily in shallow waters near shore and are caught using stationary traps attached to buoys.[52] These sedentary, equipment dependent, and therefore highly visible fishing techniques enable local lobster cartels to impose their own internal discipline, both to prevent overfishing by their members and to police their boundaries against outside encroachment by other gangs or by unaffiliated fishermen. Gangs use the threat to destroy vulnerable equipment as their principal means of achieving these goals. Legal scholars (and others) refer to such informal mechanisms of social coordination and enforcement as "social norms." The study of norms and their interaction with formal legal systems has spawned an enormous literature, a great deal of it touching on questions of property law.[53]

Generally speaking, where it is possible to limit access to an unowned resource, and where tools exist to prevent too much of the sort of opportunistic behavior that can undermine people's willingness to cooperate, users of common pool resources

[48] See Dahlman, *Open Field System and Beyond,* 23–4, 101.
[49] Gordon, "The Fishery," 99; see also Dahlman, *Open Field System and Beyond,* 120.
[50] Gordon, "The Fishery," 97.
[51] James M. Acheson, *The Lobster Gangs of Maine* (1988).
[52] Ibid., 12–22.
[53] See, for example, Robert C. Ellickson, *Order without Law* (1991); Lior Strahilevitz, "Social Norms from Close-Knit Groups to Loose-Knit Groups," *U. CHI. L. REV.* 70 (2003): 359.

can successfully prevent the Tragedy of the Commons from arising. Ostrom cites seven features she has consistently observed in successfully managed commons: (1) clearly defined boundaries, including clear definitions of who is entitled to use the resource; (2) appropriation rules tailored to the resource and to local conditions; (3) participatory mechanisms for making or modifying the rules governing the resource; (4) monitors who actively police the resource and identify rule violations; (5) graduated sanctions against those who violate the rules; (6) rapid and inexpensive conflict resolution mechanisms; and (7) relative autonomy from outside interference.[54]

As the lobster gangs demonstrate, a commons regime possessing most or all these features can form without Hardin's or Demsetz's proposed remedies of private ownership or coercive state regulation. The recognition of these other mechanisms for avoiding commons tragedies helps make utilitarian analysis of property both richer and more interesting than the more brittle models employed by Hardin and Demsetz. The difficulty of gathering the information necessary to know which solution is optimal in a particular case, however, makes utilitarian theory far less determinate in its implications for actual property regimes than its proponents have sometimes claimed.

Private Benefits

Finally, it is the interaction between privately enjoyed benefits and widely shared (or externalized) costs that drives the Tragedies of the Commons and the Free Rider. If individual actors (even rational actors) must share all or some of the benefits they receive from using a resource, their incentive to overuse that resource will be partially (or even completely) mitigated. And if they cannot share in the benefits of others' labors, they lose the incentive to free ride. In other words, these tragedies are not a consequence of common resources alone. They are the product of the interaction between common and private resources.[55] This observation does not radically change the story because systems of private ownership are nearly universal. But it does have some significance. To take Hardin's example of the herd grazing on a common pasture, in addition to privatization of the field or centrally regulating its use, another obvious option for avoiding the Tragedy of the Commons in the field is to collectivize the herd of livestock. Collectivizing the livestock does not solve the commons problem. It simply relocates it to the livestock themselves. Who will care for the animals? Who will be entitled to consume them? As we have seen, the problem of the free rider makes these questions as challenging as the classic commons

---

[54] See Elinor Ostrom, *Governing the Commons*, 91–102.

[55] This interaction is an example of a problem that Carol Rose has called "imbalanced propertization." Carol M. Rose, "The Story of Lucas: Environmental Land Use Regulation between Developers and the Deep Blue Sea," in *Environmental Law Stories*, ed. Richard J. Lazarus and Oliver A. Houck (2005), 236, 278.

tragedy. But, in certain contexts, there may be a reason to prefer focusing on the problem of free riding rather than on overconsumption.

The Content of Utilitarian Property: The Bundle of Sticks versus Exclusion

One of the strengths of utilitarian property theory, particularly when its practitioners are attentive to rigorous empirical methods, is its great flexibility. Utilitarian theorists admit that creating private property rights is not free. Thus, rather than supporting private ownership rights across the board, utilitarian theory favors them in some contexts while recommending communal property arrangements (or collective regulation) in others. Economic historian Carl Dahlman, for example, argues that the open fields system that developed in medieval villages across Europe – with its scattered plots for cultivation and shared grazing land – was a relatively efficient way of using the same land to produce both crops and livestock. When the emergence of national markets for agricultural products began to reward greater specialization in agricultural production, enclosed farms became the more efficient model.[56] "[T]he question of the relative efficiency of the two systems," he says, "is a perfectly idle one. They were equally well suited to different tasks."[57] Similarly, Demsetz discusses how the Algonquin Indians in Labrador developed a system of private ownership in response to the changing economic value of beaver pelts. Where economic pressures to hunt pelts for an export market threatened the beaver population with extinction, Demsetz argues, what had been a functional commons became a potential tragedy, resulting ultimately in the Indians' adoption of a private property solution.[58] Although Demsetz's specific parable has been subjected to a great deal of criticism concerning its descriptive accuracy,[59] his analysis demonstrates that – in contrast with libertarian, rights-based property theories – utilitarian property theory is potentially extremely sensitive to context.

But utilitarianism's contextual sensitivity generates its own concerns, even on utilitarian grounds. In fact, the potential costs of failing adequately to cabin this flexibility has been the subject of one of the most fertile areas of utilitarian property theorizing in recent years. On one side of this debate is traditional utilitarian-economic analysis of property rights, which explores different facets of ownership institutions to determine whether some particular change in the system of property rights, large or small, would be utility enhancing. This approach has been associated with a conception of property rights that views property as a bundle of sticks, that

---

[56] See Dahlman, *Open Field System and Beyond*, 130–41, 173–8.
[57] Ibid., 178.
[58] Demsetz, "Toward a Theory of Property Rights," 350–3.
[59] Demsetz has also been criticized for his failure to explain how a community of rational actors, confronted with costly externalities, gets a system of property rights off the ground. See Krier, "Evolutionary Theory," 142–3.

is, as a discrete and flexible set of specific rights with respect to things, the precise content of which is largely indeterminate and subject to constant (re)evaluation.[60]

In a pathbreaking article published in the *Harvard Law Review* in 1972, Guido Calabresi and A. Douglas Melamed provided a powerful conceptual framework for describing the various sticks in this bundle of property rights and for thinking about how to allocate them.[61] From a utilitarian standpoint, particular legal rights (including specific rights with respect to property), which Calabresi and Melamed referred to as "entitlements," should be allocated to the person who values them most highly. Generally speaking, these entitlements should remain in the hands of the person to whom they are allocated unless that person consents to transfer them to someone else. Calabresi and Melamed called this way of protecting an entitlement – allowing it to be taken from the owner only with the owner's consent – a "property rule." Property rule protection should be the norm where there is a great deal of confidence as to who values the entitlement most highly or where the market is likely to do a good job of facilitating the transfer of the entitlement to that person. Thus, Calabresi and Melamed say, "[i]n our framework, much of what is generally called private property can be viewed as an entitlement which is protected by a property rule."[62] Sometimes there is reason to think that the market will not do a particularly good job of reassigning the entitlement efficiently, such as when transaction costs remain high, even after a system of private property has been established. Where high transaction costs are likely, Calabresi and Melamed suggest permitting entitlements to change hands without the consent of their current holder upon payment of some amount of compensation. Calabresi and Melamed refer to this less robust way of protecting an entitlement as a "liability rule." Within bundle-of-sticks approaches to utilitarian property theory, how to allocate any particular property right and, once allocated, whether to protect that right with a property rule or a liability rule is – at the outset – an open question.

In recent years, a growing number of scholars have expressed the worry that such right-by-right utilitarian evaluation, if taken too far, risks undermining a core logic of exclusion that defines property institutions. These exclusion theorists, such as Thomas Merrill and Henry Smith, focus on the costs of information, particularly on the way in which property institutions employ what they view as an architecture of exclusion, which rewards information gathering and economizes on the cost of obtaining the information necessary to navigate through a world of private rights.[63]

[60] See Thomas W. Merrill and Henry E. Smith, "What Happened to Property in Law and Economics?" *Yale L. J.* 111 (2001): 357, 360–83.

[61] Guido Calabresi and A. Douglas Melamed, "Property Rules, Liability Rules, and Inalienability: One View of the Cathedral," *Harv. L. Rev.* 85 (1972): 1089.

[62] Ibid., 1105.

[63] See Merrill and Smith, "What Happened to Property?" 389.

The exclusion approach is not without its difficulties, as we will discuss in greater depth in Chapter 7. But by reorienting the focus of economic analysis of property toward the question of how property functions as a coherent institution, rather than as a disaggregated collection of individual entitlements, exclusion theorists have provided a valuable contribution to utilitarian property theory.

Problems with Utilitarian Approaches to Property

Utilitarianism and the Individual

A frequent objection to utilitarian moral theory in general, and one that applies with equal force to utilitarian property theory, is that it does not give adequate weight to the interests of individuals. Although utilitarian-economic analysis is methodologically individualistic in the sense that it understands utility as something experienced by individual human beings, it has long been criticized for a willingness to trade on individual well-being in order to enhance aggregate utility. This critique has particular bite when levied against additive principles of aggregation. As Jeremy Waldron has put it, "[w]hen we impose a Kaldor-Hicks improvement, we are not in any way honoring the voluntary consent of the losing party."[64]

Less frequently acknowledged, however, is the way in which even the more protective Pareto standard trades on the well-being of individuals. At first glance, the Pareto criterion appears to robustly respect individuals in a way that Kaldor-Hicks does not. In theory, it requires unanimous consent for a social choice to satisfy its demanding standard. In practice, however, as even those who employ the standard admit, unanimity is impossible and is therefore not demanded. There are never enough time and resources to ask each individual whether a particular social choice will make her better off. Moreover, the risk of strategic holdouts means that policy makers would be unlikely to believe a respondent when – absent certain conditions (like a decline in wealth) – she claims that a particular policy has made her worse off. Thus, according to Gordon Tullock, most economists only gesture vaguely in the direction of Pareto, while actually engaging in a far more aggregative evaluation of winners and losers.[65] Even the most exacting Paretian will necessarily use idealized conceptions of what it means for someone to be better or worse off, most often by reducing well-being to objective measures such as, for example, an individual's net worth or share of aggregate social wealth. And it is these measures – and not the actual stated preferences of the affected individuals – that the Paretian theorist will use to determine whether a choice constitutes a Pareto improvement. Some attempt to ensure that people are not harmed by social choices is more respectful of individuals than the utter lack

---

[64] Waldron, "Nozick and Locke," 101.
[65] See Gordon Tullock, "Smith v. Pareto," ATLANTIC ECON. J. 27 (1999): 254, 254–9.

of concern in the Kaldor-Hicks standard of social choice, but the Pareto criterion only honors individuals to the extent that their actual preferences match those of the idealized model of human well-being that is used. We will revisit the difficulties that utilitarianism confronts when individual interests are at stake in our discussions of redistribution in Chapter 6 and of eminent domain in Chapter 8.

The Incompleteness of Utility

The standard utilitarian and welfarist models of human well-being also have some shortcomings. For the utilitarian, a commitment to a unitary measure of value means that goods are *always* substitutable; the challenge is simply in determining the proper rate of exchange. The more multivalent concepts of human well-being at work within other property theories, however, recognize that individuals or groups experience the components of that well-being in ways that defy substitution. As Margaret Radin has correctly noted (and as we will discuss in Chapter 3), human beings form connections with particular pieces of property such that the property becomes inextricably bound up with their pursuit of the well-lived life.[66] Consider the example of a parcel of land. Once a person (or a community) has sufficiently incorporated a piece of land into her life plans, exchanging that land for some other good (even a good of very great economic value) or for some other piece of land can hinder, in some cases irreparably, her ability to flourish. Losing the land can short circuit long-term plans, deeply held commitments, and carefully constructed identities in ways that resist compensation.

Because human well-being is a phenomenon of actual, living human beings with physical needs and finite life cycles, and not disembodied collections of utility, there is an organic integrity and coherence to its individual experience that resists limitless disassembly and substitution. The structure of well-being extends along at least two dimensions. First, it has breadth as an expression of the need simultaneously to enjoy a number of distinct and nonsubstitutable goods. To thrive in a distinctively human way within a given society one must have access to a particular basket of material and social goods. And many of these goods, such as socialization and the material resources necessary for social participation, moral training, language acquisition, and the nutritional resources necessary for physical and mental development, must come in the correct form at the right time in one's life, or a person's prospects to thrive may be permanently impaired. To be sure, the countless ways to pursue and enjoy these goods leave ample room for human freedom by, say, emphasizing one good (e.g., knowledge) over others.[67] But the scope for such

---

[66] See, for example, Margaret Jane Radin, "Property and Personhood," *Stan. L. Rev.* 34 (1982): 957, 994–6.

[67] See John Finnis, *Natural Law and Natural Rights* (1980), 93–4; John O'Neill, *Ecology, Policy, and Politics* (1993), 87–90.

specialization is not limitless. Since both political freedom *and* adequate nutrition are required for human well-being, for example, we will not be able properly to compensate a person forced to live under political tyranny by giving her extra units of food or money.

Second, the coherence of well-being extends temporally as a pattern of cultivation and enjoyment of particular goods over the course of one's life. Even though well-lived human lives may take a plurality of individual forms, and even though those forms may themselves vary (even for a particular individual life) over time, well-lived lives are not constituted by a series of disconnected mental states or satisfied preferences, as utilitarian theorists sometimes seem to imagine, but will necessarily have a certain experiential integrity.[68] This integrity will sometimes make it impossible to substitute one good for another. For example, someone who has committed her life to the mastery of a particular art form cannot flourish if, at the apex of her career, we destroy her finest productions. Her loss will be tragic and irreparable, no matter how much money or pleasure or preference satisfaction we give her in a misguided effort at compensation. The foregoing discussion suggests that a complete account of human well-being is not possible using a single value, such as utility or welfare. And, because property law implicates such a wide range of human interests, the same objection likely holds for efforts to craft a property theory on the basis of a single master value.

CONCLUSION: THE VALUE OF UTILITARIAN ANALYSIS, BUT THE NEED FOR MORE

Utilitarian theory provides a set of powerful tools for thinking about property. The problems we have identified with the utilitarian analysis of property (indeed, with utilitarian analysis in general) do not mandate the conclusion that utilitarian considerations are utterly without merit. While they present serious challenges to the notion that these considerations can *fully* capture the complex human interests at work in our institutions of property, they do not mean that welfare or wealth or utility is irrelevant to those institutions. In other words, these criticisms do not call for a total rejection of utilitarian or economic analysis of property but only for a rejection of the most extreme claims that welfare or utility enhancement is all that matters in structuring property institutions.[69] The challenge for property theorists is to find

---

[68] Bernard Williams has famously converted this point about the integrity of the well-lived life into a powerful critique of utilitarian moral theory. See Smart and Williams, *Utilitarianism: For and Against*, 114–17; see also Daniel Markovits, "Legal Ethics from the Lawyer's Point of View," YALE J. L. & HUMAN. 15 (2003): 209, 228–33.

[69] See, for example, Kaplow and Shavell, *Fairness versus Welfare*, 3–4 (arguing that welfare is the only value that ought to matter in public decision making).

ways to put the valuable insights of utilitarianism to use while restricting the reach of those insights to their proper scope. Meeting this challenge suggests the need to resort to a broader moral framework. As we will argue in Chapter 5, a theory of owner obligation rooted in the Aristotelian tradition provides one such inclusive vision.

2

Locke and Libertarian Theories of Property

No single person has had more of an impact on property thought in the English-speaking world than John Locke.[1] Among contemporary theorists, however, Locke's influence is felt most directly among property rights libertarians. This is somewhat ironic, because these libertarians are able to rely on Locke only by excising from his theory several of its foundational elements. In this chapter, we will describe the outlines of Locke's theory and explore some of the debates over its cogency and meaning.

LOCKE'S CONTEXT

Locke's theory of property is laid out in his *Two Treatises of Government*, with the bulk of the relatively brief discussion appearing in the fifth chapter of the second treatise. (There are, as we will see, important elements of his discussion in the first treatise as well.) In thinking about Locke's theory, it is helpful to understand something about the debates in which he likely understood himself to be participating. Although the *Two Treatises* was not published until 1689, in the immediate aftermath of the Glorious Revolution, most commentators agree that the work was actually written several years earlier, between roughly 1679 and 1682, during the Exclusion Crisis, in which the Whigs, led by the First Earl of Shaftesbury (Locke's patron), attempted to prevent the Catholic James, Duke of York, from inheriting the throne.[2]

Commentators differ over where to place Locke on the ideological spectrum of his day. Peter Laslett has argued that Locke's political commitments were those of a moderate, establishment Whig.[3] This view of Locke's politics generally corresponds

---

[1] Cf. Christopher Tomlins, *Freedom Bound* (2010), 339.
[2] See Peter Laslett, introduction to *John Locke, Two Treatises of Government*, ed. Peter Laslett (1960); Richard Ashcraft, *Revolutionary Politics and Locke's "Two Treatises of Government"* (1987).
[3] Laslett, "Introduction," 103–4.

to an interpretation of his theory of property as largely seeking to justify the status quo at the time he was writing. In contrast, Richard Ashcraft, with the qualified agreement of Jeremy Waldron, has argued that Locke's politics were significantly more egalitarian and has attempted to place Locke's views on private ownership on par with those of earlier radical groups such as the Levellers.[4] In support of this reading, Locke's attack on primogeniture in the ninth chapter of the first treatise is particularly significant (I, 81–93).[5]

Whatever disagreement there is over Locke's politics, there is no doubt that Locke understood one of his principal intellectual opponents to be Robert Filmer, whose works were republished in the 1670s to provide intellectual support for claims of royal absolutism by James II's supporters.[6] One of Filmer's arguments was that God had given to Adam title to the entire world, which Adam then bequeathed to certain of his descendants exclusively, and they to certain of theirs, and so on. Modern monarchs, he argued, derived their authority from (among other sources) this line of property grants. As part of this argument, Filmer asserted that it was impossible to justify a system of private property on the foundation of the more egalitarian assumption that God had given the world, not just to Adam individually, but to the entire human race in common. Locke's argument in the fifth chapter of the second treatise constitutes, among other things, his attempt to refute Filmer's anti-egalitarian claims.

Although Locke's theory of property plays an important role in the overall flow of his argument in the second treatise, he did not write the treatises as a defense of private ownership. The treatises are foremost a defense of democratic self-government against pretensions of monarchical absolutism. Locke's theory of property is instrumental, but ultimately subservient, to this project of constructing a democratic political theory. Contemporary libertarian readings of Locke invert this relationship.

LOCKE'S NATURAL LAW FRAMEWORK

As Waldron has observed, the discussion of property in the second treatise "adds up to a natural law argument."[7] For Locke, the natural law is the constellation of rights and duties that God has built into the fabric of the universe. It is binding on

---

[4] See Ashcraft, *Revolutionary Politics*, chap. 9; Jeremy Waldron, *God, Locke, and Equality* (2002), 84.

[5] John Locke, *Two Treatises of Government*, ed. Mark Goldie, Everyman's Library (1993). All quotations and references to Locke's *Two Treatises* are taken from this source.

[6] See Waldron, *Equality*, 16–20; Tomlins, *Freedom Bound*, 367–8.

[7] Waldron, *Equality*, 95; see also Gopal Sreenivasan, *The Limits of Lockean Rights in Property* (1995), 21 ("Locke writes in the language of seventeenth century natural law and natural rights discourse and his theory of property is informed by the intellectual matrix constituted by that tradition.").

all human beings, and the content of it is accessible to them through the use of their rational faculties.[8] This natural law confers rights and duties prior to any social arrangements people make. It imparts moral force to – and constrains – the positive legal arrangements they devise. Although positive law can give precise form to the indeterminate law of nature, the precepts of natural law continue to operate in civil society, and, as Locke says, "[t]he rules that [legislatures] make for other men's actions, must, as well as their own and other men's actions, be conformable to the law of nature" (II, 135).

The first, and most fundamental, precept of this natural law is that human beings, as God's "property," are to be preserved (II, 6, 16). Individuals are therefore bound by duty to preserve themselves and, where this obligation of self-preservation would not be undermined, they must help others to survive as well (I, 86; II, 6). God created the world in order to allow human beings to fulfill this duty (I, 86), and, because the duty is one that each person possesses in equal measure, each person is equally entitled "to the use of those things, which were serviceable for his subsistence, and given him as means of his preservation" (I, 86; II, 25). This equal right and duty of self-preservation plays a crucial role throughout Locke's argument for private ownership: It is the point of departure for his discussion of property (II, 25), the motive for affirming the institution of private property (II, 26), and an important qualification to the rights that the institution confers on individual owners (I, 42).

LOCKE'S ARGUMENT FOR PRIVATE PROPERTY

Locke's argument for private property differs in fundamental ways from the utilitarian approaches we discussed in Chapter 1. Unlike those theories, which focus on the instrumental value of property rights to some further end (e.g., aggregate welfare or utility), Locke's theory is built around notions of moral desert.[9] Though at first glance simple, Locke's account is both rich and complex. The argument proceeds as a sort of narrative involving three interrelated stages of human existence.[10] The first is the state of nature, which is the stage in which private ownership first develops. The second stage arises with the introduction of money, which facilitates inequality in the possession of property. In the third and final stage, communities form governments, which regulate and formalize property rights.

---

[8] Waldron, *Equality*, 158–60; James Tully, *A Discourse on Property* (1980), 62–3; Sreenivasan, *Limits of Lockean Rights*, 71–3.
[9] See Stephen R. Munzer, *A Theory of Property* (1990), 255.
[10] Jeremy Waldron, *The Right to Private Property* (1988), 222.

Stage One: State of Nature

Locke begins his argument for property with a story about the state of nature prior to the formation of political society or the emergence of positive legal systems. Locke's state of nature is not an anarchic, Hobbesian dystopia of constant warfare.[11] Rather, because of his conception of natural law as binding on and rationally cognizable by human beings (II, 6) and because of his complex views on human character (e.g., II, 128), Locke describes the state of nature as relatively social and tranquil, at least in its earliest stages (II, 51). As Locke puts it, "[m]en living together according to reason, without a common superior on earth, with authority to judge between them, is properly the state of nature" (II, 19).

The state of nature is, for Locke, "[a] state also of equality, wherein all the power and jurisdiction is reciprocal, no one having more than another" (II, 4). In concept, such initial equality is ambiguous between two possible states of affairs: (1) so-called negative communism, in which no one has any initial rights to resources and therefore no one owes anyone else any duties (e.g., duties to allow access to valuable resources); and (2) a more affirmative original communism in which everyone has equal rights to access the world's natural resources, and in which people therefore owe duties to one another from the outset.[12] A number of early modern thinkers (most famously Thomas Hobbes, but also Hugo Grotius) described the original position as one of negative communism. This does not appear to have been Locke's conception. Instead, following the main channel of the seventeenth-century natural law tradition, he asserts that God has "given the earth to the children of men, given it to mankind in common" (II, 25 [internal quotation marks omitted]), though, as we will discuss, less probably turns on this distinction than some commentators suggest.[13]

This starting point of affirmative original communism, in which individuals have rights to enjoy the world's natural resources, highlights the foundational problem with which Locke grapples when he discusses private property in the fifth chapter of the second treatise. How can people make private use of the resources that God has given them (collectively), as they must if those resources are to sustain them (as God intended), without violating the affirmative and equal rights that every other human

[11] See Thomas Hobbes, *Leviathan*, ed. Richard Tuck (1988).
[12] Waldron, *Private Property*, 148–57.
[13] Ibid., 155; Tully, *Discourse on Property*, 68; Sreenivasan, *Limits of Lockean Rights*, 24–5. In adopting this position, Locke puts himself in the same line of property thinking occupied by Thomas Aquinas, see St. Thomas Aquinas, *Summa Theologica*, trans. Fathers of the English Dominican Province, 5 vols. Christian Classics (1981), IIa IIae, Q. 66, art. 2; and the sixteenth-century neo-Thomist, Francisco Suarez, *Tractatus de legibus ac deo legislatore*, trans. Gwladys L. Williams, et al. (1944), Bk. 2, chap. 14, § 16.

being enjoys over those same resources (II, 25–6)? As Locke puts the problem, "[t]he fruit, or venison, which nourishes the wild Indian, who knows no enclosure…must be his, and so his, i.e., a part of him, that another can no longer have any right to it, before it can do him any good for the support of his life" (II, 26).

Thus, affirmative original communism underscores what Gopal Sreenivasan has dubbed the "paradox of plenty." Given initial rights enjoyed by all, it would seem that we need everyone's consent before we can make private use of anything, but (Locke says) if actual universal consent were necessary to the individual enjoyment of natural resources, "Man had starved, notwithstanding the Plenty God had given him" (II, 28). Although some have interpreted this stark statement of the problem to constitute a part of Locke's argument for private ownership,[14] others read it as merely crystallizing the problem that Locke aims to solve by other means.[15] For reasons we will explain later, we think the latter position is the correct one.

To solve the paradox of plenty, Locke turns to the well-known labor theory of appropriation. Early in the chapter on property, Locke says:

> Though the Earth, and all inferior Creatures be common to all Men, yet every Man has a Property in his own Person. This no Body has any Right to but himself. The Labour of his Body and the Work of his Hands, we may say, are properly his. Whatsoever then he removes out of the State that Nature hath provided, and left it in, he hath mixed his Labour with, and joined to it something that is his own, and thereby makes it his Property. It being by him removed from the common state nature placed it in, it hath by this labour something annexed to it, that excludes the common right of other man. (II, 27)

This annexation of something that excludes "the common right of other man" to something that was previously held in common does not, Locke argues, violate the rights of other commoners so long as the position of those others is not impaired by the acts of private appropriation. To ensure this, Locke discusses three constraints.

First, no one may appropriate more than he can use before it spoils. "Whatever is beyond this, is more than his share, and belongs to others. Nothing was made by God for man to spoil or destroy" (II, 31). Indeed, if property "perished, in his possession, without their due use, [the appropriator] offended against the common law of nature, and was liable to be punished; he invaded his neighbour's share" (II, 37).

Second, Locke says that appropriation out of the commons is only permissible where "there is enough, and as good left in common for others" (II, 27). This limitation has been the subject of some controversy. Foremost are questions about what

---

[14] See, for example, Seana Valentine Shiffrin, "Lockean Arguments for Private Intellectual Property," in *New Essays in the Legal and Political Theory of Property*, ed. Stephen R. Munzer (2001), 138, 145–6; Waldron, *Private Property*, 168.

[15] Sreenivasan, *Limits of Lockean Rights*, 28–30.

actually constitutes "enough, and as good" and whether this sufficiency condition, which Locke believed was obviously satisfied in the era of primitive appropriation, constitutes an ongoing constraint on ownership once appropriation occurs. That is, does the condition guarantee nonowners an ongoing right to appropriate out of the commons, and would their inability to do so in developed systems of private ownership deprive already appropriated private property of its legitimacy? We will return to these questions later in the chapter.

Finally, in a frequently overlooked passage in the first treatise, with strong echoes of Thomas Aquinas,[16] Locke says that "[a]s justice gives every man a title to the product of his honest industry, and the fair acquisitions of his ancestors descended to him; so charity gives every man a title to so much out of another's plenty, as will keep him from extreme want, where he has no means to subsist otherwise" (I, 42).[17] Waldron refers to this condition as the "principle of charity."[18] He treats it as a constraint on private property rights once they have been established, but it can also serve as a further justification for at least some acts of initial appropriation. Recall that the problem Locke aims to solve through his theory of appropriation is how to reconcile acts of private use and appropriation with existing communal property rights. Since at least some acts of use and appropriation are necessary to human survival, the principle of charity requires human beings, as "owners" (collectively) of communal property rights, to acquiesce to the private use and appropriation sought by individuals seeking the resources they need to survive. As long as the waste and sufficiency provisions are satisfied, these acts of private appropriation will only take from the community's surplus, leaving "enough, and as good" behind in order to meet the needs of others.

The principle of charity therefore seems to mean not only that private appropriators do not violate the rights of the community when they take out of the common surplus the resources they need to survive, but that the community would gravely violate appropriators' rights by trying to stop them. This interaction between the principle of charity and the "enough, and as good" proviso suggests that the "paradox of plenty" cannot be Locke's principal argument for private property or even, as Seana

---

[16] See Aquinas, *Summa Theologica*, IIa IIae, Q. 66, art. 7.

[17] Nor, on Locke's view, can an owner use his property to extract excessive concessions from those in need. "[A] man can no more justly make use of another's necessity, to force him to become his vassal, by with-holding that relief, God requires him to afford to the wants of his brother," Locke says, "than he that has more strength can seize upon a weaker, master him to his obedience, and with a dagger at his throat offer him death or slavery" (I, 42).

[18] Waldron, *Equality*, 177; Sreenivasan, *Limits of Lockean Rights*, 102–3; Tully, *Discourse on Property*, 131–3. As Waldron notes, Locke's use of the language of "charity" does not mean that he understands this limitation as operating only on the level of private conscience. His language, that "charity gives every man title," suggests a legally enforceable property right in the surplus of others' property when a person has "no means to subsist otherwise."

Shiffrin has argued, a preliminary limitation on the scope of that argument. The rights of appropriation it justifies would be limited to property necessary for survival, and Locke clearly thinks appropriation can go farther than that (II, 48).

Stage Two: The Introduction of Money

After the first acts of appropriation in the state of nature, the next significant development in Locke's narrative is the emergence of money. Money enters the picture as a mechanism by which owners avoid violating the spoilation condition. Allowing perishables to spoil while in one's possession violates the natural rights of others to enjoy the fruits of the earth, but Locke says that an appropriator can voluntarily "exchange his sheep for shells, or wool for a sparkling pebble or diamond, and keep those by him all his life" without violating anyone else's rights (II, 46). "And thus came in the use of money," Locke explains, "and that by mutual consent men would take in exchange for [money] the truly useful, but perishable supports of life" (II, 47).

Money breeds inequality and conflict. "Where there is not something both lasting and scarce, and so valuable to hoard up," Locke says, "there men will not be apt to enlarge their possessions of land" (II, 48). Thus, in that era before money, limitations on appropriation imposed by the spoilation condition left "little room for quarrels or contentions about property" (II, 31). Equality preserved social peace because "[t]here could then be no reason of quarrelling about title" where "what portion a man carved to himself was easily seen; and it was useless as well as dishonest to carve himself too much" (II, 51). Under such circumstances, there was no need for formal law, because "[t]he equality of a simple poor way of living confining their desires within the narrow bounds of each man's small property made few controversies and so no need of many laws to decide them" (II, 107, 110–12). By permitting extensive accumulation that did not risk spoilation, however, the introduction of money facilitated the emergence of dramatic inequalities of possessions in the state of nature. The accumulation of property, made possible for the first time by the introduction of money, increased the potential for conflict as ambitions and claims began to butt up against one another.

Thus, once money arrived, along with the inequality and concentrations of property that it facilitates, conflict over property became more common and ownership more insecure. Although Locke justifies this unequal ownership on the dubious ground that, by participating in monetary transactions, people consent to inequality (II, 50), he expresses mixed feelings about the institution of money. On the one hand, he acknowledges that the desire for gain, however questionable its merit, encourages productive behavior and leads to a material abundance in monetary, commercial societies that could not be achieved without the opportunities to accumulate that money unleashes (II, 41, 48). But he expresses doubts about the ultimate value of this prosperity and also repeatedly notes that the consequence of money's introduction is a cycle of growing acquisitiveness and conflict (II, 107). He therefore repeatedly refers to its utter lack of intrinsic value – he derides it as "a sparkling pebble" or "a piece of metal" (II, 46) – and implicitly questions the wisdom of those who labor in order to "heap up" (II, 46) and "hoard" (II, 50) it.

Stage Three: Civil Society

Despite its many virtues, Locke observes that the state of nature lacks three things: a formally elaborated law to which all parties can look to ascertain the precise boundaries of their rights; a neutral magistrate to adjudicate between people when conflicts arise; and the organs of state power to enforce the judgments of those magistrates (II, 123–6). The conflicts generated by the introduction of money therefore threaten to overwhelm the limited dispute resolving capabilities of the communities that exist in the state of nature. It is these shortcomings of the state of nature that make ownership of property (at least once money is introduced) insecure. And it is in order to overcome that insecurity that people form governments. Although Locke describes the move from the informal communities of the state of nature to life under a civil government as a departure from "freedom," he views the state of nature as one that already imposes significant limits on human freedom. Though the state of nature "be a state of liberty," he says, "yet it is not a state of license" (II, 6). "The state of nature has a law of nature to govern it" (II, 6). This law of nature includes obligations not to harm others or oneself as well as positive obligations to assist others when possible (II, 6).

Importantly, the strictures of natural law do not become irrelevant once a civil society is formed. Instead, they set the boundaries for the power enjoyed by civil government. Since government exercises its authority as a delegation from the governed, it cannot wield any more power than individuals enjoyed in the state of nature, and this means that government can no more justly contravene the law of nature than individuals could before the formation of civil government (II, 135). In the context of property rights, the state's power is therefore limited by natural rights of property which exist at the time the government is formed. These include the right to continue in possession of rightfully appropriated property unless the owner consents to lose it (II, 138).

This simple assertion, however, masks a number of important points. The first involves the limitations on property rights that Locke believes already exist within the state of nature. These include the aforementioned prohibition on waste through spoilation and, on most readings, the requirement that enough and as good be left available to others. In addition, the law of nature entails affirmative obligations as well as negative rights. Among other things, it requires owners to make available their surplus resources for the subsistence of others when they cannot provide for themselves (I, 42). Along with other elements of the natural law, these affirmative obligations continue into civil society.

Perhaps the most potent qualification on natural property rights within civil society, however, concerns Locke's capacious theory of consent. Although the term *consent* is suggestive of actual, individual agreement to a loss of property, Locke repeatedly makes clear throughout the second treatise that a person "consents" to subject her property to laws enacted by the governing majority.[19] Thus, he says, "every man, by consenting with others to make one body politic under one government, puts himself under an obligation to everyone of that society, to submit to the determination of the majority, and to be concluded by it" (II, 97–8; see also II, 88, 132). And, again, in discussing taxation, he says that, "'tis fit every one who enjoys his share of the [State's] Protection, should pay out of his Estate his proportion of the maintenance of it. But still it must be with his own Consent, i.e., the Consent of the Majority, giving it either by themselves, or their Representatives chosen by them" (II, 140).[20]

Locke's notion of consent can also help to make sense of the "enough, and as good" limitation's role in a developed system of private ownership. It is natural to read that proviso as a requirement that others will not be made worse off in any significant respect because of acts of appropriation. The correct interpretation of this limitation (if it is a limitation) on appropriation is an important challenge because, if the limitation is read in a way that is too demanding, it has the potential to undermine all acts of private appropriation. With this problem in mind, Robert Nozick ruled out those interpretations of the proviso requiring that nonowners continue to enjoy unimpeded opportunities to appropriate. In his view, such a condition would only have been satisfied under conditions of very primitive appropriation. And, as he says, "if the proviso no longer holds [outside of those conditions], then it cannot ever have held so as to yield permanent and heritable property rights."[21] This is because if, at any point, an act of appropriation violates the proviso by depriving some later person of an opportunity to appropriate, then the appropriation immediately prior to that invalid one must also have violated the proviso (by making it impossible for

---

[19] See Jacqueline Stevens, "The Reasonableness of John Locke's Majority," POL. THEORY 24 (1996): 423, 439 ("In the state of nature, property can be parted with only by direct individual consent; in political society, that individual consent is implied by political membership in a community that follows the will of the majority. Consent in political society refers to the prerogative to elect an assembly, not to decide when it is OK to follow laws regulating one's property.").

[20] See Willmoore Kendall, *John Locke and the Doctrine of Majority Rule* (1959), 90–111 (arguing that Locke's position in the second treatise is that "the commonwealth's judgments are the individual's own judgments, and…they are the individual's judgments even when he consciously disagrees with them").

[21] Robert Nozick, *Anarchy, State, and Utopia* (1974), 176.

the subsequent appropriator to appropriate) and so on, until the objection zips back all the way to the first appropriation.

Nozick attempts to solve this problem by watering down the sufficiency restriction so it means only that – all things considered – nonappropriators must be better off under a system of private property than they would have been without such a system.[22] The problem with Nozick's interpretation is that it only works to avoid the zipper problem by ignoring the very real ways in which the loss of the ability to appropriate can make nonappropriators worse off than they would have been in a state of nature with no system of property. As Stephen Munzer has observed, "someone is worse off if previous acquisitions have generated powerful rights of ownership while he can now obtain only rights of use."[23] Nozick simply helps himself to the assumption that it is possible to determine that the ways in which nonappropriators are better off (due to the existence of a system of property) outweigh (on the same scale) the ways in which nonappropriators are worse off.

In addition to this assumption of some unitary metric to measure what it means for a system of property to make us "better off," Nozick's comparison of modern capitalism with a propertyless state of nature in our distant past derives at least some of its force from the opacity of the historical record. For all we know, the immediate consequence of individual acts of appropriation may have been to make many nonappropriators worse off, a situation that might have persisted for a significant period of time, perhaps even for several generations, before the existence of a mature system of private ownership began to pay dividends for society as a whole. Nozick's argument ignores the possibility that the material progress facilitated by a system of private ownership might not move in a steady upward trajectory for all the people subject to it.[24]

Waldron offers a different way to avoid the zipper problem. He argues that Locke did not intend the "enough, and as good" restriction as a limitation on justified appropriation at all, but rather as merely descriptive of early acts of appropriation.[25] Still, the requirement that appropriation not impair the position of others does seem to be a crucial part of Locke's argument for the permissibility of taking property out of the commons. That argument depends not only on the creation of

---

[22] Ibid., 176–7.
[23] See Munzer, *Theory of Property*, 270 (emphasis omitted).
[24] This observation does not make Nozick's reading incoherent. After all, it might be that acts of appropriation that were (on Nozick's reading) illegitimate at the time they occurred can become legitimate once conditions improve. But this possibility raises considerable complications for Nozick's strict historical-entitlement theory of distributive justice. To take just one example, assuming that transactions that occurred during the time when the appropriations were not yet legitimate continue to have some impact on the distribution of property today, are we obligated to respect the validity of those transactions, and therefore their distributive consequences?
[25] Waldron, *Private Property*, 209–18.

moral entitlement in the laborer, but also on the permissibility of extinguishing the community's rights to the raw materials on which she labors. And, since private property rights persist indefinitely and therefore constitute ongoing limitations on the community's previously unfettered access to the commons, it is difficult to cabin the "enough, and as good" limitation to the first generation of appropriators.

A third possibility exists, one that simultaneously avoids the difficulties of Nozick's watered down, aggregative reading of the proviso and Waldron's refusal to treat it as a limitation at all. In this approach, each person would remain entitled as a matter of natural law to appropriate the means of subsistence. But, within a civil society where there is no longer as much and as good left to appropriate from the commons, individuals may consent (via the decision of their democratically elected representatives) to the substitution of alternative mechanisms for satisfying the entitlement to self-sufficiency. On this view, property rights within civil society are consistent with natural law (i.e., they do not violate the "enough, and as good" proviso) even where new acts of original appropriation are no longer possible, but those property rights rest – at least in part – on a foundation of positive law rather than flowing directly from property rights established in the state of nature.

The state's power to substitute positive law for natural rights is not unlimited, however. Locke's theory of consent does not, for example, permit a majority within civil society to extinguish the right to self-sufficiency altogether. This is because, within Locke's theory of civil society, the duty of self-preservation constrains the power of the democratic commonwealth over individuals in a very special way.[26] A majority may only modify an individual's entitlements in ways that the individual could actually agree to (if so inclined). Thus, a majority might legitimately weaken someone's property rights (e.g., by regulating the use of property or imposing a new tax), because an individual can freely agree to forego claims to property. But it does not follow that a majority can deprive someone of the right to acquire for herself the means of subsistence, because the obligation to work (where necessary) for one's subsistence is an essential component of the broader duty of self-preservation, which Locke views as nonderogable and inalienable (II, 6). That duty is owed to God, and a democratic majority may not act on God's behalf. Nor, for the same reason, can the majority deprive someone of the right to assistance from those with surplus resources when she cannot provide for herself.

The majority can, however, legitimately substitute mechanisms for satisfying one's duty to self-preservation in place of the opportunity to appropriate those means of

---

[26] In failing to recognize the importance of duties, Leo Strauss's reading of Locke seems to go too far in identifying the democratic commonwealth with Hobbes's Leviathan. See Leo Strauss, *Natural Right and History* (1950), 231; see also Tully, *Discourse on Property*, 63; Eric Claeys, "Natural Property Rights and Privatization," Sᴛ. Lᴏᴜɪs L. J. 50 (2006): 721, 732–3.

subsistence from the commons. Wage labor would appear to be one such option.[27] But if a system of property is not to violate the right (and duty) of self-preservation in a context where it is not possible to appropriate the means of subsistence from the commons, the state must ensure that jobs exist for everyone willing and able to work or supply some other means of subsistence. Moreover, in light of Locke's views about the duties of owners not to use their property to drive others into vassalage (I, 42), the sort of wage labor that could legitimately satisfy one's natural right of subsistence must also include a meaningful right of exit. These sorts of nonwaivable limitations on wage labor suggest a significant role for the state to monitor and regulate labor markets, both to safeguard rights of exit and to ensure that wages and working conditions do not fall below minimally acceptable levels.[28]

SOME COMPLICATIONS FOR LOCKE'S THEORY

The usual reading of Locke's labor theory understands him as saying that, by mixing something she owns (her labor) with something she does not own (the raw material on which she labors), a person comes to acquire a private property right to the object of labor. This interpretation is subject to numerous questions concerning the scope of the rights created. What rights do I acquire in the land if I merely encircle an unimproved plot with a fence? How much land do I come to own if I have cleared but not enclosed? Do the rights so created include the right to exclude recreational users? To exploit mineral wealth or to leave the property by will upon my death? Perhaps most fundamentally, however, the argument is subject to Nozick's justly famous critique:

> [W]hy isn't mixing what I own with what I don't own a way of losing what I own rather than a way of gaining what I don't? If I own a can of tomato juice and spill it in the sea so that its molecules (made radioactive, so I can check this) mingle evenly throughout the sea, do I thereby come to own the sea, or have I foolishly dissipated my tomato juice?[29]

As Sreenivasan has observed, in addition to relying on a non sequitur (for the reasons Nozick's juice example brings out), the traditional understanding of Locke's labor

---

[27] See Sreenivasan, *Limits of Lockean Rights*, 50–4.

[28] But see Tomlins, *Freedom Bound*, 373 ("Patriarchy, hierarchy, and coercion to the very lintel of slavery were all...quite compatible with Locke's account of nonpolitical relations."). Our difference with Tomlin's reading is perhaps more a matter of emphasis. Even his interpretation admits that Locke endorses limits to what justice will permit with respect to the content of formally voluntary agreements. This is enough to rule out attributing to Locke the sort of pure libertarian position that Nozick favors, one in which an individual could, through force of want, legitimately sell himself into slavery. See Nozick, *Anarchy, State, and Utopia*, 331.

[29] Nozick, *Anarchy, State, and Utopia*, 175.

argument does not on its face explain why it is that we should understand a human being to own his or her own "Person" and, by extension, the "Labour of his Body and the Work of his Hands." The key premise of the argument is, on the traditional interpretation, simply assumed.[30]

The strength of Nozick's objection – or at least the hypothetical responses available to Locke – will depend on exactly what it is that we understand Locke to be trying to justify. For Nozick, as for other property rights libertarians, the goal of any interesting theory of appropriation is the establishment of full ownership in the underlying object, the sort of ownership on which he can build his robust, historical entitlement theory of distributive justice.[31] Thus, for Nozick's purposes, responses to the tomato juice objection that are compatible with the creation of only limited and contingent property rights are not worthy of serious consideration. For those who do not share Nozick's libertarian project, however, the burden is significantly less onerous.

In light of this, consider a reinterpretation of Locke's argument, which was initially advanced by James Tully and which aims to avoid the force of Nozick's juice objection. Tully's reading takes the labor mixing argument less literally than the traditional understanding.[32] Instead, it views the property argument as an instance of Locke's broader commitment to the principle that a maker is entitled to ownership of the things she intentionally brings into being. This idea of makers' rights is one that appears throughout Locke's thought. It is most conspicuous in his explanation in the *Two Treatises* of God's rights over creation. As Locke puts it, "men being all the workmanship of one omnipotent, and infinitely wise Maker…they are his property" (II, 6). The makers' rights principle also does crucial work in Locke's argument against Filmer's claims on behalf of Adam's absolute paternal rights over his children (I, 52–5).

One of the virtues of the makers' rights reading of Locke's appropriation argument is that the principle that one owns what one makes helps to explain not only why productive labor would confer ownership rights over the thing made, but also why Locke assumes that we own our own labor in the first place. A person owns her own labor because the labor, a self-generated, intentional action, is something the person makes through the exercise of her intellect and will.[33] In a sense, both a person's ownership of labor and ownership of the products of that labor fall within the ambit of the same principle of acquisition.

Of course, a laborer does not make the products of that labor in the same way that Locke understands God to have created human beings out of nothing. Laborers,

[30] Sreenivasan, *Limits of Lockean Rights*, 60–1.
[31] Nozick, *Anarchy, State, and Utopia*, 175.
[32] Tully, *Discourse on Property*, 107–9; Sreenivasan, *Limits of Lockean Rights*, 62–9.
[33] Sreenivasan, *Limits of Lockean Rights*, 65–6.

after all, work with the raw material provided by God's act of creation. The logic of the analogy between productive labor and creation suggests that, while God, who creates out of nothing, has absolute rights over his creation, human makers, who must labor on natural resources created by God, enjoy more limited rights.[34] But how limited are they? While it avoids the juice objection, the makers' rights argument raises its own difficult questions concerning the precise extent of the property rights created through productive labor.

In responding to this difficulty, both the traditional interpretation and the makers' rights interpretation of Locke's argument seem to gain some traction by relying on another assertion that Locke presses at various points. This is his claim that the greatest part of the value in things is the result of human labor. "For 'tis labour indeed," Locke asserts broadly, "that puts the difference of value on everything" (II, 40). In Locke's view, "of the products of the earth useful to the life of man nine tenths are the effects of labour: any, if we will rightly estimate things as they come to our use, and cast up the several expenses about them, what in them is purely owing to nature, and what to labour, we shall find, that in most of them ninety-nine hundredths are wholly to be put on the account of labour"[35] (II, 40).

Within the context of the makers' rights reading, the more convincing Locke's assertion about the source of value, the stronger the property rights it seems to justify, and the less significant the gap between creating ex nihilo and making something out of existing natural resources. Returning to Nozick's juice example, if the individual laborer's work contributes much more to the value of the final product than the raw materials taken from the commons, the juice in the ocean comes to resemble soup in a pan, perhaps mixed with a little water taken from a stream. Because human labor is almost always cooperative, this assertion on behalf of *individual* labor will often be a big "if," as we will discuss at greater length in Chapter 9, even if Locke is right about the (collective) contribution of human labor to a product's value.

The common law of accession provides a useful analogy. According to that doctrine, when someone takes an existing item of personal property belonging to someone else (say, a piece of wood) and innocently transforms it beyond recognition (into, for example, a fine violin) such that the bulk of the value of the transformed item is the result of the appropriator's efforts, the law will usually recognize as superior the laborer's claim of ownership, even though the laborer did not own the original item of personal property. Importantly, however, even under these circumstances, the rights provided by accession are not unqualified. The rights the maker

---

[34] Ibid., 75.
[35] Locke later expands his claim to suggest that 999/1000 parts of the value of property comes from human labor (II, 43).

acquires do not wholly supplant the rights enjoyed by the owner of the original raw materials. The law of accession grants the maker possession of the final product, but it also imposes an obligation on her to compensate the original owner of the raw material.[36]

Of course, Nozick would not be content with this response to his juice objection or with the comparison to accession. He is intent on generating what he calls "full ownership," not merely ownership of the "added value one's labor has produced."[37] For Nozick, the problem is that, even if the residual common increment of value is vanishingly small, it is enough to open the door (however slightly) to the sorts of social claims on private ownership that he wants to rule out.

Although the notion that human labor, and not natural resources, is responsible for the bulk of the value in the things we use initially seems like a compelling response to the soup objection, considering it a bit further reveals some difficulties. Foremost among these is the problem that, in many of Locke's examples of primitive appropriation, the labor involved does not really add much value to the natural resources themselves. If someone is merely gathering acorns, picking apples, or hunting deer, how can she claim that the bulk of the value of these items is provided by her labor? Locke's answer would presumably be that the intrusions of these primitive acts of appropriation on communal ownership rights are so minor in nature that only slight additions of value are required to justify them.

But problems arise even in the case of agriculture or industry, where the increment of value attributable to human labor is no doubt greater (particularly if we include within the relevant labor preparatory work, such as the domestication of plant and animal species, the acquisition of knowledge about local climate, and the development of skills in husbandry). To see why, it is important to remember that Locke's discussion is in terms of *use value* of the objects rather than *exchange value*. That is, his claim about the dependence of value on labor is a claim that the *usefulness* of products to those who consume them is mostly due to human labor that went into their production. It is not a claim about the market value of their constituent parts.[38] And it is not clear that the market value of raw materials approximates their contribution to the use value of the consumed product. As the tremendous rises and falls in oil prices demonstrate, the exchange value of a raw material when ample supplies or substitutes are present is (at best) an indirect measure of use value; the latter may not be revealed until scarcity arises in the absence of an adequate substitute. Natural abundance yields low exchange values for raw materials, but this abundance can

---

[36] See, for example, *Wetherbee v. Green*, 22 Mich. 311 (1871) (Cooley, J.) (discussing the doctrine of accession).

[37] Nozick, *Anarchy, State, and Utopia*, 175.

[38] Waldron, *Private Property*, 192.

mask that much of the use value of the objects we consume ultimately depends on the raw materials from which they are made. Thus, even if we were to use price data to confirm that, under most circumstances, the exchange value of raw materials amounts to only a small percentage of useful products' production costs, this would not constitute a successful defense of Locke's strong assertion.

With this in mind, how are we to weigh that portion of the value contributed by human labor on, say, a corn field? What portion of the use value of corn is contributed by photosynthesis within plant cells? What portion is contributed by the unique chemical properties of water, by the soil-generating activity of earthworms, and by the light and warmth created through nuclear fusion in the sun? While human labor is surely necessary to the earth's successful exploitation, that labor is sterile when it is cut off from the gratuitous generosity of nature.

This is one of the powerful insights behind Cormac McCarthy's novel *The Road*. In that story, a father and son struggle to survive in a landscape barren of plants or animals. In this environment, human choices are reduced to barbaric cannibalism or a relentless search for the few scraps of preserved food that survive from better times. Writer and environmental activist George Monbiot has called the novel "the most important environmental book ever written," describing it as a prolonged meditation on human dependence. McCarthy's story, Monbiot argues, "exposes the one terrible fact to which our technological hubris blinds us: our dependence on biological production remains absolute. Civilisation is just a russeting on the skin of the biosphere...."[39] What Monbiot asserts is true of civilization as a whole is arguably true of the individual acts of human labor on the products of nature. And, as we will discuss in connection with intellectual property in Chapter 9, the task of isolating the value contributed by individual human effort is not simplified when we move to types of consumption for which natural raw materials serve merely as the conduits of communication, as is the case with cultural products. No doubt for reasons such as these, Nozick observes that "[n]o workable or coherent value-added property scheme has yet been devised."[40]

As Matthew Kramer has observed, the situation is not changed if we shift our attention from value to the likelihood that "[w]hen a human being produced useful goods, she brought forth items that would never have materialized if her work (or corresponding work by someone else) had not proceeded."[41] This but-for causation still requires the extinguishment of the claims of all other persons to the raw materials from which the laborer has created the new "useful goods." And it provides no independent reason for denying those claims, since the raw materials were also

[39] George Monbiot, "Civilisation Ends with a Shutdown of Human Concern. Are We There Already?" *The Guardian*, October 30, 2007.

[40] Nozick, *Anarchy, State, and Utopia*, 175.

[41] Matthew H. Kramer, *John Locke and the Origins of Private Property* (1997), at 180–81.

but-for causes of the new goods. Any attempt to prioritize the laborer's rights over those with a claim to the commons on which she labored will depend on something like the value arguments we have already discussed.

In the end, the force of Locke's labor theory of appropriation seems quite uncertain. If we are not interested in using it to defend exceedingly powerful private rights, these complications are probably not too much of a problem. Locke himself did not seem intent on establishing an extremely robust system of private property rights. Nor did he need to establish such absolute rights in order to provide the foundation for his critique of arbitrary government. This is perhaps why he does not discuss in any great detail the actual content of rights acquired when one appropriates property – for example, the "incidents" of ownership. He assumed democratic governments could do the hard work of spelling out the contours of property rights. Indeed, when he does talk about specifics, it is more often to limit private prerogatives than to affirm them. Thus, in the first treatise, he challenges the system of primogeniture by attacking the notion that property owners have the right to direct their entire estates to their oldest sons upon their deaths. Younger children, he says, have "an equal Title with [the oldest son] founded on that Right they all have to maintenance, support and comfort from their Parents," a title that trumps the father's own wishes (I, 81–93). In addition, as we have seen, Locke held that, along with their duties to support their children, owners owe duties of charity to those who cannot provide for themselves. And, perhaps most expansively, Locke said that owners were obligated to submit their property to those regulations and taxes supported by the majority.

Locke's majoritarian conception of consent fits comfortably with his incomplete defense of private appropriation. As we will see in the next section, however, contemporary Lockeans want to defend extremely robust rights of private ownership against collective intervention. For contemporary Lockean libertarians, unlike Locke, private property rights must be powerful enough to constrain the state, even when the state acts with the consent of the majority. And so, for them, the absence of a decisive argument in favor of unqualified entitlement generated by original private appropriation is substantially more problematic than it was for Locke himself.

THE LOCKEAN TRADITION SINCE LOCKE

In the eighteenth and nineteenth centuries, Locke's theory of property was deployed primarily in support of populist arguments to put land into the hands of small farmers and settlers over both (1) Native Americans and (2) absentee speculators. The use of Locke's theory to undermine Native American claims was an easy fit. Indeed, some commentators, such as Barbara Arneil and David Armitage, have argued that one of Locke's principal goals in writing the fifth chapter of the second treatise was precisely to justify English colonial activities in North America, an issue with which he was intimately familiar since he served as the secretary to the proprietors of the Carolina colony from 1669 to 1675.[42] Locke's valorization of labor (by which he meant primarily cultivation) as the mechanism for appropriating land simultaneously weakened the apparent moral legitimacy of claims by native hunter-gatherers and justified the appropriation of tribal lands by agriculturalist settlers.

At first glance, using Locke to argue against absentee ownership requires more of a stretch. Once money has been introduced and civil government established, absentee ownership seems consistent with the contours of Locke's theory, provided that other restrictions – such as spoilation and duties to ensure that others have opportunities to obtain the resources for their subsistence – are satisfied. Nevertheless, in the nineteenth century, settlers on the frontier of the United States frequently drew upon Locke's theory, arguing that in order to validly appropriate wilderness lands, a putative owner "must not only claim it, but annex his labor to it, and make it more fit for the use of man; till this be done it remains in the common stock, and anyone who needs to improve it for his support, has a right."[43] Similarly, the Radical Republicans, whose views were exemplified by Elizur Wright's proposed "Soil to the Tiller" policy, freely drew upon Lockean property theory to argue for the confiscation of slaveholders' property and its redistribution to freedmen.[44] In doing so, they grasped onto an important and very real feature of Locke's theory. Although Locke does not rule out other ways of acquiring property once money and laws are in place, there is no denying the affirmative, almost theological value he places on labor as a source of entitlement.[45] And, as Ashcraft has noted, this role of labor in Locke's theory gives it a radical anti-rentier valence.[46] This rhetorical feature of Locke's thought makes its appeal to nineteenth-century radicals perfectly understandable.

In the wake of the Industrial Revolution, however, the dominant interpretations of Locke underwent a dramatic revision. In the early twentieth century, the most salient property disputes revolved around the efforts of industrial property owners to resist state regulation and redistribution at the hands of the majority. Twentieth-century interpreters of Locke began to understand his discussion of private appropriation primarily through the lens of these conflicts. This focus led them to emphasize Locke's defense of property against (arbitrary) government (which they now took to refer to government more generically) and to downplay his majoritarian political

[42] See Barbara Arneil, *John Locke and America* (1996); David Armitage, "John Locke, Carolina, and the *Two Treatises of Government*," POL. THEORY 32 (2004): 602.

[43] Gregory H. Nobles, "Breaking into the Backcountry," WM. & MARY QUARTERLY 46 (1989): 655 (quoting a 1798 pamphlet by Maine settler and pamphleteer James Shurtleff).

[44] See Richard J. Ellis, "Radical Lockeanism in American Political Culture," WESTERN POL. Q. 45 (1992): 825, 835.

[45] See Eric Claeys, "Jefferson Meets Coase," NOTRE DAME L. REV. 85 (2011): 1399.

[46] Ashcraft, *Revolutionary Politics*, 281–3.

theory. In contrast to the earlier nineteenth-century readings of Locke's labor theory as supporting egalitarian and redistributive policies, twentieth-century interpreters began to paint a picture of Locke as a defender of capitalist accumulation and rights of property. Leo Strauss, for example, ignored Locke's discussion of owners' duties to share, concluding that "Locke's doctrine of property is directly intelligible today if it is taken as the classic doctrine of 'the spirit of capitalism'" in which limitless and self-interested accumulation is both just and desirable.[47] C. B. Macpherson agreed with this assessment, famously asserting that Locke had tried to make the case, not for the justice of limited appropriation within the bounds set by the correlative needs of others, but rather limitless appropriation and boundless accumulation.[48]

In adopting this reading of Locke as a proto-capitalist, Locke's critics from the left, whose interests were in making room for regulation and redistribution, found common ground with libertarian conservatives, who wanted to protect private owners from that same regulation and redistribution. Over the course of the past hundred years, this libertarian reading of Locke has become the dominant one. Credit for this dominance goes to Nozick and, especially among American property scholars, Richard Epstein. Particularly in his early work, Epstein drew heavily on Locke's authority in support of his own classical liberal conception of private property rights and limited government.[49]

Although their theories differ in a number of respects, Nozick and Epstein both do away with Locke's theistic, natural law framework with its affirmative obligations of self-preservation and assistance to others. Instead, they favor a strictly negative community in which people merely owe one another duties of noninterference. Thus, they dramatically modify Locke's starting point of God's grant of the world to everyone in common, with its overlapping original common rights, supplanting it with a world in which all resources are originally unowned.

Epstein believes that these modifications open the door to a more robust conception of private ownership rights and, consequently, a more constrained civil government. He says, for example, that Locke would have reached the "proper" position if he had "dispensed with the idea of divine justification for private property" and adopted the view that "no one owned the external things of the world until the first possessor acquired them."[50]

As Nozick recognizes, very little changes if one begins with the assumption of a negative community. Even in a world of unowned resources, he says, "an object's coming under one person's ownership changes the situation of all others. Whereas

---

[47] Strauss, *Natural Right and History*, 246.
[48] C. B. Macpherson, *The Political Theory of Possessive Individualism* (1961), 194–262.
[49] See Richard A. Epstein, *Takings* (1985).
[50] Epstein, *Takings*, 11.

previously they were at liberty (in Hohfeld's sense) to use the object, they now no longer are."[51] This restriction on the liberty of nonowners still generates a need to explain how unilateral acts of appropriation can create rights worthy of respect by others. Remarkably, while Nozick acknowledges the problems Locke's labor theory of appropriation has in trying to solve this puzzle, he never provides his own alternative. Neither does Epstein.

Perhaps the reason for this omission is that they both believe that the restrictions on liberty entailed by private acts of appropriation do not make nonowners worse off. This is because, on their view, the creation of a system of private ownership on the basis of that appropriation "increase[s] the social product by putting the means of production in the hands of those who can use them most efficiently."[52] Epstein takes what is implicit in Nozick and makes it explicit, arguing that private property rights are justified whenever they make nonowners better off than they would have been in the state of nature.[53] This argument, however, has far more in common with Paretian welfarist theories than with Lockean natural law.

Although Epstein embraces this connection,[54] Nozick denies that his approach to justifying private acquisition makes his theory a utilitarian account of property. "These considerations enter a Lockean theory to support the claim that appropriation" does not violate the rights of nonowners, "not as a utilitarian justification of property."[55] But, as Sreenivasan correctly observes, Nozick's argument relies heavily (though implicitly) on a welfarist account of what it means for an appropriation to make nonowners worse off, one that shares a great deal with the utilitarian modes of analysis we discussed in Chapter 1. It avoids the charge of utilitarianism only by operating on an individual-by-individual basis rather than focusing on aggregate well-being.[56] But the significance of this difference is substantially mitigated by three features of Nozick's account: (1) his narrow conception of what it means to be worse off; (2) his choice, as his baseline of comparison, of the state of nature without a system of private ownership; and especially (3) his assertion that a system of private ownership is justified, even if it makes someone worse off compared to the low baseline of the state of nature, provided that it compensates her for the harm.

None of these moves, however, is uncontroversial, particularly for someone who embraces individual liberty and rejects welfarist assumptions about its exchangeability with other values. It is arguable, for example, that a nonowner is made worse off, even as compared to the nonownership state of nature, because in the world of

---

[51] Nozick, *Anarchy, State, and Utopia* 175.

[52] Ibid., 177.

[53] Epstein, *Takings*, 11. For a discussion of the Pareto criterion of social choice, see Chapter 1.

[54] See Richard Epstein, "One Step Beyond Nozick's Minimal State," Soc. & Pol. Phil. 22 (2005): 286.

[55] Nozick, *Anarchy, State, and Utopia*, 177.

[56] Sreenivasan, *Limits of Lockean Rights*, 130–9.

private property, she loses access to the means of obtaining her subsistence. In the state of nature, she has access to those resources without needing the permission of others, whereas in the modern ownership society, she must obtain permission from private owners in order to make a living. Although she may be better off if we confine our focus to the material domain, it would be a perfectly plausible position for someone to claim that she is worse off nonetheless. Moreover, as Kramer has correctly observed, even in narrowly material terms "any number of people could do better in a regime of bare privileges-without-concrete-rights than in a regime of private property.... [P]eople endowed with certain characteristics would be apt to secure more goods in a state of nature unmarked by any proprietary rights than in a state of nature bestrewn with such concrete rights...."[57] Only by abstracting from the actual individual (i.e., denying that this sort of tradeoff may plausibly be experienced as a loss) or by forcing the individual to accept externally determined monetary compensation for this loss can Nozick rule out this objection to his argument for private appropriation. To his credit, Epstein is far more forthright than Nozick about the coercive and ultimately utilitarian nature of these tradeoffs.[58]

Nozick and Epstein both follow Locke in proposing a contractarian account of the move from property owning individuals in a state of nature to a civil society whose principal justification is its superior ability to safeguard that property. But both Nozick and Epstein reject Locke's majoritarian conception of consent within civil society, and therefore reject Locke's apparently permissive attitude toward state-sponsored regulation and redistribution. Nozick appears to believe that what he calls the "minimal state," and only the minimal state, can form through the consent of property owners.[59] Within this minimal state, no redistribution will be permitted, and regulation will only be permissible to the extent that it prevents property owners from violating one another's rights. Although critical of Locke's majoritarianism, Epstein also rejects Nozick's demand for actual consent before the state may alter private property rights. He argues instead that the state is justified in coercing the acquiescence of private owners in its activities, but only if it provides them with in-cash or in-kind compensation as well as a fair share of the surplus generated by the "taking."[60] Nevertheless, Epstein views this compensation requirement as constraining the state from undertaking the sorts of redistributive acts that Locke's theory of consent would seem to permit. On his view, the government must ensure that individuals retain their relative share of the society's wealth.

Having jettisoned Locke's assumption of original common ownership, his theistic natural law framework (with its obligation of charity), and his majoritarian theory of

[57] Kramer, at 126.
[58] See Epstein, "Beyond Nozick."
[59] See Nozick, *Anarchy, State, and Utopia*, chap. 4–5.
[60] See Epstein, "Beyond Nozick, at 289–96; 334–8.

consent, Nozick and Epstein – Locke's foremost contemporary disciples – seem to have taken us very far from the circumstances that motivated Locke to write the *Two Treatises*. Instead of a theory of limited private property rights in the service of an argument for majoritarian government, twentieth-century Lockeans have offered us a theory of limited majoritarian government in the service of private property rights. Locke's egalitarian and democratic theory, which he conceived to protect individual property owners from the arbitrary acts of an absolute monarch and its aristocratic allies, has become a theory for protecting property owners (no matter how powerful) from the redistributive acts of a democratic legislature.[61] To paraphrase Karl Polanyi, however, only by serious misconception could Locke's seventeenth-century meanings be applied to our twenty-first century ideological conflicts.[62] This is not itself an argument for or against Nozick's or Epstein's particular answers to these twenty-first century questions, but it is an argument against the claim that Locke's position is the one typically ascribed to him within contemporary property scholarship.

[61] See Tully, *Discourse on Property*, 172.
[62] See Karl Polanyi, *The Great Transformation* (1944), 233.

3

Hegelian Property Theory

Probably less familiar and perhaps less intuitive than theories based on liberty and utility, or welfare, is a third strand of property thought. This line of thinking about property steers away from the social contract-based individual rights of libertarianism as well as an emphasis on aggregate social utility or welfare which seemingly sacrifices concern for the individual. Instead, it focuses our attention on the ways in which property contributes to development of the self, or personality.

This chapter will examine the personality theory in both its classical and modern iterations. We begin with a brief and necessarily truncated account of Georg W. F. Hegel's theory, commonly considered the source of property theories that stress property's role in self-realization. We then turn to a modern variation of the personality theory, Margaret Jane Radin's "personhood" theory. Radin's theory owes certain elements to Hegel, but her theory differs from the classical personality in several important respects. Finally, we will evaluate both versions of the personality theory, identifying some problems and discussing ways in which Hegel's and Radin's theories make valuable contributions to understanding property as a concept and as an institution.

HEGEL'S PERSONALITY THEORY OF PROPERTY

The personality theory of property, or personhood theory, as it is commonly known today, is usually traced to Hegel's discussion of property in the *Philosophy of Right*.[1] Hegel's account of property, unlike that of utilitarians, is a rights-based theory rather than a consequentialist theory.[2] Its justification for property has nothing to do with promoting a collective good such as happiness (which Hegel regarded as ephemeral)

---

[1] Georg W. F. Hegel, *Hegel's Philosophy of Right*, trans. T. M. Knox (1952). All quotes and references from Hegel will be taken from this translation.

[2] Accord Jeremy Waldron, *The Right to Private Property* (1988), 343–51; Alan Brudner, *The Unity of the Common Law: Studies in Hegelian Jurisprudence* (1995) 30–8. Waldron characterizes Hegel's theory

or social utility. Rather, its reasons are rooted in a concern with the individual's free will. Hegel's theory shares with libertarian accounts of property a fundamental concern with promoting individual freedom, but the similarity between the two theories ends there.

It has become common to describe the difference between the Lockean and Hegelian conceptions of freedom in terms made famous by Isaiah Berlin, who called attention to the distinction between "negative" and "positive" liberty.[3] The former refers to the absence of interference or constraints, particularly from the state; the latter means acting, or at least being able to act, in such a way that one controls one's own life and is able to experience self-realization. As we saw in Chapter 2, the libertarian conception of individual freedom focuses solely on the enjoyment of a sphere of noninterference. This is not how Hegel conceived of freedom or liberty. For Hegel, freedom is inextricably linked with personality. He defines a *person* as "a unit of freedom aware of its sheer independence." What Hegel means by that is that a person is able to develop a consciousness of self-awareness. This consciousness is a matter of detaching one's self mentally from one's needs and wants in such a way that one is able to regard these as not one's own, at least not entirely. Through this process of self-constitution a person is able to acquire a more purely abstract awareness of herself, developing what J. E. Penner terms the will that is "free *for itself*."[4] This is the crucial step in the process of self-development, for in Hegel's account, freedom is important not for instrumental reasons, but for its own sake. Freedom *is* the end.

Having once developed the will that is free for itself, a person is then able to relate it back to her particular needs and wants so that she now perceives those needs and wants, not as given attributes of herself, but as chosen. This is the point at which a person realizes true freedom. This is also the point at which personality is fully realized, for being a person is the ability to understand oneself in this way. Both steps – detaching from the particular to the abstract or universal, and then from the abstract back to the particular – are necessary for the development of the personality.

---

as a "GR [for general right]-based" theory, which he distinguishes from an "SR [for special right]-based" theory. The distinction is useful. Waldron defines a rights-based theory for private property as one "which takes an individual interest to be sufficiently important in itself to justify holding others (especially the government) to be under duties to create, secure, maintain, or respect an institution of private property." Waldron, *Private Property*, 115. An SR-theory regards an interest as having this importance not in and of itself, but by virtue of some contingent event or set of circumstances. Waldron, *Private Property*, 116. A GR-based theory conversely does not take the interest's importance to depend on the existence of any contingent facts. Rather, the importance it ascribes to the interest is a result of the character of the interest itself. Waldron, *Private Property*, 116.

3   Isaiah Berlin, "Two Concepts of Liberty," in *Four Essays on Liberty* (1969; new ed. 2002). The distinction between positive and negative senses of liberty actually can be traced back at least to Kant.

4   J. E. Penner, *The Idea of Property in Law* (1997), 171.

A person is a subject who self-consciously realizes freedom by realizing her needs and wants as chosen rather than given.

We said that a will that is free of itself is a will that makes choices, with freedom as the purpose of such choices. This was not an abstract concept for Hegel. The whole point of his theory of personality and freedom was to show how a person develops into a member of an ethical community in the actual world. Hegel believed that the will that is free of itself is intelligible only in the context of concrete human existence. As Penner states, "Freedom is situated in human society."[5]

Rejection of the Social Contract

Hegel's interest in the personality or will, its development, and the realization of freedom arose for very nonlibertarian reasons. First, Hegel has no truck with any sort of contractualist view of the state. He states, "The intrusion of this contractual relation, and relationships concerning private property generally, into the relation between the individual and the state has been productive of the greatest confusion in both constitutional law and public life" (par. 75). Although he does share with Locke a desire to establish a theoretical basis for a commitment to the individual's sovereignty over things acquired in isolation, Hegel rejects the entire social contract tradition. His starting point in *Philosophy of Right* – the individual willing subject who is the bearer of abstract rights – holds some resemblance to the starting point in many social contract theories, including Locke's, but this does not reflect any ontological assumption that the willing individual is an atom who is the basic building block from which society is constructed. Rather, its purpose is to show how the simple willing individual becomes determinate only by becoming embedded, through property, in more complex and ethically higher social contexts. The development of personality is far more communal for Hegel than it is for any social contract theorist.

Hegel's Concept of "Right"

The actual social relations that result from the choices made by free wills hold the key to understanding Hegel's concept of right. Hegel defines *right* as "freedom as Idea."[6] An "Idea," in Hegel's sense, is what a concept comes to mean for us as we encounter it in the real world.[7] So freedom as idea is freedom fully realized or actualized. Hence, right is some phenomenon in the actual world that embodies free

---

5 Ibid., 172.
6 Hegel, *Philosophy of Right*, par. 29.
7 See ibid., translator's notes, par. 1, n. 2.

will (Hegel calls this an "*existent*.").[8] Hegel regards right as "something sacrosanct" because it is "the embodiment of... self-conscious freedom."[9] Stated differently, the importance of right for Hegel lies in its role in developing and sustaining the free will, or personality: It is a necessary condition for personality.

Just as, for Hegel, the self conceived of as simple and abstract gains determinacy only once it is situated within a social context, so also the right develops. We begin with abstract right, the first stage. Abstract right is a logical construct, not a historical stage. Similarly, the human subject at this stage is a logical construct, abstracted from actual human. At this stage "right" is understood in purely formal terms. It is abstracted from particulars of human lives and from the contents of their wills. It includes only what is necessary to sustain the personality of the subject holder of the right. As Hegel states, "[T]he imperative of right is: 'Be a person and respect others as persons.'"[10] In this form, the right is essentially negative in the sense that it protects the will's capacity to detach from particular aspects of the actual world. We are not yet engaging with the world. At this stage the right is only a capacity for engagement with the actual world; it is a sort of preparatory stage for entering and engaging with the actual world, the next stages in the development of the self. This is why Hegel says that "abstract right is... only a possibility, and to have a right is therefore to have only a permission or a warrant."[11] Only in later stages of the free will's development, which Hegel called "Morality," and the final stage, "Ethical Life," does the individual become fully integrated with all of the concrete details of her life. Before she arrives at that final stage of ethical development, however, the individual must first encounter the external world in order to begin the process of reintegrating her personality as bare universality with the particularities of her life. For, as Hegel states, "A person must translate his freedom into an external sphere in order to exist as Idea."[12] Existence as idea is the endpoint in the entire process of development of the personality that Hegel sets out in *Philosophy of Right*.[13]

Externalizing Personality through Property

But just how is it, according to Hegel, that a person goes about this process of translating bare universal freedom into the actual? How does the personality develop from the cold abstract form into a form that is concrete and more familiar to us? The

---

[8]   Hegel, *Philosophy of Right*, par. 29, n. 1.
[9]   Ibid., par. 30.
[10] Ibid., par. 36.
[11] Ibid., par. 38.
[12] Ibid., par. 41.
[13] See Waldron, *Private Property*, 355.

answer is, simply, property. As Hegel states, "Personality is that which struggles...to claim th[e] external world as its own" (39[3]). Property is the necessary medium through which the process of individual and social development occurs.[14] As Penner succinctly puts it, "Property is the relation of personality to the external sphere of things, understood in terms of free will."[15]

To grasp Hegel's concept of the relationship between personality and property, we need first briefly to consider his notion of externalizing the free will. A fundamental element of Hegel's theory is the concept that the free will, at every stage of its development, necessarily is embodied in something. The notion of a disembodied or transcendent free will made no sense to Hegel. Initially, embodiment begins in individual human beings and develops from there into higher forms of embodiment, but free will must always proceed from the initial stage of embodiment in subjects or individuals, into the external world. It is in the external world that universal embodiment can be realized.[16] For the individual subject, the evolution begins more prosaically, with the individual locating her personality in the world of things. Through the (seemingly) simple processes of possessing, controlling, and owning material goods, the individual subject transcends the initial stage at which her will is merely an aspect of her inner life, extending the will as an objective feature of the external world.

What Can Be "Things"?

Now, what is the nature of the things of the external world that may objectify the free will? What is Hegel's idea of things? In a famous passage, he states, "A person has as his substantive end the right of putting his will into any and every thing making it his, because it has no such end in itself and derives its destiny and soul from his will" (par. 44). This statement not only identifies a person's destiny; it also provides a large clue regarding Hegel's notion of the nature of things. Things have no will in and of themselves; hence, unlike persons, they have no ethical status. This is why in the next sentence Hegel is able to say that a person has "the absolute right of appropriation...over all 'things.'"

The things that Hegel has in mind are quite wide-ranging. They certainly include objects of nature. Hegel emphasized man's domination over nature.[17] He says that the "determinate character assigned to nature...is inherent externality" (par. 42). That is, nature is absolutely external to itself; it cannot be conscious of

---

[14] See ibid., 348.
[15] See Penner, *Idea of Property in Law*, 173.
[16] See Waldron, *Private Property*, 355.
[17] See Peter G. Stillman, "Property, Freedom, and Individuality in Hegel's and Marx's Political Thought," in *Nomos XXII: Property*, ed. J. Roland Pennock and John W. Chapman (1980) 130, 137–40.

its concept. Nature is the logical opposite of the subject and cannot be external to itself because it is not and cannot be conscious of itself.[18] In Hegel's philosophical idealism, nature, and all of the external world, has no reality apart from its reality for individual subjects' minds. Whatever reality the external world has it gets from the human mind.

This suggests that things extend far beyond objects in nature. Anything other than another individual is potentially a thing for Hegel. Hence, he states:

> Mental aptitudes, erudition, artistic skill, even things ecclesiastical (like ser-
> mons, masses, prayers, consecrations of votive objects), inventions and so forth,
> *become subjects of a contract, brought on to a parity, through being bought and
> sold, with things recognized as things....* Attainments, erudition, talents, and
> so forth, are, of course, owned by free mind and are something internal and
> not external to it, but even so, *by expressing them it may embody them in some-
> thing external and alienate them... and in this way they are put into the category
> of things.* Therefore they are not immediate at the start but only acquire this
> character through the mediation of mind which reduces its inner possessions to
> immediacy and externality.[19]

This passage requires some unpacking. The emphasized portions of the passage make clear the importance that Hegel places on contract and alienation generally as the basis of things. Only through alienation in contract does property truly become manifest, according to Hegel; it is only through contract that property becomes fully externalized.[20] Hegel states, "Contract brings into existence the property whose external side, its side as existent, is no longer a mere 'thing' but contains the moment of a will (and consequently the will of a second person also)" (par. 72).

Once it is clear that alienation is the key to thingness, it becomes apparent that certain interests internal to the self cannot be things, for they cannot be alienated in the way Hegel describes and prescribes. Notably, such interests include those substantive internal characteristics that constitute the self. Such interests cannot be alienated because alienation requires, according to Hegel, that a person withdraw her will from the thing, and one cannot withdraw her will from the very consti-tutive internal characteristics of her personality. Hegel states, "[T]hose goods, or rather substantive characteristics, which constitute my own private personality and the universal essence of my self-consciousness are inalienable and my right to them is imprescriptible" (par. 66). Hegel identifies these inalienable characteristics as "my personality as such, my universal freedom of will, my ethical life, my religion."

---

[18] See Hegel, *Philosophy of Right*, translator's notes to par. 42.
[19] Hegel, *Philosophy of Right*, par. 43 (emphasis added).
[20] James Penner has trenchantly critiqued Hegel's error here in conflating *in personam* and *in rem* rights, rendering all of them as *in rem* rights. See Penner, *Idea of Property in Law*, 177–8.

It would seem, then, that all other interests, including intellectual property, are capable of being treated as things.[21]

Three Modes of Embodying the Will

We have seen that for Hegel a person's destiny is to embody her will in external objects. Exactly how, though, does a person go about embodying her will in the things of the world? There is an apparent similarity between Hegel's notion of embodiment and Locke's method of acquiring ownership by mixing one's labor with unowned things. But the similarity is misleading. One way of seeing the difference between the two is to understand Locke as saying that a person places her labor, and so, an aspect of herself, into the object, whereas for Hegel, the person-object relation is reversed, that is, the external is internalized. There is no loss of the will, or self, into the external thing; rather, the will is made objective through the self's appropriation of the thing for the purpose of controlling it.

Hegel identifies *possession* as the means by which one embodies one's will in an object (par. 53). He describes three modes of taking possession: (1) directly *grasping* it; (2) *forming* it; and (3) *marking* it (par. 54). Hegel states that grasping a thing is "the most complete" of these modes "because then I am directly present in this possession, and therefore my will is recognizable in it" (par. 55). The value of this mode is limited, however, because it lasts only so long as the act of grasping itself does. Moreover, the mode is available only if the object grasped is *res nullius*, meaning not already owned by another. More important is the second mode, imposition of form. The basis for this method of acquisition is rewarding investment of time and labor. It is the idea that the gap between the subjectivity of the will and the external world has been bridged.[22] Hegel states, "When I impose a form on something, the thing's determinate character as mine acquires an independent externality and ceases to be restricted to my presence here and now and to the direct presence of my awareness and will" (par. 56). So if I make a sculpture out of a piece of raw bronze, then that aspect of the bronze that cannot be understood except in relation to my will's having worked on it becomes a characteristic of the bronze itself.

The third mode of embodying the will is that of marking an object. The notion here is that the will is not actual but rather is represented.[23] Hegel states, "The meaning of the mark is supposed to be that I have put my will into the thing" (par. 58). One way of understanding how marks on objects perform this function is to interpret a mark such as one's signature on some object that one claims to own as publishing

[21] See Jeanne L. Schroeder, "Unnatural Rights: Hegel and Intellectual Property," *U. Miami L. Rev.* 60 (2006): 453.

[22] See Waldron, *Private Property*, 364–5.

[23] See Dudley Knowles, "Hegel on Property and Personality," *Phil. Q.* 33 (1983): 45, 51.

that claim for the rest of the world to see. The mark does not prevent loss by theft, but it does announce to the world the maker's intended claim to ownership.

After discussing the three modes of taking possession, Hegel turns to the *use* of an object. The crucial sentence in Hegel's discussion is a bit obscure (like much of Hegel): "The use of the thing is my need for being externally realized through the change, destruction, and consumption of the thing" (par. 59). What Hegel seems to emphasize here is action. He indicates just two paragraphs later that *having* something is not enough, in and of itself, to establish a true property relation with the thing: "The relation of use to property is the same as that of substance to accident" (par. 61A). Action is needed to perfect the will's relation with the object and to externalize the will. The action may be negative, as in eating the object so that it no longer exists, or positive, as in building it, but some form of affirmative action is necessary.

Finally, Hegel turns to alienation of property. We have already discussed the great weight that Hegel placed on alienation of property. We have also seen how Hegel defined the limits of property's alienability. Those limits mean that alienability is not essential for something to be mine, for Hegel clearly believed that some goods that one owned could not be alienated. Generally speaking, however, Hegel considered alienability essential for the ethical importance of (external) goods. The question is, why?

The answer is not clear. Jeremy Waldron argues that the relationship between property and alienability in Hegel's theory is historical rather than conceptual.[24] That is, since Hegel believed that what is actual is rational and what is actual in Hegel's society is alienability of property, he simply took it as given. This means, Waldron argues, that although Hegel shows that property is necessary for development of the free will, he fails to show that *alienable* property is so necessary.[25]

Hegel's contribution to explaining and justifying private property is quite distinctive. As Alan Ryan states, "The attractions of Hegel's development of the concept of property depend on our everyday feelings about our need to identify with and express ourselves in things that we make, control, and use."[26] Hegel took seriously the idea of the self as free will in a way that no one else did. His greatest contribution to our understanding of property was to show not only how property anchors our free wills in the actual world of objects but, more fundamentally, to explain how property does the work of establishing social relationships. Hegel's self, the self that becomes realized through property, is not an atomistic being. The whole point of the self becoming realized is movement toward high stages of ethical development that lead to membership in ethical communities – the family, then civil society, and

[24] See Waldron, *Private Property*, 368–9.
[25] See ibid., 369.
[26] Alan Ryan, *Property and Political Theory* (1984), 131.

eventually the state. As the free will becomes realized in property, others are then able to relate to the self. Property is not the basis for withdrawal from others but precisely the opposite: It is the foundation for socialization with others.[27]

The Modern Significance of Hegel's Theory of Property

Hegel's theory of property is important for more than just historical reasons. Its modern significance is twofold: First, it provides the basis for both justifying and limiting private ownership of property on the idea of self-development; second, it establishes a constitutive relationship among private property, personal identity, and community. These themes have as much resonance today as they did in Hegel's time, and no other property theory emphasizes them to the degree that Hegel's does.

Hegel offers us a property theory that, unlike utilitarianism and its cognates, does not reduce private ownership to the common good of the community but at the same time allows modifications of property rights in service of the common good consistent with preserving property as a right. This is a perspective from which to repudiate legal realist-inspired understandings of ownership as purely a nominal construct that can be manipulated in virtually any way one wishes in the interest of some ultimate collective goal. From the Hegelian perspective, the determination of property rights precedes considerations of the common good. Possession, use, and alienation are property rights that exist prior to the common good and to public regulation. Moreover, these rights should be treated as parts of a unitary whole rather than as separate elements that can be removed or destroyed without affecting the whole itself.[28]

At the same time, considerations of the common good are hardly irrelevant to property in Hegel's theory. Property rights, once determined, may be modified in the interests of the common good. As Alan Brudner aptly puts it, the common good, in Hegel's formulation, overrides property but does not define what it means.[29] So long as it does not undermine the existence of the property right itself, the legislature may modify the property right in the interest of the community. This is because the owner is not an isolated self, but situated within an ethical community and, as a member of that community, obligated to act in the community's general well-being. This is a perspective from which to see that the ethical community – the state – is not rights-abrogating when it regulates the use of property or exercises the power of eminent domain for public use (so long as compensation is paid).[30] It strives to provide a *via media* between extreme rights theories and rights denying collectivist theories, dissolving the apparent antagonism between individual rights and community goals.

[27] See Stillman, "Property, Freedom, and Individuality," 143.
[28] See Brudner, *Unity of the Common Law*, 83.
[29] Ibid., 82.
[30] See Waldron, *Private Property*, 348.

THE MODERN PERSONHOOD THEORY OF PROPERTY

The most influential contemporary property theory that draws inspiration from Hegel is Margaret Jane Radin's "personhood" theory.[31] Although, Radin claims inspiration from Hegel, her theory departs from Hegel's in important respects.[32] This section will briefly summarize her personhood theory.

Like Hegel, Radin's concern is with the relationship between property and self-development. At the outset of her article, "Property and Personhood," she states, "The premise underlying the personhood perspective is that to achieve proper self-development – to be a *person* – an individual needs some control over resources in the external environment."[33] Property rights, she argues, provide the requisite assurance of control. But, although Radin shares Hegel's insight into the relationship between property and self-development, her understanding of self-development differs significantly from his.

Radin terms her theory an "intuitive" personhood perspective.[34] The core intuition is this:

> Most people possess certain objects they feel are almost part of themselves. These objects are closely bound up with personhood because they are part of the way we constitute ourselves as continuing personal entities in the world.[35]

She gives such examples of these objects as family heirlooms, wedding rings, and the like. A measure of one's boundedness to an object is whether its loss can be relieved by some replacement.[36] Radin's insight about being bound to objects in this way leads her to develop a dichotomy between two kinds of property, which she calls "personal property" and "fungible property."[37] *Personal property* is property bound

---

[31] Radin first developed her personhood theory in her seminal article, Margaret Jane Radin, "Property and Personhood," STAN. L. REV. 34 (1982): 957. She later elaborated on the theory in a series of articles. See, for example, Margaret Jane Radin, "Market-Inalienability," HARV. L. REV. 100 (1987): 1849. See generally Margaret Jane Radin, *Contested Commodities* (1996); Margaret Jane Radin, *Reinterpreting Property* (1993).

[32] Radin notes that her personhood theory departs from Hegel's personality theory in important respects. Notably, she rejects Hegel's initial conception of the self, the self that is abstract and has yet to confront the external. She criticizes Hegel for "thus initially assum[ing] away those characteristics that render individuals unique beings – particular commitments and character traits, particular memories and future plans, particular relationships with other people and with the world of external objects." See Radin, "Property and Personhood," 971–2. But Radin overlooks the fact that Hegel's abstract self is a logical construct only, not a real person, created for the purpose of showing what is necessary for ethical development of the free will.

[33] Radin, "Property and Personhood," 957.

[34] Ibid., 959.

[35] Ibid.

[36] Ibid.

[37] Ibid., 960.

up with a person; *fungible property* is property the loss of which can be relieved through substitutes.[38] Stated more accurately, personal property is bound up with an individual's personhood in a constitutive sense.[39] It is "part of the way [people] constitute [them]selves as continuing personal entities in the world."[40] Radin's primary thesis is that because some goods constitute a person's identity in this sense, goods that promote healthy self-development, what Radin later calls "human flourishing," should be given greater legal protection than fungible property.[41]

Radin concedes that self-identification of personhood through property is subjective, varying from person to person. But Radin is eager that her theory not be reduced to a matter of personal preferences, so she needs some objective index by which to distinguish good from bad identification with objects. She originally located such an index in the concept of person itself, and later substituted the concept of human flourishing to do this work. She characterized her conception of human flourishing as pragmatic, seeking thereby to skirt the problem of locating a foundation for an objective conception of human flourishing.[42] Armed with such a (pragmatic) conception of human flourishing, Radin argues, we can rationally distinguish between those object relations that deserve greater legal protection (because they contribute to human flourishing) and those that do not.

Radin argues that the personhood theory is "implicit in our law."[43] It explains, for example, why in the context of Fifth Amendment takings claims, courts are more willing to let legislatures "destroy the expectation of gain from fungible development rights than [they are] to let the legislature destroy the personality ties someone had invested in a home or land."[44] In later work Radin used the theory to explain and justify controversial programs like rent control.[45]

---

[38] Having introduced these terms as a dichotomy, she later relaxes their relationship with each other by saying that they constitute a continuum. Radin, "Property and Personhood," 986.

[39] Meir Dan-Cohen develops a somewhat similar conception of ownership, one that emphasizes the constitutive aspect of ownership. His analysis explores the connection between ownership and possessive pronouns. He states, "Ownership, as signaled by the application of a possessive pronoun to an object, consists in the permissible inclusion, on a sufficiently enduring, continuous, and exclusive basis, of that object, within the scope of the personal pronouns used by the putative owner." Meir Dan-Cohen, "The Value of Ownership," *J. Pol. Phil.* 9 (2001): 404, 428–9.

[40] Radin, "Property and Personhood," 959.

[41] See Radin, "Market-Inalienability."

[42] Radin had originally sought to base an objective conception of the person in prevailing social consensus. See Radin, "Property and Personhood," 969. Subsequently, however, she disavowed her reliance on consensus and self-consciously embraced modern philosophical pragmatism. See Margaret Jane Radin, "Lacking a Transformative Social Theory: A Response," *Stan. L. Rev.* 45 (1993): 409, 422 n. 42, 423.

[43] Radin, "Property and Personhood," 991.

[44] Ibid., 1007 (footnote omitted). An example of such a distinction might be *Penn Central Transp. Co. v. New York City* 438 U.S. 104 (1978).

[45] See Margaret Jane Radin, "Justice and the Market Domain," in *Nomos XXXI: Markets and Justice*, ed. John W. Chapman and J. Roland Pennock (1989), 165.

CRITIQUING THE PERSONALITY AND PERSONHOOD THEORIES

Perhaps Hegel's greatest contribution to property theory is his insight into how *private* property contributes to self-identification and self-development. A fundamental aspect of what it is to be a person is to see oneself not as isolated, but as nested in various sets of relationships with others. More accurately, personality is constituted in large measure by the reciprocal rights and duties existing between oneself and others. Private property contributes importantly to defining the parameters of this network of rights and duties. In a world where all resources, including scarce resources, are owned in common, the self owes no duties to others (nor they to her), and she may take as much as she wishes, regardless of the effect on others. It is a world of all wants and no duties; the self pays attention only to itself, which is unbounded and ill-defined. But in a world where scarce resources are privately owned, the self is bounded and more clearly defined. A system of private property confers on the self rights and duties that define the self in relation to others vis-à-vis scarce resources. As Waldron states, "[P]roperty protects the development of will by erecting normative fences around the objects in which wills have become embodied."[46]

It is one thing for a theory to justify private property in general terms; it is quite another for a theory to specify the types of private property rights that ought to exist. Hegel's theory falls short of the latter objective. He did not identify in any detail what types of property rights the state ought to recognize, but left the matter to practical reason.[47] He did provide some general parameters of what sort of property right was needed. His system of property was bourgeois and antifeudal.[48] He rejected the old feudal limited forms of ownership and seemed to require a robust form of full ownership that permitted free alienation.[49] Beyond that, it is far from clear whether his system was one that could be adapted to late-stage capitalism as opposed to the bourgeois economy of small business owners in which he lived.[50] An argument that depends strongly, as his does, on owner control of objects seems ill-suited for an economy in which extensive division of labor attenuates the relationship between workers and objects.

Radin's personhood theory has perhaps greater salience for modern society than does Hegel's. Her intuitive view that people are constitutively bound up with certain

---

[46] See Waldron, *Private Property*, 377.

[47] See Schroeder, "Unnatural Rights," 454.

[48] See Ryan, *Property and Political Theory*, 129.

[49] An important qualification must be noted here. These features were necessary at the stage when the abstract will was first becoming actualized. At the later stages when the abstract right has been subsumed within the spheres of morality and ethical community, other considerations become paramount. For example, family property takes precedence over individual property, so that freedom of testation is limited. See Hegel, *Philosophy of Right*, par. 169–71, 178–9.

[50] See Waldron, *Private Property*, 374.

objects appears to have empirical support in social psychology.[51] Of course, it is one thing to say that a human phenomenon exists but quite another normatively to justify its entrenchment in the law. Can we justify giving greater legal protection to those objects that are constitutive of personal identity than to those that are not? One basis for doing so is utilitarian: We defer to people's special attachments to particular objects or interest because of our respect for their personal preferences. This clearly is not Radin's theory. Her basis for according greater legal protection to objects that are constitutive of self-identity is not utility or welfare but human flourishing. A core difficulty with that theory, however, is the notable absence of any rigorous account of what human flourishing means.[52] Waldron provides one possible approach that is consistent with a human flourishing theory. He argues that private property rights can be justified on the basis of the way in which they contribute to the owner's moral development. Private ownership, Waldron contends, "assigns enduring objects to the exclusive control of individuals" who then experience the effects of willing, not only at one time but over a period of time. The individual learns how to act consistently and stably with respect to that object over time.[53] This argument provides a basis for justifying private property rights in general, but it does not explain why greater protection is needed for some objects than for others.

Apart from this problem there lies a deeper problem with the personhood theory. Unlike Hegel's theory which, as we previously noted, stressed how externalizing the will in objects provides a foundation for relationships with others, the personhood theory focuses solely on the autonomous self and its relationship with objects. It has nothing to say about the relational aspect of property. It is true that Radin criticizes Hegel's concept of the abstract person for emptying the self of all content, including relationships with others, as Immanuel Kant did. But beyond conceiving of persons as concrete rather than abstract, Radin has nothing to say about social relationships or the important role that property rights play in creating and fostering relationships. As we discuss in Chapter 5, any adequate concept of human flourishing must pay close attention to the relational dimension of self-development.

---

[51] See Helga Dittmar, *The Social Psychology of Material Possessions: To Have Is To Be* (1992).
[52] See Stephen J. Schnably, "Property and Pragmatism: A Critique of Radin's Theory of Property and Personhood," STAN. L. REV. 45 (1993): 347, 357.
[53] See Waldron, *Private Property*, 372–4.

4

Kantian Property Theory

Among American legal theorists, interest in Immanuel Kant's theory of property has never been as strong as it has been in the theories of Locke, the utilitarians, and even Hegel. Nevertheless, a brief look at Kant's approach to property is appropriate not only because of Kant's general philosophical importance, but also because there are signs of awakening interest in Kant's private law theory among North American legal theorists.[1]

For Locke and Hegel, property is in some sense an extension of the person. Hence, for both, initial acquisition is the normative basis of ownership.[2] Kant's concern, including his consideration of property, is individual freedom, defined as "independence from being constrained by another's choice."[3] The key question in terms of property is, how can free persons interact with one another in using and possessing property while remaining independent?

Kant's view of individual freedom is noninstrumental. It is not a means to some further end – utility, welfare, human flourishing, or whatever – but is an end in itself. Kant supposes that freedom of choice is a universally shared human characteristic. All humans enjoy transcendental freedom by virtue of the mere fact that they are rational beings. Respecting and protecting individual freedom to choose is paramount in Kant's political philosophy.

---

[1] See, for example, Arthur Ripstein, *Force and Freedom: Kant's Legal and Political Philosophy* (2009); Ernest Weinrib, *The Idea of Private Law* (1995).

[2] See Ripstein, *Force and Freedom*, 57 n. 2.

[3] Immanuel Kant, "The Doctrine of Right," part 1 of the *Metaphysics of Morals* in *Practical Philosophy*, trans. and ed. Mary Gregor (1996), 6:237. All references are to the Prussian Academy pagination appearing in the margins of the Academy version.

THE UNIVERSAL PRINCIPLE OF RIGHT

Kant defines the universal principle of right in this way:[4] "Any action is right if it can coexist with everyone's freedom in accordance with a universal law, or if on its maxim the freedom of choice of each can coexist with everyone's freedom in accordance with a universal law."[5] By this Kant means that each person is entitled to be his or her own master, "not in the sense of enjoying some special self-relation, but in the contrastive sense of not being subordinated to the choice of any *other* particular person."[6] Kant describes this universal principle as a "postulate incapable of further proof."[7] But Kant does provide normative arguments for the universal principle, normative arguments that address the problems of the relationships among free persons who can and do come into conflict with one another. For Kant, a person is free and independent insofar as she decides which goals, which ends she will pursue, not encumbered in her choices by the constraints of others, except to the extent necessary to preserve mutual independence. As we will see, this is a strictly formal conception of freedom, devoid of specific content and independent of context or circumstance.[8] Kant aims for a system of equal freedom as an end in itself, a system in which individual freedom means that each person is his or her own master and no one is master of anyone else.

THE INNATE RIGHT — FREEDOM

Kant considers freedom to be the only innate right. He states that freedom "is the only original right belonging to every human being by virtue of his humanity."[9] Protecting this right is, in his view, the only legitimate basis for the state: not welfare, not happiness, only freedom. A general concept of happiness is, he believes, too vague to form the basis of a universal principle of right, and any specific conception of happiness would be only contingent, not universal. The same is true, he argues, of any other empirical good. Only freedom is truly universal.

---

[4] This is the first and most familiar statement of the universal principle. Kant later restates it as an imperative: "[S]o act externally that the free exercise of your choice could coexist with everyone's freedom in accordance with a universal law." Ibid., 6:231.

[5] Ibid., 6:230.

[6] Ibid., 4.

[7] Ibid., 6:231.

[8] As Lewis Beck has pointed out, Kant has at least five different conceptions of freedom. The conception in "The Doctrine of Right" is a negative conception. See Lewis W. Beck, "Five Concepts of Freedom in Kant," in Stephan Körner, *Philosophical Analysis and Reconstruction*, ed. Jan T. J. Srzednicki (1987), 52.

[9] Kant, "The Doctrine of Right," 6:237.

For purposes of securing independence, the innate right of all humans to be free is incomplete in Kant's view. This is so because the innate right only entitles each person to pursue her own purposes through her own body. The innate right is purely formal. It fails to take into account entitlements that apply to a wide array of interests, interests that extend beyond bodily integrity and reputation. More specifically, it does not entitle individuals to pursue their goals through external things, such as objects of property, the actions of others, and the like. Other sorts of rights are needed to implement the innate right in the external world. The need for such wider entitlements, or "acquired" rights, leads to Kant's system of *private rights*. Such a system – which includes the legal areas of property, contract, tort, and other relations between persons – is required if the human capacity for free choice is to be meaningfully exercised. These acquired rights in turn need to be secured and enforced by a common mechanism with the power to establish a "condition of right." The need for such an enforcement agency gives rise to Kant's system of *public rights* and the state.

ACQUIRED RIGHTS

The basis for Kant's system of acquired rights is what Kant calls a postulate of practical reason,[10] a postulate which he treats as an extension of the universal principle of right.[11] According to this postulate,[12] consistency with the innate right requires that each person can rightfully use usable things in pursuit of some end that he or she has.[13] With respect to property rights, in Kant's view, a right to some external object is a right to use that object as a means to some personal end. The problem, Kant says, is that unlike using one's own body, any external object of choice could be yours or it could be mine.[14] This could-be-yours-could-be-mine outlook structures Kant's approach to the whole topic of acquired rights. From the perspective of free choice, every single external object of choice could in theory be yours or mine. Who has the right to the object depends, for Kant, upon which of us performed the

---

[10]   Ibid., 6:246.
[11]   Ibid.
[12]   It is a postulate insofar as it is not deductively demonstrable. But as Paul Guyer explains, "Kant expounds the conditions that make it possible to acquire property consistently with the general principle of right given the fundamental conditions of actual human existence – namely, in the spatio-temporal circumstances of life on the surface of a naturally undivided sphere – without attempting to prove that such conditions can actually be fulfilled otherwise than by means of the practical certainty provided by the moral possibility and indeed necessity of the acquisition of property." Paul Guyer, "Kant's Deductions of the Principles of Right," in *Kant's Metaphysics of Morals: Interpretive Essays*, ed. Mark Timmons (2002), 56.
[13]   See Ripstein, *Force and Freedom*, 19.
[14]   Kant, "The Doctrine of Right," 6:246.

requisite affirmative act, for acquired rights can be established only through some affirmative act.

Kant wants to show that having objects at your disposal as means to pursue your ends is consistent, in a formal sense, with the freedom of others. Unlike Locke, Kant focuses on what it means to have objects as your own rather than on how to acquire them.[15] Acquired rights represent extensions of the universal principle of right so that people can use external objects to pursue their own ends. If people could pursue their own ends solely with their own bodies, there would be no need for acquired rights; the innate right to freedom would be sufficient. But so long as there are usable external objects through which people can pursue their ends, the universal principle of right must be applied so that people have the rightful power to make use of such objects, that is, use that coexists with the freedom of everyone else.[16] Kant states:

> If it were nevertheless absolutely not within my *rightful* power to make use of it [the object], that is, if the use of it could not coexist with the freedom of everyone in accordance with a universal law (would be wrong), then freedom would be depriving itself of the use of its choice with regard to an object of choice, by putting *usable* objects beyond any possibility of being used.... [17]

In this passage Kant underscores the formality of an entitlement to a thing by emphasizing that before an object can be rightfully used, it must first rightfully be subject to one's own choice. He also explains how, by not depriving you of anything you already have, my exercise of my acquired right to property is fully consistent with your freedom.[18]

Kant achieves this consistency by giving the concept of choice a strictly formal meaning. This means that my choice must not depend upon the content of my choice, that is, the specific ends for which I have chosen the external object, but is valid for any possible particular end. External objects are integrated into a formal system of universal freedom insofar as people are physically capable of using those objects as their chosen means for pursuing whatever ends they wish to pursue.

Kant understands property in an external thing, that is, anything external to one's body, in terms of a right to have the thing at one's disposal in pursuing one's own ends.[19] Property in this sense, Kant believes, requires full ownership, and Kant

---

[15] Arthur Ripstein notes that this approach to establishing ownership contrasts with Locke's and Hegel's theories of property. Both Locke and Hegel begin by treating property as an extension of the self; that is, initial acquisition is the normative basis of ownership. By contrast, Kant first establishes the rightfulness of ownership on the basis of the postulate; initial acquisition is a secondary matter on this view. Ripstein, *Force and Freedom*, 57 n. 2.

[16] Kant, "The Doctrine of Right," 6:246.

[17] Ibid.

[18] See Ripstein, *Force and Freedom*, 67.

[19] See ibid.

analyzes ownership in terms of two components: possession and use. Possession is the dominant component in Kant's analysis.[20] He distinguishes between "sensible" and "intelligible" possession. *Sensible possession* is bare physical possession. If I hold a pencil and you snatch it from my hand without my permission, then you have committed a wrong against me by taking the pencil from my physical possession, thereby depriving me of the opportunity to use the pencil to further my ends. Kant thinks that sensible possession is an inadequate conception of rightful possession of an object. An adequate conception of rightful possession must be broader, recognizing that if someone else uses an object that is mine, her use harms me even though I did not physically possess the object or use it at the time. Her use infringes on my freedom by robbing me of the ability to put it to use toward my chosen ends. When I say that I am in rightful possession of the object, I mean not just that I hold it (I might be away from home temporarily), but that I can put it to use for whatever ends I have in mind. Kant wants to show that the idea of being in rightful possession of some object must include the idea of possessing the object regardless of its location in space.[21] He calls this more capacious, nonspatial conception of possession "intelligible" possession.[22] He defines *intelligible possession* simply as "possession of an object *without holding it* . . . ."[23] From his discussion of it, intelligible possession seems tantamount to ownership.[24]

The distinction between sensible and intelligible possession reflects a more fundamental point at the core of Kant's theory of property. In Kant's terms, property is a noumenon, not a phenomenon. This means that property is not a fact that can be empirically discovered or established. Reason alone establishes its reality. What Kant means is that property is not an object but an institution that regulates relationships between and among persons. From this perspective, the validity of the statement that this ball is mine and not yours cannot be established empirically in the way that the statement the earth is round can.

Kant derives this broader conception of possession from the notion of free choice. He bases it on what he argues it means for a person to be able to choose a purpose and to choose the means by which to pursue that purpose. Kant's conception of free choice is strictly formal. You are entitled to set and pursue whatever purposes you choose, however you choose them, if usable objects are available to you through your choice as means to secure those purposes. Regardless of what your purposes are, if you are capable of using the object to secure your purposes, and if it is subject to your choice as a means to set and pursue your purposes, then you have freedom

[20] See Alan Ryan, *Property and Political Theory* (1984), 80.
[21] See Mary Gregor, "Kant's Theory of Property," REV. OF METAPHYSICS 41 (1988): 757, 774.
[22] Kant, "The Doctrine of Right," 6:246.
[23] Ibid. (emphasis in original).
[24] See Howard Williams, "Kant's Concept of Property," PHIL. Q. 27 (1977): 32.

of choice over that object, and your exercise of that freedom does not compromise anyone else's freedom of choice. My freedom of choice with respect to an object is compromised only if your having a property (or contract) right over that object deprived me of something I already had.[25]

TYPES OF ACQUIRED RIGHTS

Kant refers to external things that are possible subjects of acquired rights under the term *objects of choice*. The term is far-reaching. He defines it as anything external to me that I have the ability to use. It includes (1) physical things; (2) other persons' freedom of choice regarding performance of an act; and (3) other people's status in relation to me.[26] So objects of choice include not only corporeal assets but also contract relations and status relations. Arthur Ripstein points out that "[u]nderlying these divisions is the intuitive idea that separate persons who are free to set their own purposes can interact in three basic ways."[27] If people pursue their own purposes without the aid of others, acting autonomously, then the relative relationship is person to object. More commonly perhaps, people pursue their purposes in conjunction with other people, that is, relationally. If those relationships are established consensually, then the people involved give each other contract rights. If, however, the relationships are established nonvolitionally, then rights are acquired by virtue of status.

Property

Acquired rights in property are concerned with external things and how I may possess and use them. I have a property right in an apple (or land) if I have control over it whether or not I physically possess it or use it. That is, so long as I have the right to have the apple at my disposal, to use it to pursue whatever ends I choose, I have a property right in it, or we would say, I own it. So there are two elements, or components, to ownership at work here: possession and use. These need not be actual but may be only potential or entitled. To own something external to me I must be entitled to possess it (e.g., hold the apple in my hand) and use it (e.g., eat it). Bare possession alone doesn't advance my program of securing my chosen ends.

A property right initially looks to be a strictly person-to-thing relation. On closer inspection, however, it does have a relational dimension, one that Kant certainly did not ignore. For Kant is really concerned with the conditions under which it can be said that another has wronged me. Clearly, if I physically hold an apple and you wrest

---

[25] See Ripstein, *Force and Freedom*, 63.
[26] Kant, "The Doctrine of Right," 6:248.
[27] Ripstein, *Force and Freedom*, 66.

it from my hand, Kant says, you have wronged me. Specifically, you have wronged me "with regard to what was *internally* mine (freedom)."[28] But you have not violated any acquired right of mine, only my innate right. What Kant wants to establish is that you wrong me when you take an apple that I possess even without holding it.[29] Any external object creates a potential for incompatibility between your choice and mine. Because it is an object of an acquired right, it could in theory be yours or mine. If the object of choice is mine, it must be subject to my choice if it is in my physical possession. This is so because if I physically possess the object and you interfere with my physical possession, then you have interfered with my person, thereby violating my innate right. But of course I am not always in physical possession of the objects of choice that are mine, and it is possible for you to interfere with my acquired right to such objects without violating my innate right to my person. This is the violation of the acquired right of property. From the perspective of pursuing my chosen ends, it matters not whether I physically possess the apple. Either way, you have wrongfully interfered with the means through which I will pursue my ends. Indeed, you have appropriated that object (the apple) and used it as a means to pursue ends that are not of my choosing whatsoever, ends that may be at cross purposes with mine. Even if I had no set plans for using the object, you still wronged me because you deprived me of the opportunity of using it as an instrument for realizing possible future plans.

This discussion underscores why Kant treats his analysis of property as metaphysical, independent of particular societies or cultures. For the core of property to Kant is the link between having *means* at one's disposal and pursuing one's own *ends*. And that relationship, for Kant, transcends any particular context.

In Kant's scheme, property is not merely relational; it involves a special kind of relationship. If I own an apple, your duty with respect to my property rights to that apple is negative in nature, namely, not to interfere with my opportunity to put that apple to use to pursue some end of my choosing. The wrongdoing is of a special sort. It is not just that you interfere with my plans but that, as Ripstein puts it, "[y]ou wrongfully limit my external freedom because you limit the means I have with which to set and pursue my own ends."[30] With property rights, then, duties are negative: You may not injure or trespass upon me or my external objects. Kant treats contract and status rights differently, as we shall see.

Contract

Property sets boundaries of noninterference among persons with respect to objects. Contract allows people to adjust those boundaries. Through contract, I am entitled

[28] Kant, "The Doctrine of Right," 6:248.
[29] Ibid.
[30] Ripstein, *Force and Freedom*, 68.

to depend upon your performing some act. As Kant describes them, contract relations are more interdependent than property relations. This interdependency becomes clearer when we look at the character of wrong involved in contract. If you and I are in a contractual relationship and you have breached the contract, your wrong consists of your failure to promote my ends in some way to which you consensually agreed and to which I am entitled to have you act. This is interference of a sort, but not the same sort as with property rights. The interference consists of a failure to perform some affirmative act rather than to desist from some act. So if duties in property relations are negative in nature, contract duties are affirmative.

Status

Status is the category of interdependent relationships in which consent is impossible or insufficient. One party in the relationship cannot exit the relationship or modify it because of some disability (physical or legal). Contract between the parties is impossible for this reason. If *A* cannot give her consent, *B* is not entitled, for this reason, to use *A* to pursue *B*'s own ends. Examples that Kant gives of such status relationships are husband-wife, parent-child, and master-servant.[31] Other relationships involving dependence might fit the same structure. Thus, fiduciary-beneficiary, doctor-patient, even teacher-student might qualify as Kantian status relationships.

   The key aspect of status relationships for Kant is the nature of the wrong involved due to the absence of consent by one party. Consent makes rightful what would otherwise be wrongful interferences with human freedom. This is why through contract, I may enlist you or your means to pursue ends that I, not you, have chosen. But if you cannot give consent, I may not use you to pursue my own ends. Indeed, as the example of the parent-child relationship makes clear, I may have a duty to act for your benefit so that you can develop as a purposive being.[32]

   Property, contract, and status relations can be compared and contrasted in the following terms.[33] Property rights include possession and use of the object. Contract rights are weaker in the sense that only a use right, not possession, is conferred. In status relationships, Kant treats the rights holder as in possession of the nonconsenting party but not entitled to use that person to further the rights holder's own ends. The wrongs involved in the three relationships are similarly distinguishable. With property rights, wrongs to rights holders consist of interference with their ability to pursue their own chosen goals. With contract, however, the wrong consists of your failure to further my ends, after you had consented to do so. Wrongs in status relationships consist of nonconsensual use of me to advance your ends.

[31] Kant, "The Doctrine of Right," 6:248.
[32] Ibid., 6:281–2.
[33] Ripstein, *Force and Freedom*, 76.

ACQUISITION OF PROPERTY RIGHTS

After analyzing the types of acquired rights, Kant turns to the question of how property rights can be acquired. This reverses the traditional strategy, followed by Locke and others, of understanding property through an analysis of how property is first acquired. Kant views this traditional strategy as mistaken, rejecting it as the "guardian spirit" theory of property.[34] For Kant, acquisition cannot drive the basic or normative theory of property; it can only serve to identify which objects get into the system of property. The reason it cannot serve a greater theoretical function is that property rights constrain the conduct of others, and acquisition poorly serves to explain why property legitimately constrains others. Of course, one person can unilaterally acquire an external unowned object, but the question is, how does this act bind others?

Locke's error, Kant believes, was to confuse necessary and sufficient conditions of original ownership acquisition. Physical appropriation of an object is a necessary condition, but it is not a sufficient condition. In Kant's view, conclusive ownership in unowned objects cannot be acquired without authorization by some public right.[35] Kant considers that my appropriation of an external object can bind all others only through some form of social contract through which consent is given.

Kant uses the state of nature device to explicate the initial acquisition of property rights, seemingly like Locke's argument. Both Kant's conception of the state of nature and his use of that device, however, differ markedly from Locke's. Kant uses the concept as a device with which to analyze the status of rights prior to the creation of a civil constitution. Kant considered that in such a state of nature, property rights could exist, but they would be only provisional. The basic structure of property, including possession and use rights, that one person is able to assert against others may be explained in terms of a state of nature or prepolitical conditions, but enforcement of such rights cannot be so explained. The right's security awaits the creation of a civil constitution.

Prior to the civil state, possession of objects can only be provisionally rightful under the circumstance that the possessor does not come into conflict with others.[36] It is fortuitous and empirical. To perfect this possession, the possessor's will must accord with the wills of all others. As Kant puts the point, "[O]nly in accordance with this principle of the will is it possible for the free choice of each to accord with the freedom of all, and therefore possible for there to be any right...."[37] In fact, Kant contends, individuals are under a duty to enter into a civil condition so that the property rights of all may be defended.[38]

[34] Kant, "The Doctrine of Right," 6:260.
[35] Ibid., 6:255. See Ripstein, *Force and Freedom*, 97.
[36] Kant, "The Doctrine of Right," 6:267.
[37] Ibid., 6:264.
[38] Ibid., 6:267.

The need for universal consent that can be enforced leads to Kant's justification of the state. We cannot go into this important but complex topic here, but suffice it to say that Kant regards the state as necessary for the existence of real freedom. State power is required if all individuals are to be guaranteed access to property in order to realize their personal freedom. The existence of the state is what distinguishes merely empirical or provisional rights in property (that is, property that is only contingent) from what Kant calls intelligible (or conclusive) rights in property.[39] It is in the second basic part of *The Doctrine of Right*, titled "Public Right," that Kant specifies the conditions under which the state makes provisional rights conclusive. These conditions need not detain us here, except to say that Kant sanctions the use of force when necessary to protect property rights and, ultimately in his view, freedom. This, of course, leaves us with the familiar paradox – a paradox to us, but not to Kant – of sanctioning the use of coercion in the name of freedom.

---

[39] Ibid., 6:257.

5

Property and Human Flourishing

This chapter sets out a theory of property that aims at realizing the ideal of human flourishing. The theory draws inspiration from the political and moral theories of Aristotle and Thomas Aquinas. Though it departs in significant ways from those classical theories, enough debt to Aristotle remains that we will sometimes refer to the theory simply as "Aristotelian." As background, we first briefly examine the historical ancestry of this theory, notably in Aristotle's and Aquinas's discussions of property.

ARISTOTLE

Human Nature

We begin with Aristotle's famous statement, which he repeated seven times,[1] that "a human being is by nature a political animal."[2] This statement contains both empirical and normative claims.[3] Empirically, part of his meaning is that humans are social creatures and that we characteristically choose to live with others. As he states in the *Nicomachean Ethics*, "[n]o one would choose to have all good things all by himself, for man is a social and political being and his natural condition is to live with others."[4] Beyond this general inclination toward the company of others (at least sometimes), Aristotle also means that we have a deeper need to be part of a political community within which we experience richer and more complete lives than are available to us either alone or within small family units.

[1] See Richard Kraut, *Aristotle* (2002), 247 n. 10.
[2] Aristotle, *Politics*, trans. Ernest Barker (1982), I.2 1252a2–3. All quotations and references to Aristotle's *Politics* will be taken from this translation. Where referenced in the text, this work will be indicated with *P* preceding the citation.
[3] See Kraut, *Aristotle*, 247.
[4] Aristotle, *Nicomachean Ethics*, trans. Martin Ostwald (1962), IX.9 1169b17–19. All quotations and references to Aristotle's *Ethics* will be taken from this translation. Where referenced in the text, this work will be indicated with *E* preceding the citation.

The normative message of his statement that we are by nature political animals is that it is good for us to live with others in such broad communities. In the *Ethics* Aristotle says that "the final and perfect good seems to be self-sufficient" (E: I.7 1097b9–10). He then quickly adds:

> However, we define something as self-sufficient not by reference to the "self" alone. We do not mean a man who lives his life in isolation, but a man who also lives with parents, children, a wife, and friends and fellow citizens generally, since a man is by nature a social and political being.[5]

Our proper human development requires that we live with others, especially at certain crucial stages of life. Living in isolation prevents us from realizing what is distinctive about us as human beings. We cannot have a well-lived life except in cooperation with others.

In saying that we are *political* animals, moreover, Aristotle means that our need for others is only satisfied within certain kinds of complex social organizations (the polis) within which we carry out our lives. In the *Politics*, Aristotle argues that "every polis [city] exists by nature."[6] Proper human development requires the polis, a form of social and political organization where people can best live good lives.

Practical Reason

Aristotle offers a theory of the good that is objectivist. That is, he intends that his account of what is good for human beings holds true for all human beings, regardless of cultural or other differences. For Aristotle, the ultimate end of the good human life is happiness (*eudaimonia*), or flourishing.[7] Every other good is sought because it is part of or leads to happiness, Aristotle argues. Aristotle recognized that there is disagreement about what constitutes happiness (flourishing), and he dismisses several plausible candidates, including pleasure. Flourishing is an irreducibly complex concept that is constituted by numerous plural and incommensurable goods.

An important part of the good life for a person consists of those activities that make effective use of the function that distinguishes humans from other species: our capacity to reason (E: 1098a10–12).[8] By *reason*, Aristotle does not mean speculative intelligence alone. In addition, he means our capacity to deliberate about

---

5 Ibid., I.7 1097b10–15.
6 Aristotle, *Politics*, I.2 1252b30.
7 Aristotle, *Ethics*, I.4 1097b16–18. The term *flourishing* is a better translation of Aristotle's term *eudaimonia*, which is sometimes translated as "happiness." "Flourishing" more accurately captures Aristotle's meaning because *eudaimonia* does not connote a mood as "happiness" does. See Kraut, *Aristotle*, 53 n. 4.
8 Ibid., I.7 1097b92–94.

our everyday actions, reflecting on our emotional responses and where appropriate adjusting their strength, examining facts, developing theories that explain them, and then critiquing those theories. Well-being, in Aristotle's account, "consists in the skillful deployment of our capacity to give and respond to reasons...."[9] It is true, of course, that not all persons exercise this capacity for practical reason equally. The extent to which we do so depends on our innate abilities and upon the degree to which our capacities have been nurtured by those around us from the time of infancy through adulthood.[10] But every adult whose capacity for rational thought has been nurtured has acquired (in some degree) the skill of practical reasoning, that is, the ability to give reasons for her actions, to deliberate about alternative plans and goals, and to productively interact with others about common concerns. The activity of practical reasoning is, for Aristotle, objectively good for us.

The Virtues

Virtues are acquired, stable dispositions to engage in certain characteristic modes of behavior conducive to human flourishing. The well-lived life is therefore, among other things, a life of virtue.[11] Because of the difficulty involved in acquiring the virtues, Aristotle by no means contemplates that a person can flourish at just any age. Human flourishing unfolds over the course of a person's lifetime as, supported by those around her, she gradually acquires the requisite skills and resources for living well. The virtues necessary for flourishing are not genetically endowed talents. They are dispositions that one acquires over time through careful cultivation, nurturing, and support from families, friends, and communities. Aristotle thought that the idea of a virtuous child is an oxymoron, for only in adulthood can one have acquired the requisite excellence to engage in virtuous activity. Human flourishing therefore has an ineliminable developmental dimension, one closely tied to the human life cycle of birth, childhood, adulthood, aging, and, ultimately, death.

Justice

The virtue that receives the greatest amount of attention in the *Nicomachean Ethics* is justice. Aristotle's basic conception of justice as a virtue, developed in book five of the *Ethics*, is active participation in the political life of one's community. The just person is a social being conversant in the norms, rules, customs, and issues of

---

[9] Kraut, *Aristotle*, 85.
[10] Ibid., 59–63.
[11] See Philippa Foot, "Virtues and Vices," in *Virtues and Vices* (2002), 2–4; Rosalind Hursthouse, *On Virtue Ethics* (1999), 167.

the political aspects of her community and who participates in the community's political life to improve the well-being of her fellow citizens. Aristotle distinguishes between different types of justice.[12] For property theory – concerned as it is with the allocation of rights in things – what is most relevant is Aristotle's discussion of distributive justice, which he saw as a kind of equality. Aristotle believed that the proper basis for the distribution of goods is merit. If all recipients are of equal merit, they should receive equal shares, but if some are superior to others, their shares should be proportionately larger.[13] What kind of merit should count? Aristotle thought that this was a matter to be determined on the basis of what would contribute to the common good of the entire community.

PROPERTY

Aristotle begins his discussion of property in the *Politics* by listing three possible ownership regimes: one in which land is owned individually but crops are communally used; a second in which land is owned and farmed communally but crops are distributed for private use; and a third in which both land and crops are communal in all respects.[14] The regime he endorses is the first. He deploys a variety of arguments against the second and third options. He rejects the third option, the full communal regime defended in Plato's *Republic*, because he thinks it both unworkable and unjust.[15] One of the reasons Aristotle gives for favoring the system of private ownership/communal use anticipates the kind of utilitarian arguments we discussed in Chapter 1.[16] Private ownership, he argues, creates incentives for individuals to take better care of what they own than they would if resources were communally owned (P: 1263a28–29). Another reason he gives in favor of private property is that it promotes friendship (P: 1263a28–29). Aristotle's thinking here seems to be that through proper education individuals will learn that property, though privately owned, is to be shared with friends. Relatedly, private ownership facilitates the exercise of such virtues as generosity and moderation (P: 1263b5–14). His point here ties in with the one just raised. Aristotle means to say that the possibility of generosity depends upon the existence of some degree of private rights. Generosity presupposes a voluntary act of sharing, so that the owner must willingly transfer to

[12] Many scholars refer to this distinction in terms of "universal" and "particular" justice. As Richard Kraut points out, that terminology is misleading, for it mistakenly implies that the former applies in all (or nearly so) communities whereas the latter applies only on a much more restricted basis. That is not Aristotle's meaning. See Kraut, *Aristotle*, 102 n. 6.
[13] See Aristotle, *Ethics*, V.3 1131b28–32.
[14] See ibid., VII.5 1263a3–8.
[15] See Robert Mayhew, "Aristotle on Property," REV. OF METAPHYSICS 46 (1993): 803, 807.
[16] See Jeremy Waldron, *The Right to Private Property* (1988), 6–9.

someone else the power to use and enjoy the resource. And her act can only be voluntary, and therefore praiseworthy, if she was entitled not to share.

In describing his ideal city in the *Politics*, Aristotle divided land into two basic parts, one being public property, the other given over to private ownership.[17] Public land was to be used for the common good, including growing crops necessary to provide common meals (the right of dining at common tables was open to all citizens).[18] As to privately owned land, each citizen would be allotted two parcels, one near the city center, the other in the city's outskirts. Private landownership had a political purpose – to support virtuous citizenship. Land was to be owned "by the class which bears arms and the class which shares in the conduct on government" (*P*: VII.10 1329b41–42). Aristotle thought that private landownership should not include the unrestricted power to buy, sell, or exchange land. Restrictions on the power of market alienation were necessary, in his view, to prevent citizens from undermining the very purpose of private landownership.

AQUINAS

Aquinas built on Aristotle's ethics to further elaborate a conception of property focused on the virtues and human flourishing. Aquinas thought that the only reasons we have for choices and actions are the goods to which the first practical principles point us.[19] Among the most important of the first practical principles, which Aquinas takes to be self-evident, is the duty to love one's neighbor as oneself.[20] The love of neighbor principle is foundational for Aquinas, for he says that all moral principles and norms, especially those concerning relations among people, can be derived from it.[21] And it expresses why, for Aquinas more so than for Aristotle, the common good is truly *common*. As John Finnis explains, "[T]o love a person volitionally...is to will that person's good."[22] And this applies, Aquinas believes, not just to a few individuals, but universally. He states:

> For...if the good for one human being is the same good as the good for a whole *civitas*, still it is evidently a much greater and more perfect thing to procure and preserve the state of affairs which is the good of a whole *civitas* than the state of affairs which is the good of a single human being. For: it belongs to the love

[17] See Aristotle, *Politics*, VII.10 1330a14–16.
[18] Ibid., VII.10 1330a6–7.
[19] Examples of the first practical principles are "life is a good to be pursued" and "good is to be done and pursued, and evil is to be avoided." St. Thomas Aquinas, *Summa Theologica*, trans. Fathers of the English Dominican Province, 5 vols. Christian Classics (1981), I-II q. 94 a. 2.
[20] Ibid., I-II q. 99 a. I ad 2, q. 100 a. 3 ad I, q. 100 a. IIc, II-II q. 44 a. 2.
[21] See John Finnis, *Aquinas* (1998), 127.
[22] Ibid.

which should exist between human persons that one should seek and preserve the good of even one single human being; but how much better and more god-like that this should be shown for a whole people and *for a plurality* of *civitates*. This good, *the good common to one or many civitates*... is what the theory... has as its point. And so it is this theory, above all... that considers the ultimate end of human life.[23]

The common good of which Aquinas speaks here is, in Finnis's apt phrase, "integral human fulfillment,"[24] the integral fulfillment of persons and communities.

In Aquinas's view there are intelligible, not merely emotional, bases for the duty to love one's neighbor. They are, first, that other people may, by virtue of their very humanity, experience and share in the human good. In Aquinas's view, our shared humanity leads us to want others to participate in the human good. A second basis is that the human good includes, as a constituent element, the good of friendship.[25] At the most generalized level, this is necessarily an extremely thin and greatly attenuated form of friendship, predicated on each person's likeness with all other humans in their specific nature.[26] But the important point is that the relationships are noninstrumental. As Finnis explains:

> The essence of any friendship... is that A is interested in B's well being for B's sake; and B is interested in A's well being for A's sake; and A is interested in A's own well being not only for its own sake but also for B's sake; and B likewise. Thus the interest of neither person comes to rest solely on that person's own well being, nor solely on the other person's well being. So their relationship of interest... is, and is directed towards, a truly common good – not simply two individual goods of the same "common" type, nor the sum of those goods.[27]

What is true of the friendship between A and B can be extended to many and even to all human beings, Aquinas believed. In saying this, he is not claiming a sort of universal intimate friendship, but rather that each of us affirms the basic equality among all persons based on our very status as human beings, entitling all of us to certain human goods.

The obligation to love our neighbors requires us to support the social and material preconditions for their (and our own) flourishing. One important point in this regard is that the flourishing of each of us depends on the existence of political communities promoting the common good. In addition, because property exists in

[23] Thomas Aquinas, *Sententia Libri Ethicorum* (Commentary on Aristotle's *Nicomachean Ethics*) (Busa 1992; Spiazzi 1949; first publ. 1271–2), I. 2. nn. 11–12 [29–30]. Citations refer to the 1992 edition.
[24] Finnis, *Aquinas*, 115.
[25] See ibid., 116–17.
[26] Aquinas, *Ethics*, VIII. I n. 4 [1541].
[27] Finnis, *Aquinas*, 116.

order to promote human well-being, property rights are (for Aquinas) subordinate to the human goods that constitute human flourishing. Thus, Aquinas closely follows Aristotle in justifying private ownership primarily in instrumental terms and in insisting that, while property should (for those instrumental reasons) be private, the use of things should remain common and owners should be "ready to communicate them [property] to others in their need."[28]

Aquinas drives home the limited nature of property rights with particular force in his discussion of theft. He begins by asking whether it is lawful to steal through force of need, but he ends up going substantially further than offering an affirmative answer to the question. He redefines the terms of the discussion to show that taking someone else's property in a situation of dire need is not theft at all. He quotes St. Ambrose's admonition to owners who do not share with those in need: "It is the hungry man's bread that you withhold, the naked man's cloak that you store away, the money that you bury in the earth is the price of the poor man's ransom and freedom."[29] Private ownership exists to ensure the ability of human beings (collectively) to flourish. Most of the time, this is accomplished by people using their own property to satisfy their own needs and sharing their surplus with others. But when that system fails, Aquinas says, and someone stands in dire need of resources, the one in need is entitled to take what she needs from the private holdings of others. "It is not theft, properly speaking," Aquinas says, "to take secretly and use another's property in case of extreme need: because that which he takes for the support of his life becomes his own property by reason of that need."[30]

Indeed, Aquinas goes even further still. Consistent with his idea of the obligation to love one's neighbor, Aquinas says that, not only is it permissible to take what you need from others, "a man may also take secretly another's property in order to succor his neighbor in need."[31] Combining all of these principles, it is clear that Aquinas thought that, since need gives title to the one in need, it is just for third parties, including presumably the state, to openly take property from someone with an abundance of resources in order to give to those in society who lack the resources to satisfy their basic needs. Although what Aquinas says about necessity and theft is dramatic, the more important point is the conceptual one. Property rights are, in the Thomistic account, instrumental to deeper and more fundamental human goods. And they must give way at the appropriate moments if they are not to undermine their proper goal of promoting human flourishing.

---

[28] Aquinas, *Summa Theologica*, IIa IIae, Q. 66, art. 2.
[29] Ibid., art. 7.
[30] Ibid.
[31] Ibid.

A MODERN HUMAN FLOURISHING-BASED THEORY OF PROPERTY

The Aristotelian and Thomistic conceptions of human flourishing and of the common good provide the foundations for a modern, nonutilitarian theory of property, but one that shares with utilitarianism a concern about the consequences of property law for human welfare, broadly understood.[32]

Human Flourishing

We begin, as Aristotle did, with a conception of human flourishing. The theory builds on the Aristotelian and Thomistic insights that humans are social animals and that the human condition is marked by dependency on (and friendship with) others. It stresses the fact that although human beings value and strive for autonomy, dependency and interdependency are inescapable aspects of well-lived lives.

Contrary to the understandable tendency to equate flourishing with individual self-realization, we, following both Aristotle and Aquinas, stress its inherently social character. Flourishing is an unavoidably cooperative endeavor rather than an individual pursuit or purely personal project. Our ability to flourish requires certain basic material goods and a communal infrastructure that themselves depend upon contributions from all members of the relevant society. However much we may value our personal independence, it is quite literally impossible for a person to flourish without others. To see why this is so, we need to explore the meaning of flourishing a bit more fully.

As Aristotle explained, human flourishing has two aspects: faring well (well-being) and doing well (virtue). To flourish, humans first must live under the right circumstances, or at least under certain acceptable circumstances. We cannot live the lives that are the best possible lives for us if we live in conditions of extreme deprivation and in want of basic human needs. Perhaps one might occasionally choose to forgo certain basic requirements, such as by fasting, but, however else we may wish to define flourishing, it requires, minimally, that basic human necessities be available to us at certain crucial times. As we shall see, it further requires the availability of external goods beyond those needed to provide for our basic physical survival.

The other aspect of human flourishing is doing well, or virtue. And our ability to live a life of virtue depends on the cultivation of our specifically human capacity to reason in cooperation with others. Humans are both social and rational creatures.

---

[32] See Gregory S. Alexander, "The Social-Obligation Norm in American Property Law," CORNELL L. REV. 94 (2009): 745; Eduardo M. Peñalver, "Land Virtues," CORNELL L. REV. 94 (2009): 821; Gregory S. Alexander and Eduardo M. Peñalver, "Properties of Community," THEORETICAL INQUIRIES IN LAW 10 (2009): 127.

Putting this together, we can say that a flourishing human life is one that consists of rational and social activities expressing the human excellences or virtues and that such a life is supported by those external goods necessary for participation in such activities.

As we have already indicated, human beings develop the capacities necessary for well-lived and distinctly human lives only in society with, and indeed dependence upon, other human beings. To put the point even more directly, living within a particular sort of society, a web of particular kinds of social relationships, is a necessary condition for humans to be able to develop the distinctively human capacities that allow us to flourish.

Finally, human flourishing must include at least the capacity to make meaningful choices among alternative life horizons, to discern the salient differences among them, and to deliberate deeply about what is valuable within those available alternative choices. That is, in addition to the features we have already described, human flourishing requires authentic and robust freedom. These values – having the resources necessary for physical well-being, social life, intellectual development, and freedom – each contribute something vital to the ability of human beings to flourish, and are not fully substitutable with one another.

The patterns of human life that are consistent with human flourishing (understood as encompassing physical well-being, sociality, rationality, and freedom) are rich and diverse.[33] There is no one way in which human beings can flourish. The well-lived life is not captive to any single good or value. Finnis states the point nicely:

> Besides limitless diversity in…forms of pursuit, there is diversity in the depth, intensity and duration of commitment, in the extent to which the pursuit of a given value is given priority in shaping of one's life and character. One man's recognition of the value of truth may elicit from him the response of a lifetime of austere self-discipline and intellectual grind; another's may evoke a commitment sufficient only to enjoy the intellectual play of a good argument; another's may carry him no further than a disposition to grumble at the lying propaganda on his television set…. This diversity results not only from the fact that truth is not the only basic value, but also from the fact that human beings (and thus whole cultures) differ in their determination, enthusiasm, sobriety, far-sightedness, sensitivity, steadfastness, and all the other modalities of response to *any* value.[34]

Still, the recognition of a plurality of ways of responding to different values does not eliminate the possibility of recognizing certain features that are basic to the well-lived life, values such as friendship and knowledge.[35] The goal is to identify

---

[33] See John Finnis, *Natural Law and Natural Rights* (1980), 81–92.
[34] See ibid., 85.
[35] See ibid., 59–83.

a framework for describing human flourishing that, as Martha Nussbaum puts it, "allows a great deal of latitude for diversity, but one that also sets up some general benchmarks"[36] for evaluating the practices that prevail within a particular society as either conducive to or inconsistent with the achievement of the well-lived life.

The Capabilities Approach

Building on work by Nussbaum and Amartya Sen and drawing on their "capabilities approach," we can discuss the law's role in fostering human flourishing in terms of its facilitation of a person's acquisition of certain crucial capabilities.[37] This approach measures people's well-being not by looking at what they possess, but at what they are able to do.[38] The well-lived life requires that one possess substantive powers – capabilities – to choose a life of human dignity.

Human flourishing is not constituted solely by the possession of particular material goods, the satisfaction of particular subjective preferences, or even, without more, the possession of particular negative liberties. It is marked by attaining certain objectively valuable personal states and the performance of certain valuable activities. The objectively valuable conditions and activities may range from the very basic, such as being properly fed, to the more complex, such as participating in the community's political life. Flourishing does not necessarily require that a person actually experience all of these states or activities. Although an individual certainly must experience *certain* of them (e.g., nourishment) at the right times in order to flourish, the diversity of ways of flourishing leaves broad scope for choice.[39]

Exactly which capabilities are essential for the possibility of a well-lived life is a matter about which people may reasonably disagree. Four capabilities should be relatively uncontroversial: (1) *life*, a capability we take to include subsidiary capabilities such as health and security; (2) *freedom*, which includes identity and self-knowledge;[40] (3) *practical reason*, which Aristotle defined as "the capacity of

---

[36] Martha C. Nussbaum, *Women and Human Development* (2000), 50–5.

[37] See, for example, ibid.; Amartya Sen, *Development as Freedom* (1999); Martha C. Nussbaum, "Foreword: Constitutions and Capabilities: 'Perception' Against Lofty Formalism," HARV. L. REV. 121 (2007): 5.

[38] See Amartya Sen, *Commodities and Capabilities* (1985), 10–11.

[39] See Nussbaum, *Women and Human Development*, 87–8.

[40] The conception of freedom that includes identity and self-knowledge is more capacious than the classical liberal conception of freedom as freedom from constraints and coercion by third parties. It is one that, as Jeremy Waldron states, sees that "it is necessary for the free man not only to *be* independent of others, but actively to assert himself as a free and independent will and to be recognized as such by others." Waldron, *Private Property*, 301–2. Such a conception understands that personal freedom requires "development of a personality able to identify, pursue, and revise interests and projects." Jedediah Purdy, *The Meaning of Property* (2010), 88. One cannot freely engage with others or develop and pursue personal goals without a sense of self and one's relationship with society.

deliberating well about what is good and advantageous for oneself";[41] and (4) sociality, or what Nussbaum calls *"affiliation,"* a capability that encompasses subsidiary capabilities such as the possibility of social participation, self-respect, and friendship. As we indicated previously, the values underlying these capabilities are plural and incommensurable. It is impossible to flourish without some degree of all four, and the lack of one (below the threshold necessary for flourishing) cannot be adequately compensated by an excess of one or more of the others.[42]

Capabilities and Dependence

No individual can acquire these capabilities or secure the resources to acquire them by herself. This is because the physical process of human development mandates our dependence on others for a great deal of the time during which we are cultivating the necessary capacities. Obviously in infancy and childhood, but even in adulthood, we place at least partial physical dependence (and even emotional or psychological dependence) on others as we move through a dangerous world. And, as we reach the final years of our lives, the possibility of physical dependence begins once again to loom ever larger. In one form or another, we simply cannot escape dependence on others, and they on us, throughout our entire lives.

Life, freedom, practical reasoning, and sociality are possible, in a meaningful sense, only within a vital matrix of social structures and practices. Even the most seemingly solitary of these capabilities, freedom, depends upon a richly social, cultural, and institutional context for the presence of which the free individual must rely on others. Charles Taylor has pointed out that our status as free agents itself depends upon the existence of public debate about moral and political questions. Suppose that we were cut off from this debate, he asks. Who would help us to clarify the alternatives available to us or to remind us of similar debates of the past and decisions made and their consequences?[43]

The same is true for every single one of the other capabilities. We are not born endowed with them; rather, they are acquired over a period of time, sometimes quite extended. We cannot acquire any of them without help from others who provide various resources necessary to nurture the capabilities' development. The resources necessary to nurture development of the capabilities vary from emotional support to material goods, and both the means of acquiring resources and the persons from whom they come may be indirect or even remote. (We shall examine this point further in Chapter 6, where we discuss redistribution of resources.) But whatever the

[41] Aristotle, *Ethics*, VI 5. 1140a 25–27.
[42] See Nussbaum, "Foreword: Constitutions and Capabilities," 14.
[43] Charles Taylor, "Atomism," in *Philosophy and the Human Sciences*, vol. 2 of *Philosophical Papers* (1985), 306.

resources and whoever furnishes them, we cannot possibly avoid being dependent on others to enable our development as capable human beings. We are necessarily indebted to others.

Dependence and Obligation

If we can agree that our physical survival, our capacities to engage in practical reasoning, to participate in the social life of the community, and to make decisions about how to live our lives, are valuable components of the well-lived human life, then it would seem that we should also be able to agree that we owe some obligation to others within our communities to share our resources to support and nurture the social structures necessary for the development of these human capabilities. For if we affirm the value of these goods, and if these goods can only exist within particular sorts of social contexts and physical environments, then it would seem irrational to deny that we are obligated to participate in and contribute to the vitality of those social structures and physical environments. The facts of social dependence and interdependence prevent us from drawing clear lines between our individual well-being, or flourishing, and that of others. As Aquinas recognized, human fulfillment is not individual; it is social and communal.

Reciprocity, at least in any strict sense of that term, cannot fully account for this obligation for two basic reasons. First, the persons to whom we owe the obligation are often not the same as those from whom we received resources or help. There is no way of predicting *ex ante* the persons to whom we shall be required to give. It might be our parents, but it might be total strangers from whom we have received nothing. Second, even if the persons to whom we shall give are the same as the persons from whom we have received some benefit, what we give is often not the same as what we received. This will commonly be the case between parents and children and indeed between all persons of different generations whenever some form of nurturing is involved. What our parents gave to us to nurture us as we developed into healthy and stable adults capable of making thoughtful choices is typically quite different from the kind of care they later require of us as their dependency grows with age. Moreover, often the amounts differ, sometimes very considerably. As members of flourishing social networks, we understand that often what we give we give unconditionally, because the measure of what is expected of us is the need of others rather than what we have already received or expect to receive in the future.[44] This is most obviously true between parents and children, but it also holds true (to a limited extent) in wider relationships. We give to our friends, colleagues, neighbors, and others in the myriad of social networks that constitute our ordinary lives, and

---

[44] See Alasdair MacIntyre, *Dependent Rational Animals* (1999), 100.

we give to them because of their need rather than as repayment for the benefits they have conferred upon us in the past or that we necessarily expect from them in the future.

If we want to describe the mechanism at work here in terms of reciprocity, it is only in a kind of second order sense (expected). This second order reciprocity does not operate through a long run accounting of costs and benefits, but rather looks to the possibility of rough reciprocity built into the structure of our social relationships. Thus, while it seems likely that we can never repay our parents and while it is possible that some family members will have grave needs that mean they will receive more than they will return, the family, considered as a multigenerational social institution, nonetheless seems, at its best, well-suited to provide the possibility of a rough and ready reciprocity among its constituent members.

Flourishing and the Law

Although the human flourishing theory of property depends on a conception of the law as suffused with moral implications, it does not simply merge the categories of morality and law. Rather, it is consistent with treating the law instrumentally, as a means of achieving a more just society in which individuals have adequate opportunities to flourish. From this point of view, the law has as an important goal affirmatively facilitating human flourishing, but, for practical reasons, it often does so only indirectly. The use of the coercive tools of legal intervention in support of the opportunity for human flourishing should be reserved for situations in which that legal intervention is likely to yield better consequences than would otherwise occur.[45]

Laws can foster human flourishing in several important ways. First, they can attempt to directly enforce specific moral obligations. This aim is particularly (and on some views, exclusively) appropriate when legal enforcement of obligations is necessary to protect those whose opportunities to flourish might otherwise be impaired. In the property context, laws against theft and fraud are obvious examples. But there are many others. As we discuss in Chapter 6, we can understand redistributive taxes as an attempt to compel people to comply with their moral obligations to share their surplus resources with those in need of additional resources for their own development as human beings capable of flourishing. Title II of the Civil Rights Act of 1964,[46] which mandates a nondiscrimination norm for private owners of places of public accommodation, is arguably another example of this sort of legal prohibition of harmful use of property, one to which we will return in Chapter 7.

---

[45] In this sense, the view of law on which the human flourishing theory of property depends is very similar to Joseph Raz's service conception of law. See Joseph Raz, *The Morality of Freedom* (1986), chs. 3, 15.

[46] 42 U.S.C. § 2000a (2000).

Legal intervention can also clarify social obligations and coordinate collective actions necessary for human flourishing where private owners would otherwise struggle to do so on their own.[47] Well-crafted environmental statutes or regulations, for example, can help spread the word about best practices to property owners who lack information about the remote consequences of their behavior. Civil rights statutes provide another helpful illustration. Scholars have noted that statutes prohibiting discrimination empowered proprietors and employers who did not particularly want to discriminate but who did so out of fear of reprisals for violating social taboos or of being put at a disadvantage. By ensuring that their competitors could not obtain a competitive advantage by offering a segregated alternative, civil rights statutes reduced the cost of doing the right thing for those already predisposed to do it.[48]

It bears emphasizing that the notion that law should be used to foster human flourishing does not require embracing an unrelentingly intrusive role for the law, one that is inconsistent with a basic commitment to freedom. Even when we reach the conclusion that a citizen is not living up to her obligations in ways that harm others, the question whether coercively to enforce compliance with those obligations through the force of law will turn on a number of additional considerations.[49] It will turn, for example, on our evaluation of citizens' likely behavior in response to differing forms of legal compulsion and persuasion. This evaluation will itself require an understanding of the character of the typical citizen and of the community in which she is situated. The answer will likewise depend on the mechanisms for political decision making and law enforcement at our disposal, and the degree to which we think those mechanisms partake of the same virtues and pathologies of private decisions or are instead subject to their own context-specific strengths and shortcomings.

Finally, the independent value of individual autonomy, which is itself an important component of human flourishing, may require that the law stay its hand in certain contexts, even when it is likely that intervention would be effective to prevent harmful choices.[50] Sometimes, the law declines to intervene in individual choices because legal compulsion would be utterly inconsistent with the capability of freedom. In certain contexts, using the coercive power of law, even to prevent harm,

---

[47] See, for example, Mary M. Keys, *Aquinas, Aristotle and the Promise of the Common Good* (2006), 208–16.

[48] See, for example, John J. Donohue III and James Heckman, "Continuous Versus Episodic Change: The Impact of Civil Rights Policy on the Economic Status of Blacks," *J. ECON. LIT.*, 29 (1991): 1603, 1639; Russell K. Robinson, "Casting and Caste-ing: Reconciling Artistic Freedom and Antidiscrimination Norms," *CAL. L. REV.*, 95 (2007): 1, 33.

[49] See, for example, John Courtney Murray, *We Hold These Truths* (1960), 149–64; Christine Swanton, "Commentary on Michael Slote's 'Virtue Ethics and Democratic Values,'" *J. OF SOCIAL PHIL.*, 24 (1993): 38, 46.

[50] See Raz, *Morality of Freedom*, 408.

may sweep away a broader zone of privacy that is instrumentally necessary for agents to make other good and valuable choices.[51] This is arguably why civil rights laws exempt private clubs and owner-occupied homes from their reach.[52] They do not do so out of a belief that racist decision making in those domains is a matter of indifference, but because legal intrusion into, say, the private home, will necessarily have practical consequences for freedom across a much broader range of choices. (It is from a related concern to safeguard autonomy that Nussbaum and Sen speak of the state's obligations in terms of helping people to acquire *capabilities* rather than directly pushing them to flourish.[53] The crucial and valuable choice whether to actually put capabilities into practice remains with the individual and this freedom is itself part of what it means to flourish.)

The key point of the foregoing discussion is to make the case that there is a role for law to play in fostering human flourishing. At the same time, however, for an Aristotelian *property* theory, the determination that a particular use or allocation of property would contribute to human flourishing is only the first step in a more complex analysis. A separate question always remains about how best, if at all, the law should seek to foster human flourishing (by mandating or encouraging that use or allocation) in a way that gives due regard to the various components of human flourishing.

Flourishing and Property

The obligation to support and nurture the social structures necessary for development of human capabilities, and therefore for the possibility of human flourishing, has special meaning for property owners. Property law has long recognized that property rights are inherently relational and that, because of that character, owners necessarily owe obligations to others. For example, for centuries the common law has recognized a negative obligation of landowners not to use their land in ways that constitute nuisances for their neighbors.

But human flourishing requires the recognition that property owners will sometimes owe the various communities to which they belong obligations that are thicker

---

[51] Cf. Raz, *Morality of Freedom*, 419 (objecting to the legal prohibition of acts that do not harm others because of a concern for the impact of such prohibitions on the freedom to make even good choices). We do not need to inject ourselves into the interesting debate over whether there is intrinsic moral value to choice (even choice of that which is wrong) and whether a proper regard for the value of autonomy provides principled, rather than merely prudential, reasons to oppose legal coercion. See, for example, Robert P. George, *Making Men Moral* (1993), ch. 6. Because the subject of our concern, property law, concerns the allocation among people of legal rights over things, property wrongs invariably involve harm to others that the law is, in principle, justified in preventing.

[52] 42 U.S.C. § 2000a(e) (2000).

[53] See Martha C. Nussbaum, "Capabilities and Human Rights," *FORDHAM L. REV.*, 66 (1997): 273, 296.

than a simple duty not to harm others. Owners are responsible for the continued well-being of these communities which have nurtured and continue to nurture the development of their personal capabilities essential to their own flourishing. Taylor puts the point well, stating:

> [S]ince the free individual can only maintain his identity within a society/culture of a certain kind, he has to be concerned about the shape of this society/culture as a whole. He cannot...be concerned purely with his individual choices and the associations formed from such choices to the neglect of the matrix in which such choices can be open or closed, rich or meager.[54]

Because human flourishing depends upon social structures, the communities to which property owners belong may legitimately make demands of them to contribute out of their resources or to share their property in order to sustain those social matrices. In some societies the bonds of affection and reciprocity between members of tightly knit communities may be sufficient to ensure that each person's obligations to contribute resources and relationships necessary to sustain the capabilities requisite for human flourishing are fully satisfied. In complex modern societies, however, guaranteeing that individuals contribute the many material and social prerequisites for the capabilities we are describing is beyond the abilities of private, voluntary communities, considered either individually or in cooperation with one another. At least since the rise of modern capitalism, the voluntary actions of private entities have never been sufficient to supply all members of society with access to all of the resources necessary for the opportunity to develop the capabilities necessary for human flourishing.[55]

If the state, then, may legitimately make certain demands on its citizen-members to contribute to the maintenance of the matrices and services that nurture the capabilities necessary for human flourishing, just what implications does this have for property owners? To begin with, like all animals, human beings need access to the resources necessary for physical survival. As even some of the most stringent of property rights libertarians have acknowledged, the extreme need of some in the community trumps the property rights other people hold over their surplus resources.[56] In essence, acknowledging this right to resources necessary for physical survival constitutes an acknowledgment of the existence of an entitlement to the material assistance of others under certain circumstances, and, given the difficulty of ensuring

---

54 Charles Taylor, "Cross-Purposes: The Liberal-Communitarian Debate," in *Liberalism and the Moral Life*, ed. Nancy L. Rosenblum (1989), 159, 207.

55 See Milton Friedman, *Capitalism and Freedom* (1962), 191 ("In small communities, public pressure can suffice [to meet the needs of the poor] even with private charity. In the large impersonal communities that are increasingly coming to dominate our society, it is much more difficult for it to do so.").

56 See Richard A. Epstein, *Skepticism and Freedom* (2003), 98–100.

compliance with such obligations in the modern, depersonalized economy, to the assistance of the state, through directly redistributive measures, in obtaining survival resources. Similar arguments, founded in the protection of human health or the health of future generations, can justify the state's demand that individuals' use of their property be made in ways that do not permanently harm the environment.

In addition, the long period of intellectual and moral training necessary to function as practically rational beings within modern capitalist societies points in the direction of some minimal provision for the well-being and education of the young, irrespective of the wisdom, diligence, or luck of their parents. Almost by definition, such an entitlement will demand that the state implement a degree of economic redistribution and regulation, either in cash or in kind. Those whose parents do not wish to educate their offspring must be compelled to do so, at least to a point, and those who cannot afford education must have that education provided to them at the expense of others. Moreover, this redistributive educational process arguably entails ensuring that the parents of such children have the economic resources necessary to provide a suitable environment in which the educational effort can take root.

An intuition along these lines appears to underlie the New Jersey Supreme Court's reasoning in the *Mt. Laurel* line of cases. The court in those cases repeatedly rejected the use of zoning codes to exclude low-income housing and imposed an affirmative obligation on more affluent municipalities to do their "fair share" to admit low-income households into their communities.[57] It observed that the local funding of municipal services – particularly education – created the incentive for municipalities to exclude those who did not pay enough in property taxes to cover the costs of the services they received, but it rejected that as an adequate reason for excluding low-income housing.

Finally, resources are necessary in order to facilitate the capability of sociality. Because human beings experience sociability as an imperative and not as a choice, all societies must struggle with the challenge of providing adequate opportunities for individuals to obtain the things they need in order to function as social beings without at the same time undermining the necessary incentives for productive activity. In the context of a modern society like our own, this observation points in the direction of an entitlement to some kind of social safety net that can guarantee a substantial basket of resources.

None of this is meant to suggest that the state's power, even as it touches on the facilitation of the capabilities we are discussing, is unbounded. The limits to the state's proper domain are supplied by the same principles that justify its action: the demands generated by the capabilities that facilitate human flourishing – freedom, practical rationality, and sociality, among others. For example, the substantive

---

57   See *South Burlington County NAACP v. Township of Mt. Laurel*, 67 NJ 151 (1975).

good of human freedom limits the intrusions that the state ought to make into the sphere of private decision making, particularly in the context of intimate settings like the home or private expressive associations. Similarly, the material necessities of life are, it has been amply demonstrated, more likely to be provided in a relatively free market than in one subject to pervasive central planning. Within this framework, however, the discussion about how to allocate responsibilities among private communities, the market, and various state actors does not proceed through the lens of individual property rights in the first instance, but, rather, through pragmatic discussions about which allocations will best foster opportunities for a society's members to flourish. Property rights will, however, come into the picture at some point, because of the connection between stable entitlements and any plausible conceptions of human flourishing. Once up and running, a system of private ownership will impose its own flourishing related restrictions on the means by which the state can go about pursuing the goal of fostering the capabilities.

Because the aggregate material resources within a community will plausibly, though indirectly, affect the ability of its members to flourish, utilitarian or welfarist analyses of a particular decision's consequences for wealth are far from irrelevant within an account of property built around the concept of human flourishing. But there will always be additional questions to ask before a decision maker is warranted in concluding that the wealth maximizing move is the right one. This is because wealth maximization does not stand, in Philippa Foot's words, "outside morality as its foundation and arbiter" but rather "within morality as the end of one of its virtues."[58] A human flourishing approach to property would therefore seem to be a version of what Matt Adler and Eric Posner have called "weak welfarism." As they define it, weak welfarism is the position that "overall welfare has moral relevance but that other considerations, such as distributive or rights-based considerations, may have moral relevance as well."[59]

PLURALISM AND INDETERMINACY

The pluralist dimension of the human flourishing theory generates challenges for it as a tool of social choice. Any legal theory built around plural and incommensurable moral values cannot reduce social choice to the consideration of the consequences of that choice for a single foundational moral value.[60] This raises the possibility (and, in

---

[58] Philippa Foot, Utilitarianism and the Virtues, MIND 94 (1985): 196, 204.

[59] Matthew A. Adler & Eric A. Posner, *New Foundations of Cost-Benefit Analysis* (2006), 25–6.

[60] There is disagreement about the precise meaning of *incommensurability*. For present purposes, we will treat it as synonymous with *incomparability*. In this view, two or more goods are incommensurate goods when no positive value relation between them holds. A positive value relation means that we can say that x is *better than* y, or x is *less than* y, or x is *equal to* y. If we can say none of

a world of scarce resources, the inevitability) that plural values will come into conflict with one another. This possibility of conflict is absent in monist theories, like utilitarianism or welfarism, which recognize only one foundational value. Assuming the relevant information can be obtained (a big assumption), the reduction of all value to a single metric permits all possible consequences to be determinately compared and ranked according to their tendency to increase or reduce that one value. Welfare theorists therefore consider it a failure of pluralists that in many cases (e.g., where the situation requires tradeoffs between different incommensurable values) they cannot unequivocally endorse one uniquely correct course of action. These theorists consider pluralist theories such as human flourishing to be indeterminate and for that reason inferior to welfarism, which they consider highly determinate.[61]

This "index problem," as it has been called,[62] is a genuine challenge for pluralist theories of social choice, and therefore for a pluralist theory of property, such as the human flourishing theory. Indeed, philosophers working with pluralist conceptions of value have dedicated entire books to explaining how rational choice is possible in the face of plural and incommensurable values.[63] Although the debate among philosophers continues, we will briefly describe three interrelated responses that have been offered.

The first response is the negative move of observing that the "index problem" challenge puts the cart before the horse. This response concedes, at least for the sake of argument, that it would be preferable to have a theory of value that permitted the determinate ranking of all possible options along a single scale of value. But the question just is whether such a single scale exists, and pluralists deny that it does. Accordingly, the fact that value monists can generate a simpler decision-making process does not constitute an argument on behalf of those theories unless it is in fact true that there is such a single, all-encompassing value. If values are in fact plural and incommensurable, the difficulty of making social choices is simply a challenge that must be faced. As Martha Nussbaum has put it, to water down the moral universe in pursuit of easier mechanisms of decision making is "[e]vasiveness, not progress." "To purchase neatness at such a price," she plausibly contends, "appears irrational rather than rational."[64] And so the argument to be had is really about

---

those things about the relation between *x* and *y*, then they are incommensurable. See Elizabeth Anderson, "Practical Reason and Incommensurable Goods," in *Incommensurability, Incomparability, and Practical Reason*, ed. Ruth Chang (1997), 90.

[61] See Louis Kaplow, "Primary Goods, Capabilities...or Well-Being?," PHIL. REV. 116 (2007): 603.

[62] See ibid.

[63] See, for example, Elizabeth Anderson, *Value in Ethics and Economics* (1993); Henry S. Richardson, *Democratic Autonomy: Public Reasoning About the Ends of Policy* (2003); Henry S. Richardson, *Practical Reasoning About Final Ends* (1997); Michael Stocker, *Plural and Conflicting Values* (1990). See also the essays collected in ed. Chang, *Incommensurability*.

[64] See Martha C. Nussbaum, *Love's Knowledge* (1990), 60.

whether values are indeed plural and incommensurable, not about the difficulty of social choice if that is the case.

The pluralist usually makes the further move of treating the possibility of irreducible conflict among plural values as an attractive feature of pluralist theory, rather than a bug. Our lived experience of moral choice, whether in personal or social domains, includes the experience of conflicting values and tragic choices and of the moral regret that these conflicts and tragedies generate for us. This point flips the monists' index problem back on them, noting the difficulty monist theories face in accounting for the notion that moral choice sometimes involves the need to act even in the face of irreconcilable conflict among values.[65] When this happens, actors are often tormented by their decisions long after they have settled on a particular course of action as the best they can do under the circumstances. For the pluralist, it is rational to perceive such tradeoffs as conflicts, potentially even tragic in scope, and at times to make such choices only with the greatest degree of regret. For the monist, the idea that a rational actor might rationally regret a choice that he understood (correctly) to be the right one – because of its impact on the overall unitary measure of value – can be extremely difficult to explain.

These preliminary moves are only partial rejoinders to the index problem, though. It is at least a valid criticism for monists to argue that pluralist theories are deficient if they utterly fail to offer guidance as to how actors ought to go about choosing in a broad range of contexts. And so pluralists are under some obligation to provide an affirmative account of how reasonable decision making can occur in the face of conflicts between plural and incommensurable values.

This obligation leads to a second stage in the pluralist response to the challenge of indeterminacy. This stage, which acts as something of a preliminary to the pluralist's affirmative account of rational choice, seeks to challenge the assumption that for a choice to be fully rational, it must be specified as clearly superior to all other competing options. Joseph Raz, for example, argues that "[r]ational action is action for (what the agent takes to be) an undefeated reason. It is not necessarily action for a reason that defeats all others."[66] That is, it can be rational to make a choice between two options, neither of which the actor perceives to be clearly superior (in terms of the intrinsic value of the option itself) to the other. Indeed, this is how we understand ourselves as we go about making most decisions.[67] Moreover, the mere fact that the actor has made a choice in favor of one of the options does not imply that

---

[65] See J. J. C. Smart and Bernard Williams, *Utilitarianism: For and Against* (1973), 114–17; Michael Stocker, *Abstract and Concrete Value: Plurality, Conflict, and Maximization*, in ed. Chang, *Incommensurability*, 196, 197–205.

[66] Raz, *The Morality of Freedom* 339; see also Joseph Raz, "Incommensurability and Agency," in ed. Chang, *Incommensurability*, 110, 111 (distinguishing between "rationalist" and "classical" conceptions of human agency).

[67] See ibid., 128.

the actor perceives the option to be superior, and certainly not superior by reference to some commensurating value. To insist otherwise is to beg the questions concerning the incommensurability of value and the nature of rational choice.

The final part of the pluralists' response to the index problem is to offer an affirmative account(s) of how people in various roles can (and should) go about choosing among options that implicate incommensurable goods. The discussion of the possibility and methods of rational choice among incommensurables typically occurs as part of an elaboration of the Aristotelian conception of "practical reason," meaning the process of deliberating about both our ultimate ends and the means of achieving them.[68]

There are many ways for individuals to flourish, and these different paths to flourishing reflect many different values, or goods. The patterns of human life that are consistent with human flourishing will be diverse and varied and marked by pursuit of multiple goods.[69]

But we need not compare all of our choices according to some single scale of value in order to have a principled basis for choosing among them. This is not what rationality requires and it is not what practical reason involves. For a choice among options implicating incommensurable values to be rational, it must take seriously each of those values as values that have a rightful claim on us. What is important, according to David Wiggins, is that, in our deliberative process, we "attend to each value in its separateness and irreducibility to others."[70] The requirement to "attend to each value" will usually reveal a number of options to be inferior. And, indeed, it will often be easier to understand what attending to each value requires in the negative – as ruling out certain options that cannot plausibly be characterized as taking seriously some value or other.

Where every option is "inferior" in the sense of failing to give some fundamental value its due, we are in the zone of tragic choices. As Elizabeth Anderson observes, however, in many (most?) situations, even those that do not involve tragic choices, "[t]here may be very different and incommensurable ways of adequately expressing one's valuations of one's ends."[71] But the possibility that, having taken seriously the demands of several incommensurable values, we still find more than one acceptable option does not make rational choice among them impossible.

Among other things, when confronted with such competing options, we can look to reasons for preferring one choice over the others that do not reflect an assertion that there is a value difference among the options considered in themselves.

---

[68] See David Wiggins, "Incommensurability: Four Proposals," in ed. Chang, *Incommensurability*, 52, 62. For Wiggins's argument on this point as an interpretation of Aristotle, see David Wiggins, "Deliberation and Practical Reason," PROCEEDINGS OF THE ARISTOTELIAN SOCIETY (1975) 76: 29–51.

[69] See John Finnis, *Natural Law and Natural Rights* (1980), 85.

[70] Wiggins, "Incommensurability: Four Proposals," 65.

[71] Anderson, *Value in Ethics and Economics*, 63.

For example, as Raz observes, we can (and do) properly look to agent relative considerations of habits of character to explain our choice for one or another from among a set of acceptable but incommensurable options. An individual agent facing such a choice, for instance, is entitled to ask whether one or another of the options at her disposal fits better with her life goals and commitments, with her project of becoming the kind of person she has chosen to be.[72]

The same can be true in the context of social choice. In collective decision making, we often find that, after deliberating about our ends and the means at our disposal to achieve those ends, we still have a number of options that fail to defeat one another as clearly superior to each of the others. In such situations, we may legitimately choose one of the options simply because it fits better with the constellation of values we have already chosen to pursue through our prior collective decisions. We take it that something like this is at work when people talk about one option or another fitting better with a country's unique "national character." In the United States, for example, a long-standing commitment to individual liberty might make it rational to favor an option that gives particular priority to freedom when choosing among a number of competing (but incommensurable) options for providing access to, say, health care. Charles Taylor seems to be referring to a process like this when he talks about an option's "complementarity"– an understanding of its relative contributions to the various values in the overall scheme of justice that the choice in question reflects.[73] Henry Richardson speaks in very similar terms of a choice's "fit and coherence with other ends and commitments."[74] These bases for choice do not reflect a judgment about which good is more valuable but instead an interpretation of how the goods fit together in the decision maker's (or community's) particular vision of justice and which option best promotes that vision.

As a theory committed to a pluralist account of value, the human flourishing theory of property accepts the possibility that there are multiple ways to choose well between or among competing incommensurable moral values. It must therefore confront the index problem. In the context of both personal morality and law there are situations in which more than one right option is available, and it can be rational to choose among these options. Nevertheless, we concede that spelling out in a more satisfying way the contours of the process of applying practical reason to social choices implicating plural and incommensurable values remains an important challenge for the human flourishing theory of property, and, indeed, for pluralist theories of all kinds.

---

[72] Raz, "Incommensurability and Agency," 124–8; Gregory S. Alexander, "Property and Pluralism," *Fordham L. Rev.* (2011) 80: 101.

[73] See Charles Taylor, "Leading a Life," in ed. Chang, *Incommensurability*, 170.

[74] Richardson, *Democratic Autonomy*, 108–9.

PART II

6

Government Redistribution of Resources

Ethel Javins rents a one-bedroom apartment from Metro Rental.[1] She signs a written lease for a one-year tenancy, with a monthly payment of $800. The lease states that the tenant has inspected the leased premises and takes them "as is." When Javins moves in, she discovers that the bathroom toilet is clogged with paper and waste and will flush only by dumping pails of water into it. Moreover, windows in the kitchen and bedroom are broken, and there is no lock on the front door. The bathroom light and wall outlet don't work. Water leaks from the water pipes of the apartment upstairs. In the bedroom, sections of plaster dangle dangerously from the ceiling. She pleads with Metro Rental to make repairs, but despite repeated promises, no repairs are ever made. Javins consults a lawyer and brings legal action against Metro. Should the court enforce the lease as written or recognize that, regardless of what the parties have agreed, tenants have a right to live in dwellings that do not pose a danger to their health and safety?

In the modern regulatory state, the government frequently acts in ways designed to shift resources from the wealthier to the poorer segments of their societies. This is true not only in the social welfare states of Europe but also in the United States, where state-supported welfare programs traditionally have been less robust. Modern capitalism has become synonymous with redistributive state interventions coexisting with a background market economy. Virtually every jurisdiction in the United States, for example, recognizes an "implied warranty of habitability" in residential leases. Even when a tenant signs a lease that expressly provides for the apartment to be rented "as is," courts will disregard the agreement and require landlords like Metro to repair the apartment up to minimum habitable standards and, in the meantime, will excuse tenants like Javins from paying rent.

---

[1]   The facts of this hypothetical are drawn from *Javins v. First Nat'l Realty Corp.*, 428 F.2d 1071 (D.C. Cir.), *cert. denied*, 400 U.S. 925 (1970).

In this chapter, we will look at various types of state-sanctioned redistribution through the lenses of the property theories that we examined in Part I. Some of these programs involve obvious forms of redistribution, such as progressive taxation to fund monetary transfers to the poor. Others involve in-kind transfers of rights, such as the implied warranty of habitability, where the redistributive aspect of other programs may be less obvious. Despite their different details, all of these acts of redistribution have been controversial. The contours of the debates over their legitimacy and wisdom vary depending upon the theory of property being used to justify or critique them.

UTILITARIANISM AND REDISTRIBUTION

Utilitarian theory, in principle, has no a priori position on the justifiability of redistribution. Its goal is to maximize total utility. One way to improve utility is by shifting valuable resources into the hands of those who would derive the most utility from owning them. Accordingly, if property is allocated such that resources are not already in the hands of those who value them most highly, utilitarianism calls for redistribution of some sort. This simple description, however, leaves out an enormous amount of complexity in the utilitarian approach to redistribution.

The first element of complexity concerns how to move property from those who currently possess it into the hands of those who value it more highly. Most utilitarians agree that, all things being equal, the best way to accomplish this task is through voluntary market transactions. When, for example, a woman purchases a book for ten dollars, the utilitarian says, she gets something she values more than ten dollars (the book), improving her utility. The bookseller gets something she values more than the book (ten dollars), improving her utility. The consequence of the transaction is that things move into the hands of those who value them more highly, increasing overall utility. If this pattern is repeated over and over again, things will have a tendency to wind up where they are most highly valued, and overall utility will be increased.

Institutions and Information

The ability of the market to function properly as an allocative device, however, depends on people having the information they need in order to engage in intelligent transactions that increase their utility. If our book buyer thinks he's receiving a high-quality hardcover book but in reality the seller is passing off a shoddy book with several missing pages, the transaction may not be utility enhancing. If buyers do not have an easy way to identify which booksellers have which books for sale, they may choose to spend their ten dollars on something else. And so the utilitarian case for relying on markets depends on the availability of information as well as institutions (courts, consumer protection agencies, arbitrators) and rules (prohibitions on fraud, incentives for buyers to gather information or for sellers to voluntarily disclose it, rules concerning the enforcement of contract) to ensure that market transactions are mutually beneficial.

Wealth Effects

In addition to information and institutions, the market's ability to distribute property in ways that increase utility depends on participants in the market having the means to express their utilitarian valuations in terms that the market recognizes, typically the willingness to pay money. Substantial inequalities in the distribution of money distort market participants' ability to clearly express the utility they would derive from possessing particular items of property. One way this could happen would be if money has a diminishing marginal utility. To say that money has a diminishing marginal utility is to say that, as human beings acquire more dollars, each additional dollar is worth less to them. In other words, giving some amount of money (say, $100) to someone who has none would generate more utility than giving the same amount to someone who already has $1 million in the bank. In addition, the declining marginal utility of money would mean that the mere fact that a wealthy person is willing to pay $100 for a coat does not demonstrate that she will actually derive more utility from it than a very poor person only willing to pay $10. Thus, to the extent that money has a declining marginal utility, significant doubt arises regarding the ability of the market to distribute goods to those who will derive the most utility from them, except when the initial distribution of wealth is relatively egalitarian. The more unequal the initial distribution, the more the declining marginal utility of money will distort the market's ability to allocate goods in a way that maximizes utility.[2]

Endowment Effects

When human behavior deviates from the assumptions of rational self-interest, market transactions become a less reliable mechanism for maximizing utility. One of the oldest and most robust findings of behavioral economics is the so-called endowment

---

[2] Some theorists have questioned whether income actually shows a diminishing marginal utility. See, for example, Walter J. Blum and Harry Kalven, Jr., "The Uneasy Case for Progressive Taxation," *U. Chi. L. Rev.* 19 (1952): 417; Richard E. Easterlin, "Diminishing Marginal Utility of Income? Caveat Emptor," *Soc. Indicators Research* 70 (2005): 243. Nevertheless, across a range of social sciences, there is widespread agreement that marginal utility declines with increasing income. See ibid., (noting the consensus but questioning its soundness).

effect. According to classical rational actor assumptions, an individual should place the same dollar value on a product whether she owns it or not. That is, if I value a coat at ten dollars, I should be willing to pay ten dollars to purchase it, and I should be willing to sell it for any price over ten dollars. In experimental settings, however, economists almost universally observe that the amount people are willing to spend to obtain something they do not possess is lower than what they demand to part with that same thing if it is already in their possession. According to one early study, participants who were given money were willing to pay half as much to obtain a chocolate bar as they demanded in order to part with the same chocolate bar when it was given to them.[3] This basic pattern – of demanding more to part with property in your possession than you are willing to pay to receive the same item of property – has been replicated in scores of experiments using a wide range of resources.[4] At the margins, the presence of endowment effects acts as a kind of inertia in the market favoring existing allocations of property rights.

Transaction Costs

Even when information is accurate and wealth or endowment effects are not decisive, other factors may prevent utility-enhancing transactions from occurring. These include high transaction costs that arise when large groups of people need to work together to consummate a transaction. For example, the rational actor model assumes that, when large numbers of people must cooperate to sell a good, even if the transaction is utility enhancing overall, individuals will hold out for a larger share of the gains from the transaction. Conversely, when a large number of people must cooperate to purchase the good, rational individuals will free ride on the others and try to contribute as little as possible toward the purchase price. This sort of strategic behavior drives up the costs of successfully negotiating the transaction. Even when the numbers of people involved are very small, as when two neighbors must reach an agreement to transfer a right of way, the dynamic of a so-called bilateral monopoly (when each side knows that the other side can only deal with her) can encourage strategic behavior by rational actors that can ultimately block a mutually beneficial deal.

Recall that in Chapter 1, we described Demsetz's property theory as relying on the notion that the creation of private property generally reduces the transaction costs that stand in the way of internalizing externalities. Although this is sometimes the

---

[3]   See Jack L. Knetsch, "The Endowment Effect and Evidence of Nonreversible Indifference Curves," AM. ECON. REV. 79 (1989): 1277.

[4]   Colin Camerer, "Individual Decision Making," in *The Handbook of Experimental Economics*, eds. John H. Kagel and Alvin E. Roth (1995), 587, 665–70.

case, the plausibility of Demsetz's assertion depends on (among other things) a fit between the spatial scale of the externality and the private property rights. As Robert Ellickson has observed, when the spatial scale of an externality vastly exceeds the scale of private property rights, transaction costs will remain high and market transactions among private owners are unlikely to constitute a viable strategy for internalizing the externality.[5] Indeed, far from reducing transaction costs, in situations where there is a significant spatial mismatch between externalities and property rights, the existence of robust private ownership rights may *increase* transaction costs, generating what Michael Heller has dubbed a "Tragedy of the Anticommons."[6]

Nonmarket Values

Finally, notwithstanding the absence of other sorts of distortions or transaction costs, utilitarians acknowledge that markets do a poor job of allocating resources when people believe that market transactions for certain sorts of goods are not appropriate. Guido Calabresi and A. Douglas Melamed, whose distinction between property rules and liability rules we discussed in Chapter 1, referred to a category of preferences that they called "moralisms," which, by virtue of their particular content, "do not lend themselves to collective measurement which is acceptably objective and nonarbitrary."[7] Economists have proposed various methods for measuring or monetizing these sorts of preferences, and those methods have been the subject of a great deal of academic discussion. But setting aside the merits of those techniques, these preferences will not typically make themselves felt in market transactions, and so, where they are pervasive, they represent another reason for doubting that allocations achieved by the market will maximize utility.

Responding to Market Failure

When these sorts of forces (informational or institutional deficiencies, wealth effects, transaction costs, nonmarket values) stand in the way of ostensibly utility-enhancing market transactions, market failure can prevent property from moving toward those who value it most, and the utilitarian case for some form of involuntary redistribution is strengthened. But the utilitarian case for redistribution is more complicated than merely demonstrating that there are utility gains to be had from reallocating property from one person to another. Costs involved in coercively reallocating

---

5   See Robert C. Ellickson, "Property in Land," YALE L. J. 102 (1993): 1315, 1323–31.
6   Michael A. Heller, "The Tragedy of the Anticommons," Harv. L. Rev. 111 (1998): 621.
7   Guido Calabresi and A. Douglas Melamed, "Property Rules, Liability Rules, and Inalienability: One View of the Cathedral," HARV. L. REV., 85 (1972): 1089, 1111–13.

property must also be taken into account. And, from the point of view of evaluating costs, certain means of reallocating property will perform better than others. The utilitarian will only favor redistribution when the gains from redistribution exceed the costs of undertaking it. And, even then, she will favor the means of redistribution that generates the greatest utility gains while generating the lowest costs.

The utilitarian must consider two broad redistributive strategies. First, the party who values the property more can engage in self-help, seizing it directly from the current owner. (A similar option, which we will treat as equivalent, would be for a third party to seize the property on behalf of the person who wants or needs it.) Although context matters a great deal, from a utilitarian standpoint, this sort of self-help redistribution has the potential to generate enormous costs, both for the taker and for those from whom the property is taken. These costs include the possibility of resistance by the owner from whom the property is taken, as well as the insecurity that self-help engenders in owners more generally. In addition, the self-helper may not take the property from the owner who values it the least. Finally, even though some self-help may be utility enhancing, carving out legal space for it invites bad (or perhaps merely misinformed) actors to engage in self-help even when market transactions are available to them. Because of both the direct and indirect costs of self-help redistribution, utilitarian theory restricts it to situations in which the utility gains are highest and the costs incurred are likely to be low.[8]

The law of adverse possession, which permits a nonowner to acquire land without the owner's consent by actually and openly occupying it for a period of seven to ten years, maps onto this utilitarian account of self-help redistribution fairly well.[9] The law imposes enormous costs on adverse possessors, who must occupy property for a relatively long period of time. By engaging in the activities required to qualify for adverse possession, the adverse possessor makes it very clear that she actually places a high value on the property in question. The law also makes it very easy for the title owner to resist adverse possession during the adverse possession period. This protects other owners from becoming demoralized by successful cases of adverse possession (since they can easily avoid suffering the same fate). It also ensures that, when an adverse possessor does actually succeed, the title owner is someone who does not place much value on the property – since she could not be bothered to exercise ownership rights within the prescribed period of time. The doctrine of necessity, which permits people to take property from others in moments of dire need, also seems to make sense from a utilitarian perspective.

[8] See, for example, Henry E. Smith, "Self-Help and the Nature of Property," *J. L. Econ. & Pol'y* 1 (2005): 69, 80–92.

[9] See Lee Fennell, "Efficient Trespass," *Nw. U. L. Rev.* 100 (2006): 1037; Eduardo M. Peñalver and Sonia K. Katyal, *Property Outlaws* (2010), 148–52.

In addition to permitting self-help redistribution in certain contexts, the state may opt to step in and redistribute property in order to increase overall utility. State-sponsored redistribution is likely to be more orderly and predictable than self-help. Accordingly, the state can undertake redistribution without generating the same degree of anxiety that uncoordinated self-help might produce among current owners. Generally speaking, then, when redistribution is utility enhancing, notwithstanding its costs, state-sponsored redistribution will likely perform better, from a utilitarian standpoint, than self-help.[10]

On the other hand, state-sponsored redistribution comes with costs of its own, including the impact that redistribution may have on the incentives of owners to engage in productive behavior. In addition, there are numerous costs associated with creating the state's infrastructure of redistribution. These include sheer administrative costs. They also include the possibility that state actors may act for reasons other than the maximization of utility. Thus, given the opportunity, they may use the cover of redistributive programs as opportunities for self-dealing or, relatedly, for paying off the well-connected. This latter possibility has led some theorists to oppose redistribution on the ground that it will more often be – counterproductively – used for the benefit of the already wealthy rather than to improve the situation of the poorest.[11] These claims turn on complex and controversial empirical questions concerning the operation and consequences of particular redistributive policies.

Whenever the state opts to engage in redistribution, it must always choose between redistributing property in kind (e.g., by taking actual items of property or redefining property entitlements) and redistributing through a system of taxation and cash payments. Some theorists have argued that taxation and cash redistribution is always a superior way for the state to engage in the process.[12] But there may be circumstances in which in-kind redistribution makes utilitarian sense. One such case involves situations in which the beneficiaries of redistribution have very high subjective attachments to particular items of property such that reallocation of the thing itself is the cheapest (or perhaps the only) way to achieve the benefits of redistribution. Cases of adverse possession often match this description. In cases of in-kind redistribution, paying compensation to the party losing the item of property can help to spread more evenly the costs of achieving the benefits of redistribution.[13]

---

[10]　See Peñalver and Katyal, *Property Outlaws*, 156–8.
[11]　See Richard A. Epstein, *Skepticism and Freedom* (2003), 61; cf. Hanoch Dagan, *Property: Values and Institutions* (2011), 97.
[12]　See Louis Kaplow and Steven Shavell, "Why the Legal System is Less Efficient than the Income Tax in Redistributing Income," *J. LEGAL. STUD.* 23 (1994): 667 ("Redistribution is accomplished more efficiently through the income tax system than through the use of legal rules.").
[13]　See Thomas W. Merrill, "Property Rules, Liability Rules, and Adverse Possession," *Nw. U. L. REV.* 79 (1984): 1122.

In addition, when political constraints make taxation and cash redistribution unlikely, in-kind redistribution may be a feasible second-best solution. For instance, in a political environment where taxes are unpopular, it may still be possible to increase overall utility by, say, imposing an implied warranty of habitability or rent control on landlords. Even though it would be – let us assume – more efficient to give poor renters more cash to purchase better quality housing, it might still be utility enhancing to opt for the second-best in-kind transfer.[14]

The state must also choose at which geographic scale to engage in redistribution. This choice of scale can have a significant impact on the effectiveness of redistributive policy – whether in cash or in kind – since redistribution at smaller geographic scales may facilitate avoidance of the redistributive policy by those who are well off. For example, if a municipality engages in redistributive taxation, those from whom income would be redistributed may opt – at relatively low cost to themselves – to move to a neighboring municipality to avoid the redistribution. Redistributive polices at the metropolitan or state or provincial level may be harder to avoid. Depending on the circumstances, redistribution at the national level can only be avoided at great cost.[15] The relative ease of avoiding local redistribution has led some theorists to argue that, from a utilitarian standpoint, redistribution should normally be undertaken at higher levels of geographic or governmental scale.[16]

Scale can also have an impact on redistribution by limiting the feasibility of redistribution in certain contexts. It is likely that, in utilitarian terms, there would be substantial utilitarian gains from redistributing across national boundaries, say, from wealthy countries to poor countries.[17] Yet the fact that people from poor countries cannot participate in the political process in wealthier countries virtually guarantees that no significant international redistribution will occur.

Conclusion

Precisely which redistributive measures are (from a utility standpoint) cost justified and which redistributive strategies are most efficient constitute deeply difficult empirical questions. One can accept all the premises of utilitarian property theory and come down on different sides of the question whether a particular redistributive program is wise or just. The key point we wish to emphasize, however, is that – normatively speaking – utilitarian property theory leaves a great deal of

---

[14] See Peñalver and Katyal, *Property Outlaws*, 157–8.

[15] See, for example, Wallace E. Oates, *Fiscal Federalism* (1972); Paul E. Peterson, *City Limits* (1981), chap. 9.

[16] But see Clayton P. Gillette, "Local Redistribution, Living Wage Ordinances, and Judicial Intervention," *Nw. U. L. Rev.* 101 (2007): 1057, 1067–88.

[17] See, for example, Peter Singer, *One World* (2004).

room for redistribution. The scale of that redistribution and the precise redistributive mechanisms that utilitarian theory prescribes will be extremely dependent upon empirical questions. Despite the uncertainties, utilitarian theory provides a useful framework for thinking about the questions involved in redistributing property.

LIBERTARIANS AND REDISTRIBUTION

Perhaps the most prominent objection to state-compelled wealth redistribution has come from libertarian property theory. The connection between libertarians' opposition to redistribution and their property theory is straightforward. Libertarian theorists argue for property rights that are so robust that they do not give way to the sorts of interests that underlie demands for redistribution. Indeed, for certain libertarians, property rights seem to constitute the full embodiment of individual rights and so are the only kinds of rights worth discussing. Thus, Ayn Rand argues that "[t]he right to life is the source of all rights – and the right to property is their only implementation."[18]

More sophisticated libertarians, such as Richard Epstein, have qualified their opposition to redistribution, acknowledging that the extreme need of some in the community can trump the property rights other people hold over their surplus resources.[19] But it can be difficult to make this exception fit with their broader theory of property without introducing qualifications that undermine the larger libertarian account of property rights. Thus, Robert Nozick is more typical of the libertarian position when he concurs with Rand that property rights are the principal embodiment of individual rights – at least as they relate to external resources – and are only constrained by the negative rights of others. As a consequence, human interests, such as survival, do not give rise to affirmative redistributive claims over owned property. "Even to exercise his right to determine how something he owns is to be used," Nozick says, "may require other means he must acquire a right to, for example, food to keep him alive; he must put together, with the cooperation of others, a feasible package."[20] Thus, Nozick concludes, no one's rights are violated if they are forced to choose between working (presumably under whatever conditions the employer demands) and starving.[21]

Notwithstanding the apparent harshness of Nozick's discussion of need, even this hard-line libertarian position does not amount to the assertion that property rights

---

[18] Ayn Rand, "Man's Rights," in *Capitalism: The Unknown Ideal* (1966), 286, 288.
[19] See Epstein, *Skepticism and Freedom*, 98–100.
[20] Robert Nozick, *Anarchy, State, and Utopia* (1974), 238.
[21] See ibid., 262–4. Contrast this with Locke (I, 42) on the conditions that a property owner can demand in the face of another's necessity. John Locke, *Two Treatises of Government*, ed. Mark Goldie, Everyman's Library (1993).

are absolute. After all, libertarians acknowledge that the property rights of one owner must give way to the coextensive property rights of another. Thus, they admit the need for a law of nuisance, which prohibits using your property in a way that harms the property rights of others. In addition, libertarians usually admit that there might be certain intrinsic constraints operating within property rights as a result of the limitations on permissible appropriation from the commons. As we saw in Chapter 2, for example, Nozick viewed his version of the Lockean proviso – however watered down – as a continuing limitation on property rights. And, as we will discuss in Chapter 9, Rand believed that intellectual property rights must be limited in duration. But none of these limitations on property rights permit the state to transfer property or wealth, once defined and allocated, from one person to another when that action is taken in order to adjust the distribution of wealth or income generated by consensual transactions in the market.

Robert Nozick's Libertarian Argument against Redistribution

Nozick's argument against redistribution begins with the observation that theories of distributive justice can either be based on "patterned" principles or "historical" principles.[22] By *patterned* theories of distributive justice, Nozick refers to theories that define the justice of a particular distribution on the basis of its conformity to some ideal distributive end state. An egalitarian theory of distributive justice is patterned in this way, as is a theory that says that people are entitled to property necessary to meet their needs. In contrast, by *historical* principles of distributive justice, Nozick refers to theories of distribution that are entirely backward looking. These procedural theories assess the justice of a distribution exclusively on the basis of whether the procedures leading to the current distribution were permissible, without regard to how property is actually held.

Because property owners in a free society will undertake transactions that upset prescribed patterns, he argues, "no end-state principle or distributional patterned principle of justice can be continuously realized without continuous interference with people's lives."[23] Nozick does not fully explain what is so wrong with these interferences, which might be no more onerous than the requirement to file an annual tax return. He thinks it is self-evident that, if an existing distribution of property is just, then the distribution that results from voluntary transactions among competent, property owning adults will also be just. And he appears to believe that redistributive interventions required to maintain patterns of distribution squelch human freedom by undoing consequences people have freely chosen. But this argument

[22] Nozick, *Anarchy, State, and Utopia*, 155–64.
[23] Ibid., 163.

rests on an overly broad description of what people choose to bring about when they enter into a transaction.

Consider Nozick's famous Wilt Chamberlain example, which we will also discuss in connection with intellectual property in Chapter 9. In the example, one million people voluntarily drop a quarter in a box in order to watch Wilt Chamberlain play basketball.[24] If, at the end of the season, Chamberlain has received two hundred and fifty thousand dollars, "[c]an anyone else complain on grounds of justice?" Nozick's confidence in the answer to this question rests in part on the unfounded assumption that no one is affected by the private transactions between Chamberlain and his fans other than the participants themselves. But nonparticipants may find their circumstances changed for the worse as a result of the Chamberlain transactions in ways that justify them in objecting. They might never put their quarter in the Chamberlain box, and yet find that their standing in the community is reduced by the great rise in Chamberlain's wealth and influence.[25] Or they might be the children of a Chamberlain addict, someone who puts so many quarters in the Chamberlain box that he fails to save enough money for the family's meals. If the chain of transactions is long enough, and if we begin to introduce differences in luck and native talent, the consequences of voluntary transactions for nonparticipants can become extremely severe and might very plausibly be described as unjust.

The fact that voluntary transactions can, individually or in the aggregate, harm third parties can, even accepting many of Nozick's libertarian assumptions, justify coercive efforts to undo some of the consequences of freely chosen transactions, including through redistribution. Imagine that Ethel Javins, the tenant from our example at the beginning of the chapter, has a six-year-old child who lives with her in the apartment. Even if, on libertarian grounds, we believed that Javins could justly be held to the terms of her agreement to rent the dilapidated apartment from Metro, do either Metro or Javins have the right to subject Javins's child to those conditions? The need to protect people who do not consent to a bargain but are affected by it provides a powerful objection to libertarian arguments against interfering with the terms of voluntary market transactions on the basis of individual autonomy. The standard libertarian response to this sort of objection is to define *harm* in extremely narrow terms that exclude the objection of most people indirectly affected by a consensual transaction. The challenge then becomes how to justify embracing such a restrictive conception of harm.

---

[24] Ibid., 161. Wilt Chamberlain is one of the most dominant basketball players in NBA history. Among other things, he is famous for having scored 100 points in a single game on March 2, 1962. See "Wilt Chamberlain," in *Wikipedia* (available at http://en.wikipedia.org/wiki/Wilt_Chamberlain).

[25] See G. A. Cohen, "Robert Nozick and Wilt Chamberlain: How Patterns Preserve Liberty," *ERKENNTNIS* 11 (1977): 5, 10.

In addition to their tendency to ignore the impact of market transactions on nonconsenting third parties, libertarian arguments against redistributive government intervention overstate the intrusion of redistribution on individuals' liberty to use their property as they see fit (assuming for the purposes of discussion that such a liberty exists). This is particularly the case with taxation and cash transfers. Return to the Wilt Chamberlain hypothetical. If the state were to tax Chamberlain at a marginal rate of thirty percent on his earnings in order to fund redistributive programs of various sorts, how severely would Chamberlain's liberty be impaired, as long as he remained free voluntarily to enter into the transaction (or not) knowing that such a tax would be collected?[26] The point is even stronger for those who put the twenty-five cents into the Chamberlain box. Most of them certainly would not care what percentage of their twenty-five cents Chamberlain receives, as long as they get the chance to see him play. After all, they are engaged in a market transaction, not giving a gift.[27] But even if they did care, how significantly does it impair their liberty that Chamberlain receives eighteen cents instead of the entire quarter? Redistributive taxes do not force either the payer or the payee to enter into transactions against their wills. Although the income-leisure tradeoff means that, at the margins, taxes reduce the incentive to enter into profitable transactions, they do not force anyone to do (or refrain from doing) anything.[28] Even with the thirty percent tax, Chamberlain (who we will assume knows about the tax) plays, if at all, only voluntarily, and everyone who puts a quarter in his box also does so voluntarily.

A 100 percent tax on certain transactions – for example, gifts – would obviously constitute a restriction of liberty in the way that Nozick fears. But it is harder to make the case that a lower tax rate would have the same impact on liberty. In other words, it is implausible to argue, as Nozick does, that *any* commitment to redistribution in order to preserve some sort of distributive pattern necessitates a prohibition of voluntary, pattern upsetting acts. Even more directly intrusive forms of redistribution, like the implied warranty of habitability claim brought by Javins, sometimes only interfere with owners' liberty at the margins. Metro, after all, remains free not to enter into a residential lease with Javins. And arguments that the warranty interferes with tenants' freedoms to enter into leases for uninhabitable apartments ignore the fact that the warranty is only enforced if a tenant raises the issue.[29]

---

[26] Ibid., 15 (noting that belief in the justice of patterns does not require belief that patterns must be perfectly preserved at all times).

[27] See Barbara Fried, "Wilt Chamberlain Revisited," PHIL. & PUB. AFF., 24 (1995): 226, 240.

[28] This is the problem with Nozick's memorable claim that income taxation is morally equivalent to forced labor. Nozick, *Anarchy, State, and Utopia*, 169.

[29] In an argument that suggests that the informal coercion of landlord-tenant relations might well exceed that of the implied warranty, Lior Strahilevitz has suggested that fears of landlord retribution when tenants search for other apartments can exert a powerful disincentive on tenants to raise the implied warranty. See Lior Jacob Strahilevitz, *Information and Exclusion* (2011), 134–40. In addition to tenants'

In the end, libertarian arguments against redistribution rest on the strong assertion that rights of private property include the right to ensure that those with whom owners transact receive everything owners give them. Correlatively, they assume, rights of private property entitle each person to own all the things other people are willing to give him. On this view, the state's interference with distributions of wealth and property, even using relatively unintrusive tools like a modestly progressive income tax, impermissibly intrudes on ownership rights understood in this very serious way.

Although libertarian arguments against redistribution rest ultimately on very strong claims about the nature of property rights, their theories of property do not provide a sufficient foundation for those claims. As we discussed in Chapter 2, John Locke's theory of property, on which Nozick relies, does not support the existence of the extremely robust natural private property rights necessary to drive his arguments against redistribution. Moreover, while Locke's *political* theory rules out redistribution in the absence of democratic consent, it gives democratically elected governments wide latitude to redefine property entitlements.[30]

Redistribution within (Broadly) Libertarian Assumptions

Thoroughgoing libertarianism about property rights is an unworkable position, and therefore extremely unusual among academic theorists.[31] Without the permissibility of some coercion, no system of taxation – and hence, no state, and therefore, arguably, no private property – would be viable. Rand and her followers called for a system of voluntary taxation,[32] but it is safe to say that no such system could ever be made to work. In contrast, Epstein frankly admits that the state may coercively deprive citizens of property when it offers them something of equal or greater value in return.[33] Although not as forthright in this regard, Nozick also suggests the

---

vulnerability to landlord retribution, David Super has pointed to a number of other factors that have, in recent years, diminished the effectiveness of the implied warranty. See David Super, "The Rise and Fall of the Implied Warranty of Habitability," *Cal. L. Rev.* 99 (2011): 389–463.

[30] Locke, *Two Treatises*, II, 140.

[31] In his 1989 book, *The Examined Life*, Robert Nozick called his earlier, uncompromising libertarianism "seriously inadequate," (Robert Nozick, *The Examined Life* (1989), 286–7). In subsequent interviews shortly before his death, however, he suggested that he still considered himself a libertarian. See, for example, Julian Sanchez, *An Interview with Robert Nozick*, July 26, 2001 (http://www.trinity.edu/rjensen/NozickInterview.htm).

[32] See Ayn Rand, "Government Financing in a Free Society," in *The Virtue of Selfishness* (1964), 157. "In a fully free society, taxation – or, to be exact, payment for governmental services – would be voluntary. Since the proper services of government – the police, the armed forces, the law courts – are demonstrably needed by individual citizens and affect their interests directly, the citizens would (and should) be willing to pay for such services, as they pay for insurance."

[33] See Richard A. Epstein, *Takings* (1985), chap. 14.

permissibility of coercive takings when coupled with some kind of compensation.[34] But once the door is cracked open for such coercive takings – even with the requirement of in-kind compensation – the permissibility of redistribution becomes very hard to rule out as a matter of principle.

The difficulty of constraining the scope of these quid pro quo takings is generated by two very challenging framing issues. First, the temporal frame over which compensation is to occur is not self-defining.[35] Consequently, the state might make an argument that a particular act of redistributive taxation is justified because it will yield greater long-term economic stability and growth that will, over time, benefit even those from whom property is disproportionately taken. The plausibility of this justification will depend on extremely difficult empirical predictions.

The second framing question concerns the proper way of describing the breadth of redistributive practices. We might look at each demand for a tax payment from each individual property owner under an existing progressive tax scheme as a single redistributive act that needs to be justified on its own merits. More broadly, we might view the establishment of the progressive tax scheme as a single, composite redistributive practice that must be justified in the aggregate. Even more broadly, we might view the entire political and economic system operating in a particular community (call it the "regime") as the relevant object of justification. That regime will include the tax system, the services and public works those taxes fund, the regulations the government imposes, and the accommodations it makes. Depending on the breadth of our evaluative focus, we might see a great deal of impermissible redistribution or, alternatively, a lot of permissible give and take that offset one another.

Nozick and Epstein would like to keep the frame of reference very narrowly focused on specific redistributive actions at specific moments in time, but this is inconsistent with the position that both of them take in justifying the permissibility of private appropriation from the commons against objections by those who can no longer appropriate. In that context (their discussion of the Lockean proviso), they want to cast the net very widely and ask whether those who can no longer appropriate are better off, all things considered, living in a society that recognizes private ownership.[36] Using such a broad frame, the question we should ask is not whether each and every redistributive act that occurs as a result of a particular practice or regime constitutes (at the moment it is implemented) a Pareto improvement. Instead, the question may be whether the regime as a whole was validly implemented in the first place. In Nozick's or Epstein's terms, the question is whether that regime – considered as a whole – makes each person subject to it better off in some sense than she would be under a different regime.

---

[34] See Nozick, *Anarchy, State, and Utopia*, 119; Richard A. Epstein, "One Step Beyond Nozick's Minimal State," Soc. Phil. & Pol'y 22 (2005): 286, 300–4.

[35] See Dagan, *Property: Values and Institutions*, 102–7.

[36] Nozick, *Anarcy, State, and Utopia*, 177; Epstein, *Takings*, 15.

Moreover, in order to rule out the permissibility of redistribution, Nozick and Epstein would need to assert more than simply that shifting toward a particular regime (from, say, laissez faire to the welfare state) makes those who lose property within that regime worse off, even in the long run. They must also defend the proposition that the prior practice or regime (in this example, laissez faire) did not itself make anyone worse off when it supplanted its own predecessor, and so on. Answering this extremely challenging series of questions depends on determining the precise historical trajectory of a given society back into the origins of private ownership in prehistory. For example, one might argue that a European-style welfare state is a necessary institutional mechanism for ensuring that no one is harmed in the move from the kinds of intimate, face-to-face societies that existed before the rise of capitalist systems of production. Even if it makes those who won under the prior regime of laissez faire worse off, that loss might simply constitute the necessary byproduct of the effort to rectify even more ancient injustices. Disproving these assertions with any confidence would be a very challenging undertaking.

Conclusion

Libertarian property theories oppose most forms of government redistribution, but it is not clear that their position is sufficiently supported, either by their theories of private ownership or by their concerns with the impact of redistribution on individual freedom. Among libertarian theorists, Epstein is the most forthright about this theoretical shortcoming. Particularly in more recent work, he has tended to rest his arguments against redistributive government action more squarely on utilitarian grounds, contending that redistribution is counterproductive and utility destroying.[37]

THE PERSONALITY/PERSONHOOD THEORIES AND REDISTRIBUTION

Georg W. F. Hegel had nothing to say about taxation specifically. Nor did he directly address questions about the propriety of collective redistribution of property or wealth transfers. Nevertheless, his personality theory does have implications for property redistribution on whatever form. On the whole, the theory tends to support redistribution of property, although the argument is not straightforward.

As we saw in Chapter 3, for Hegel, property is the means to embodying individual freedom. Recall also that self-realization through mastery of things must be based on a common will, (i.e., the process through which the isolated self becomes socialized through mutual recognition with the other). The atomistic self is an inadequate foundation for embodied freedom because it is insecure and, ultimately, self-defeating: If

---

[37] See Epstein, *Skepticism and Freedom* (2003), 59–64.

the singular self is all that is necessary for freedom, then there is no basis for opposing crime. A more secure foundation for freedom requires acceptance of the common will – mutual recognition between the self and the other as ends.[38]

Acceptance of the common will as the foundation of freedom involves substantive changes in the content of individual rights. Grounded in the common will rather than self-sufficiency, the right to embodied freedom encompasses not simply the negative right of freedom from interference, but the positive right to effective autonomy as well.[39] That is, the content of the common will stems not from the content of the isolated self alone (a content that is indifferent to power relations and to the vicissitudes of the market), but a content that takes seriously the socialized self and the obligation of moral agents to recognize one another as ends. Alan Brudner refers to this content variously as "equity" and "the paradigm of moral autonomy."[40] By those terms he means "the idea of a freedom the right to which entails duties not only of forbearance but also of affirmative concern."[41]

Affirmative concern requires that, collectively, we attend to the material preconditions of autonomous actions. Hegel's claim, after all, is that all people need property to develop their personality and their freedom.[42] Now, Hegel does *not* mean that it is any single person's duty to satisfy another's material needs. Enough of the formal right remains that we, individually, are liable to others only for misfeasance (apart from contract).[43] But there is a collective obligation to alleviate poverty, and this obligation must have implications for the shape of the negative right of freedom. As Brudner states, "[A]n owner's right against takings of property is now *inwardly* limited by the equal right of all persons to the material prerequisites of self-determined action."[44] Concretely, this means that the state may legitimately – that is, consistently with the owner's negative rights – redistribute private property so long as this action is taken for the purpose of securing the freedom of all. Redistribution does not violate the owner's negative right to freedom because the collective obligation to meet property needs is an internal limitation upon that right rather than being externally imposed upon the right. That is, it is one of the constitutive factors that shape the very contours of the negative right.

The same considerations lead Hegelians to view property regulations favorably, especially when the effect of such regulations is a net transfer of wealth from wealthy property owners to the less advantaged.[45] Examples of such regulations may

[38] See Alan Brudner, *The Unity of the Common Law: Studies in Hegelian Jurisprudence* (1995), 69–71.
[39] Ibid., 71.
[40] Ibid., 72.
[41] Ibid.
[42] See Jeremy Waldron, *The Right to Private Property* (1988).
[43] Ibid., 73.
[44] Ibid., 74 (italics added).
[45] See, for example, Brudner, *Unity of the Common Law*, 74.

include landlord-tenant laws like the nonwaivable warranty of habitability, wetlands regulations, and housing antidiscrimination laws. So long as these regulatory actions are undertaken for the purposes of protecting persons vulnerable to property-based power or preventing the exercise of property rights that deny human equality, they are valid measures that protect freedom from subjugation. Such measures are part of the substantive content of the common will, the set of norms that Brudner calls *equity*. The important point is, as Brudner states, "Equity has...ceased to be an external and non-legal corrective to a right based on a nonequitable principle; it has become itself the principle of law."[46]

Margaret Jane Radin's personhood theory tends to justify redistributive measures, but not in any straightforward fashion. It does not seek to justify redistribution in general but only in the context of particular categories of goods. Moreover, when it supports redistributive collective actions, it does not do so for the sake of equality, but instead in the interest of protecting and promoting the development of individual personhood.

Radin's discussion of redistribution under the personhood theory suggests that the theory favors redistribution in kind rather than in cash. Rather than effecting redistribution through progressive taxation, Radin prefers protecting specific assets that are closely tied to one's personhood. So, for example, she supports residential rent control (at least under some circumstances), not on the basis of what Nozick calls a patterned theory of distributive justice, but on the nonutilitarian view that housing should not be treated as a mere market commodity.[47] Conceding that "no general principles compel either that rent control is always justified or that it never is,"[48] Radin contends that "the real purpose of rent control is to make it possible for existing tenants to stay where they are, with roughly the same proportion of their income going to rent as they have become used to...."[49] The basis of this purpose is an intuition that she asserts as a general rule: "The intuitive general rule is that preservation of one's home is a stronger claim than preservation of one's business, or that noncommercial personal use of an apartment as a home is morally entitled to more weight than purely commercial landlording."[50] Important, protection under this general rule extends only to *existing* tenants and not to would-be tenants. That is, it is the tenant's interest in an *"established home"* for which Radin seeks protection.[51]

Radin draws upon her distinction between personal and fungible property in developing her argument. As we saw in Chapter 3, *personal property* consists of those

[46] Ibid.
[47] See Margaret Jane Radin, *Reinterpreting Property* (1993), 73.
[48] Ibid., 74.
[49] Ibid.
[50] Ibid., 79–80.
[51] Ibid., 81 (italics in original).

objects in which the owners become so self-invested that their identities or sense of themselves are intertwined with them.[52] Radin tells us, "The 'home' – usually conceived of as an owner-occupied single-family residence – is a paradigm case of personal property of our social context."[53] Residential tenancy, she argues, carries the same moral weight insofar as a tenant considers an apartment to be her home in the very same sense.

Putting aside possible objections that might be raised to the rest of the argument, what needs to be stressed here is that Radin's theory is *not* a theory of distributive justice. Indeed, she concedes that it is far from certain that residential rent control always or even usually results in a net redistribution of wealth from landlords as a class to tenants as a class or from the wealthy to the poor. The actual wealth effects depend upon a variety of market conditions such that it is difficult to generalize about the distributive consequences of residential rent control.[54] But that is not Radin's concern. Rather than offering a welfare rights argument, which would justify minimal entitlements to *some* shelter and then only based on economic need, the personhood theory justifies protection to the apartment that the tenant *already* occupies. Moreover, economic need plays no role as a filter for choosing among recipients of such protection. Still, it seems likely that under Radin's scheme some degree of wealth redistribution from landlords to tenants would occur, and it would be justified indirectly out of considerations of personhood and protection of sense of self.

REDISTRIBUTION AND FLOURISHING

Aristotle was more than passingly familiar with taxation, and he directly addressed the government's power to tax in the *Politics*. Greek cities had the power to tax, and Aristotle thought they should use it to alleviate poverty. In fact, he criticized Sparta for failing to make sufficient use of its taxing power.[55] He thought that the state could not depend solely on the generosity of wealthy individuals to take care of the problem of poverty.

Aristotle did not address the moral or political legitimacy of redistributive taxation as such, but he certainly did address the broader issue of economic equality. In general, Aristotle was not an egalitarian.[56] He did not favor equal division of land. Human flourishing, he believed, requires only that every citizen has sufficient land to live a virtuous life, no more, no less.[57] But, with respect to resources

---

[52] See Chapter 3, supra.
[53] See Radin, *Reinterpreting Property*, 83.
[54] It must be noted, however, that the consensus view among American economists is that the distributive effects of residential rent control are not, on the whole, an effective wealth redistributive tool.
[55] Aristotle, *Politics*, trans. Ernest Barker (1982), II.9 1271b10–17.
[56] Aristotle, *Politics*, II.7 1266b24–35; Richard Kraut, *Aristotle* (2002), 348.
[57] Aristotle, *Nicomachean Ethics*, trans. Martin Ostwald (1962), I.10 1101a 15.

other than land, Aristotle was more egalitarian, at least among those who counted as citizens. He favored equal education for all citizens, equal sharing of common meals, and full equality of citizen participation in public office and political assembly.[58]

Recently, scholars have disagreed about the extent to which Aristotle favored redistribution of resources. Martha Nussbaum has argued that Aristotle's ideas support social democracy of the form existing, for example, in some Scandinavian countries where collective mechanisms, including steeply progressive taxation, are used to redistribute wealth on the basis of need.[59] She does not claim that Aristotle himself explicitly advocated social democratic positions; rather, her argument is that he laid the philosophical foundation for such positions.

Her argument is straightforward: Aristotle thought that the main purpose of the political community is to provide for the good life of its citizens. Such a life requires a minimum level of material welfare. Distributive justice requires that citizens receive goods according to their material needs. We may infer, then, that Aristotle thought that it was the political community's duty to provide all citizens what they need to live a good life according to their individual needs. The basic claims of this argument are consistent with Aristotle's views, but some scholars have balked at labeling Aristotle a full-fledged social democrat.[60] Aside from the obvious problem that Aristotle, like everyone else in his culture, excluded everyone but free white males from citizenship, one scholar points out that it is not at all clear that Aristotle was so committed to distributive justice that he was willing to rectify social disadvantage.[61] For example, Aristotle says that the best flutes should be allocated to the most accomplished players, regardless of birth or beauty.[62] But the best players might be those wealthy enough to have gotten the best lessons. This interpretation would exclude those who have the best natural potential, the result that presumably would be favored by the social democrat so that persons who *would* be the best flute players but for their disadvantaged backgrounds are not excluded.

Whatever the correct outcome of this debate, it is clear that Aristotle favored requiring citizens to contribute to the common good according to their ability to do so.[63] This would certainly involve substantial collectively compelled transfers of

---

[58] See Kraut, *Aristotle*, 349.

[59] See Martha C. Nussbaum, "Nature, Function, and Capability: Aristotle on Political Distribution," *Oxford Studies in Ancient Philosophy*, supp. vol., ed. Julia Annas and Robert H. Grimm (1988), 145; Martha Nussbaum, "Aristotelian Social Democracy," in *Liberalism and the Good*, ed. R. Bruce Douglass et al. (1990), 203.

[60] See, for example, Richard Mulgan, "Was Aristotle an 'Aristotelian Social Democrat'?" *Ethics* 111 (2000): 79; Robert Mayhew, "Aristotle on Property," *REV. OF METAPHYSICS* 46 (1993): 803.

[61] See Mulgan, "Was Aristotle an 'Aristotelian Social Democrat'?" 92–3.

[62] Aristotle, *Politics*, III.12 1282b31–1283a3.

[63] See Kraut, *Aristotle*, 351.

wealth from the rich to the poor. On the question of redistribution, Aristotle may not have been a socialist, then, but he certainly was no Nozickean either.[64]

Setting aside what Aristotle himself thought, the modern Aristotelian human flourishing theory of property, although not a theory of distributive justice as such, clearly has distributive implications. Indeed, from within this approach, redistribution is something of a misnomer. The term redistribution presupposes the existence of some prior, legitimate distribution of the property entitlement, which the social obligation norm then modifies. But that way of looking at things begs the question of the legitimacy of the initial distribution of the entitlement.[65] The human flourishing theory does not redistribute entitlements so much as it defines them. State v. Shack, a case well known to law students, illustrates this point.[66]

In Shack, two individuals who worked for government-funded aid organizations entered private property for the purpose of providing medical aid and legal services to migrant workers employed and housed upon the land. When the owner/employer demanded that the defendants leave, they refused. They were then convicted of criminal trespass. On appeal, the New Jersey Supreme Court held that there was no trespass because, under New Jersey common law, ownership of real property did not include the right to bar visitors to the owner's resident employees under these circumstances.

The decision in Shack did not involve any judicial redistribution of entitlements. Rather, the court in that case defined the parameters of the landownership, finding that the rights associated with landownership did not include the right to control the people with whom workers residing on one's land associated.

Recall that the human flourishing theory draws on the capabilities approach first developed by Amartya Sen and Martha Nussbaum.[67] The capabilities approach itself is not a theory of distributive justice in the same way that, say, John Rawls's theory is. Theories of distributive justice must specify a distribuendum that they regard as the object of justice. Rawls's theory seeks justice in the distribution of what he calls primary goods. In his theory, then, primary goods, that is, "things which it is supposed a rational man wants whatever else he wants," are the distribuenda.[68] Similarly, egalitarian welfare theories use welfare as the distribuendum. Such theories are sometimes called resourcist theories. The capabilities approach is not resourcist. It does not focus on the equal distribution of some specified category of basic means. Rather than focusing on the distribution of some category of means, it focuses on what individuals may gain by such means. It is based on the insight that

[64]　See Mayhew, "Aristotle on Property," 822 n. 50.
[65]　See Liam Murphy and Thomas Nagel, The Myth of Ownership: Taxes and Justice (2002).
[66]　277 A.2d 369 (N.J. 1971).
[67]　See Chapter 4, supra.
[68]　John Rawls, A Theory of Justice (rev. ed. 1999; 1971), 78–80.

the value that any asset has to an individual depends upon, among other factors, the individual's capabilities.

Nevertheless, the approach clearly has implications for a theory of resource distribution. As critics of the approach have pointed out,[69] *capabilities* is an ambiguous concept, but to have a capability, one must have access to external resources. These external things needed to support the capabilities, which in turn facilitate human flourishing, include money as well as access to specific physical goods and services. These goods and services include obvious necessities like medical care, education, food, and shelter, as well as less obvious needs, such as access to the community's material infrastructure and its shared cultural heritage.

Once we have determined what goods and services must be distributed to individuals to enable their human flourishing, the question then shifts to who must provide these external goods. More specifically, may the state properly make demands upon property owners to foster the development of the capabilities in others? The state need not always be the provider of the requisite goods and services. In early societies, human beings' needs were met by local, or face-to-face, communities (e.g., families, churches, neighborhoods). To some extent this continues to be the case today. Other forms of communities have also emerged in recent years, including so-called virtual communities, and some of them now have begun to fulfill the same role. But at least within modern capitalist societies, a strong case can be made that guaranteeing individuals the necessary access to many of the material and social prerequisites for the capabilities we are describing is beyond the abilities of private, voluntary communities, considered individually or in cooperation with one another. Under the conditions of modern capitalism, the uncoerced actions of private entities are not adequate to ensure that all members of society have access to the resources they require to develop the capabilities necessary for human flourishing.[70]

What demands, then, may the state legitimately make on the property of its citizens, according to Aristotelian property theory? We can easily identify some demands that should be relatively uncontroversial. Acknowledgment of a right to resources necessary for physical survival constitutes an acknowledgment of an entitlement to the assistance of others under certain circumstances, and, given the difficulty of ensuring compliance with such obligations in the modern, depersonalized economy,

---

[69] See, for example, Ronald Dworkin, *Sovereign Virtue* (2000), 285–303; G. A. Cohen, "Equality of What? On Welfare, Goods, and Capabilities," in *The Quality of Life*, ed. Martha C. Nussbaum and Amartya Sen (1993), 9–53.

[70] Accord Milton Friedman, *Capitalism and Freedom* (1962), 191 ("In small communities, public pressure can suffice [to meet the needs of the poor] even with private charity. In the large impersonal communities that are increasingly coming to dominate our society, it is much more difficult for it to do so.").

to the assistance of the state, through directly redistributive measures, in obtaining survival resources or in fending off attempts by private owners to prevent those in need from taking them. Other demands also seem relatively uncontroversial. For example, some minimal provision must be made for the well-being and education of the young, even where parents cannot (for whatever reason) afford to pay. Almost by definition, such an entitlement will demand that the state implement a degree of economic redistribution and regulation, either in cash or in kind. And, as we have already observed in chapter 5, guaranteeing children a suitable education arguably requires providing parents with the resources necessary for a stable home environment.

Other demands will be far more controversial. What would be the net distributive effect of enforcing the nonwaivable warranty of habitability? Specifically, would it produce a redistribution of wealth from Metro to Javins, or, more broadly, from landlords as a class to residential tenants as a class? Opinions are divided over this question with the conventional view among economists being that enforcement of the warranty will not lead to a redistribution of wealth.[71] But other scholars have argued that under certain market conditions, a shift in wealth from landlords as a class to tenants as a class will occur as a result of enforcement of the warranty.[72] Moreover, even if the warranty does not produce a redistributive effect, it surely results in wealth redistribution in some individual cases.

Where such redistribution from landlord to tenant occurs as a result of the legally mandated warranty of habitability, is this, from the point of view of Aristotelian property theory, a legitimate demand to make of landlords as property owners? A strong case can be made that it is. The shift in wealth in this context will usually contribute to one or more of the tenants' necessary capabilities. By providing safer and healthier living conditions, the warranty, with its attendant wealth shift, directly and substantially contributes to the cluster of the tenants' capabilities grouped under the terms *life* and *affiliation*. These are very strong interests and will often be compelling, especially in those circumstances in which the tenant is poor or disadvantaged. Tenants like Javins in our hypothetical can hardly expect to live lives that go as well as possible for them when they are residing in squalid and dangerous conditions. By contrast, landlords who are in the business of renting residential property have

[71] See Edward H. Rabin, "The Revolution in Residential Landlord-Tenant Law: Causes and Consequences," CORNELL L. REV. 69 (1984): 517, 558.

[72] See Duncan Kennedy, "The Effect of the Warranty of Habitability on Low Income Housing: 'Milking' and Class Violence," FLA. ST. U. L. REV. 15 (1987): 485; Richard Markovits, "The Distributive Impact, Allocative Efficiency, and Overall Desirability of Ideal Housing Codes: Some Theoretical Clarifications," HARV. L. REV. 89 (1976): 1815; Bruce A. Ackerman, "Regulating Slum Housing Markets on Behalf of the Poor: Of Housing Codes, Housing Subsidies and Income Redistribution Policy," YALE L. J. 80 (1971): 1093.

little or no capability interests at stake. Landlords who choose to use their property for commercial purposes, renting the property to individuals who use it as their primary residence, have responsibilities that other property owners may not have. The redistribution in wealth that results from enforcement of the warranty of habitability partially fulfills those responsibilities.

As we have already discussed, utilitarian property theorists may well concur in the conclusion that redistribution is justified in a particular case. Their overriding commitment to a unitary measure of value, however, frequently leads them to favor redistribution via taxation and cash transfers over in-kind transfers or redistributive property rules.[73] In contrast, the plural values recognized by Aristotelian property theory push its commitment to redistribution in more complex and expansive directions.

To take the most basic need as an example, a person cannot flourish without the ability to occupy some physical space within which she can carry out activities essential to her existence, such as eating and sleeping.[74] If we owe an obligation to foster human flourishing among those within our political community, we owe an obligation to those without such a space to help them obtain it. In many cases, utilitarians are probably correct when they argue that the least wasteful means for fulfilling that obligation is through broad redistributive measures employing the state's power to tax and spend. But the utilitarian focus on aggregate measures of utility or welfare obscures the situations in which the nonfungibility of the goods needed to flourish (or the poor choices people sometimes make for themselves or those within their care) can render monetary redistribution ineffective or even counterproductive.

For the legal economist, a unitary measure of value means that goods are *always* substitutable; the challenge is in determining the proper rate of exchange. The more multivalent concept of human flourishing, however, recognizes that individuals or groups experience the components of that flourishing in ways that defy substitution. As Radin has correctly noted, human beings form connections with particular pieces of property such that the property becomes inextricably bound up with their pursuit of the well-lived life.[75] Land constitutes a central locus of this nonfungibility. Once a person (or a community) has sufficiently incorporated a piece of land into her life plans, exchanging that land for some other good (even a good of very

---

73 See, for example, Louis Kaplow and Steven Shavell, "Why the Legal System is Less Efficient than the Income Tax in Redistributing Income," *J. Legal. Stud.* 23 (1994): 667; Robert C. Ellickson, "Property in Land," *Yale L. J.* 102 (1993): 1357 ("To help equalize wealth, land can be periodically reassembled, repartitioned, and reallotted, although this policy is usually inferior to cash redistributions effected through tax and welfare programs.").

74 See, for example, Jeremy Waldron, "Homelessness and the Issue of Freedom," *UCLA L. Rev.* 39 (1991): 305–6.

75 See, for example, Margaret Jane Radin, "Property and Personhood," *Stan. L. Rev.* 34 (1982): 993–6 (discussing a hypothetical statute incorporating the normative judgment that tenants should be allowed to become attached to places and that the legal system should encourage them to do so).

great economic value) or for some other piece of land can hinder, in some cases irreparably, her ability to flourish by short circuiting long-term plans, deeply held commitments, and carefully constructed identities.[76]

As we discussed in Chapter 1, because human flourishing is a phenomenon of actual, living human beings and not disembodied collections of utility, there is an organic integrity and coherence to its individual experience that resists disassembly and substitution. The structure of flourishing has breadth as an expression of the need simultaneously to enjoy a number of distinct and nonsubstitutable goods. It also extends temporally as a pattern of cultivation and enjoyment of particular goods over the course of one's life.

This integrity will sometimes make it impossible to substitute one good for another. And the nonfungibility of various components of human flourishing across these two dimensions suggests that redistribution of land rights via in-kind transfers of ownership or occupancy will at times be the only appropriate way of fostering flourishing, and that exclusive reliance on an aggregated system of taxation and monetary payments will be inadequate, efficiency considerations notwithstanding. In the context of land, an obligation rooted in justice to share one's property in kind with others might arise, for example, (1) because exclusion (or, more precisely, exclusion for particular reasons) is inconsistent with the dignity of the excluded person; (2) because of the unusually acute and immediate nature of the recipient's need for access to a particular parcel of land; (3) because of the relationships the recipients have formed with the owner's land; or (4) because of the relationships of dependence or reliance that owners have formed with the recipients. In such cases, the law may (and frequently already does) appropriately intervene through the use of redistributive property rules coercively to enforce owners' obligations to share or even cede rights to a particular piece of land.

The need to protect certain crucial dignitary interests in kind, for example, is reflected in civil rights statutes prohibiting racial discrimination in housing markets and places of public accommodation.[77] A regime permitting racial exclusion from places of public accommodation but requiring owners to pay money to the victims of that exclusion would rightly be accused of misunderstanding the way in which racially discriminatory exclusion inhibits human flourishing. Similarly, the law ensures access to land through the doctrine of necessity, which permits a trespasser to make use of another's land in circumstances of dire need and prevents an owner from interfering with that use. Property law has traditionally protected the long-standing bonds land users form with land they do not own through

---

[76] See Eduardo M. Peñalver, "Land Virtues," CORNELL L. REV. 94 (2009): 821.

[77] See, for example, Fair Housing Act, 42 U.S.C. §§ 3601–3631; Civil Rights Act of 1964, Title II, 42 U.S.C. §§ 2000a – 2000a-6.

doctrines like adverse possession and prescription. More recently, it has attempted to do the same through newer devices, such as rent control and eviction protection statutes.[78] Finally, the law sometimes requires the in-kind transfer of interests in land in response to particular relationships of dependence and reliance, either using traditional equitable doctrines like estoppel[79] and constructive trust,[80] or by creating new doctrines, as in *State v. Shack*.[81]

[78] For a description of South Africa's eviction protection law, see *Modderklip East Squatters v. Modderklip Boerdery (Pty) Ltd.*, 2004(8) BCLR 821 (SCA), aff'd on other grounds 2005 (5) SA 3 (CC), in *Constitutional Property Law*, ed. A.J. van der Walt (2005).

[79] See *Holbrook v. Taylor*, 532 S.W.2d 763 (Ky. 1976).

[80] See *Rase v. Castle Mountain Ranch, Inc.*, 631 P.2d 680 (Mont. 1981).

[81] 277 A.2d 369 (N.J. 1971).

7

The Right to Exclude and Its Limits

INTRODUCTION

"A man's home is his castle." We usually understand this saying to suggest that homeownership is characterized, and perhaps even constituted, by a powerful right to exclude others.[1] But it also reflects commonly held conceptions about private ownership more broadly and its connection with the right to exclude. Are these conceptions accurate? Is the right to exclude the sine qua non of ownership, as some have argued, such that, lacking the right, there is no private property? Consider these questions in connection with the following examples, which discuss the right to exclude in several different contexts.

The Right to Exclude and the Private Home

The Jacque family owned a home on 170 acres in a rural area of Wisconsin.[2] Steenberg Homes needed to deliver a mobile home to a parcel near the Jacques' property, and the easiest way to get there was to cross the Jacques' land. (There were other ways to get there, but they involved significantly more expense.) Steenberg Homes sought the Jacques' permission to cross their land, but the Jacques refused to grant it. When Steenberg nevertheless crossed the Jacques' land, the Jacques sued. After a trial, the jury granted, and the Wisconsin Supreme Court ultimately approved, a significant punitive damages award. *Jacque* seems to affirm the veracity of the notion that a man's home is his castle, with a vengeance! But the law is more complicated than that:

> In the case of fire, flood, pestilence or other great public calamity, when immediate action is necessary to save human life or to avert an overwhelming destruction of

---

[1] But see Eduardo M. Peñalver, "Property Metaphors and *Kelo v. New London*: Two Views of the Castle," FORDHAM L. REV. 74 (2006): 2971 (proposing alternative reading of the "castle" metaphor).

[2] *Jacque v. Steenberg Homes, Inc.*, 563 N.W.2d 154 (Wis. 1997).

property, any individual may lawfully enter another's land and destroy his property, real or personal, providing he acts with reasonable judgment....

If the individual who enters and destroys private property happens to be a public officer whose duty it is to avert an impending calamity, the rights of the owner of the property to compensation are no greater than in the case of a private individual. The most familiar example of the exercise of this right is seen in case of fire. The neighbors and fireman freely trespass on the adjoining land, and houses are even blown up to prevent the spread of the conflagration.[3]

Similarly, the Restatement (Second) of Torts provides:

One is privileged to enter or remain on land in the possession of another if it is or reasonably appears to be necessary to prevent serious harm to

(a) the actor, or his land or chattels, or
(b) the other or a third person, or the land or chattels of either, unless the actor knows or has reason to know that the one for whose benefit he enters is unwilling that he shall take such action.[4]

A man's home is not always his castle, and even a homeowner does not have an *absolute* right to exclude others from entering upon her property. What is the status of the right to exclude with respect to businesses open to the public?

The Right to Exclude and Businesses Open to the Public

"We reserve the right to refuse service to any person." Walk into a corner deli in almost any city in the United States and you will likely find a sign with those words. May the owner of a business exclude anyone for any reason? Is the business owner's right to exclude as broad as that of the private homeowner's? The short answer is no. In Title II of the Civil Rights Act of 1964, Congress prohibited exclusion from "places of public accommodation" on the basis of "race, color, religion, or national origin." What constitutes *public accommodation* is defined by the statute itself and the category includes a great deal of privately owned property. According to the statute, a public accommodation is:

(1) any inn, hotel, motel, or other establishment which provides lodging to transient guests, other than an establishment located within a building which contains not more than five rooms for rent or hire and which is actually occupied by the proprietor of such establishment as his residence;

---

[3] 1 Nichols on Eminent Domain §§ 1.43[1], 1.43[2], at 1–841 to 843 (3d ed.1989) (footnotes omitted).
[4] Restatement (Second) of Torts §197.

(2) any restaurant, cafeteria, lunchroom, lunch counter, soda fountain, or other facility principally engaged in selling food for consumption on the premises, including, but not limited to, any such facility located on the premises of any retail establishment; or any gasoline station;

(3) any motion picture house, theater, concert hall, sports arena, stadium or other place of exhibition or entertainment; and

(4) any establishment
    (A) (i) which is physically located within the premises of any establishment otherwise covered by this subsection, or (ii) within the premises of which is physically located any such covered establishment, and
    (B) which holds itself out as serving patrons of such covered establishment.[5]

Although controversial when first proposed, Title II has become a fixture in the American legal landscape. For most people, the legal prohibition of racial discrimination on most commercial property constitutes a settled limitation on rights of private ownership.

Apart from public antidiscrimination laws, are there other restrictions on the business owner's right to exclude? The answer depends on the jurisdiction. To get a better view of the options, we need to take a short detour through the world of high-stakes blackjack.

Card Counting

When properly practiced, the card counting method of playing blackjack can give its practitioners a slight statistical advantage over the casino. If the card counter has the resources to place large bets and overcome short-term variations in luck, she can impose significant financial losses on casinos. According to the rules of blackjack, however, card counting is not cheating. Nevertheless, and for obvious reasons, casinos do not want capable card counters playing high-stakes blackjack at their tables.

Kenneth Uston was a pioneer of card counting in blackjack. Uston, who died in 1987, was so successful that casinos began to ban him from their tables. He responded by donning disguises in order to ply his trade incognito. He also sued casinos in Las Vegas and Atlantic City, arguing that it was unlawful for them to exclude him from their tables for engaging in a lawful card playing strategy. The casinos responded that, under the common law of property, they could exclude any person from their premises for any reason, as long as the reason was not specifically prohibited by a civil rights statute such as Title II.

Uston's suits yielded dramatically different results. His lawsuit against Nevada casinos was dismissed by the federal district court on the ground that a casino had no legal obligation to permit Uston to play at its tables. The court reasoned that,

[5]   42 U.S.C. § 2000a.

although innkeepers and common carriers have historically had some common law duties to do business with patrons, casinos – at least in their capacity as places for gambling – are not inns and so are not similarly constrained and can exclude someone for any reason (no matter how frivolous) not specifically prohibited by, say, civil rights laws.[6]

This account of the common law of trespass is not uncontested. Although it does correctly describe the law as it came to be in most states by the late nineteenth century, prior to that, both in the United States and in England, businesses that held themselves out as open to the public were required to serve anyone willing to pay unless the owner could point to some reasonable basis for refusing service.[7] In Uston's New Jersey lawsuit, the state supreme court was more faithful to this earlier common law tradition when it ruled in his favor. "When property owners open their premises to the general public in pursuit of their own property interests," the court said, "they have no right to exclude people unreasonably." "On the contrary," it continued, "they have a duty not to act in an arbitrary or discriminatory manner towards persons who come on their premises."[8] According to the court, for a casino, which has opened its doors for people to come and gamble on its property, to exclude a gambler who is not acting disruptively or violating the rules of the game is to act in an arbitrary or unreasonable manner. As a consequence, the court concluded, casinos in New Jersey could not exclude Uston for counting cards. Under this New Jersey approach to exclusion, the business owner's common law right to exclude is narrower than that of the private homeowner simply by virtue of the commercial character of the property. Might other aspects of the character of the property also affect the scope of the right to exclude?

Beach Access

Atlantis Beach Club owned a waterfront parcel in Cape May County, New Jersey, which it made available to the general public for a substantial fee.[9] For nearly a decade before it opened up the private club in 1996, its owner had made no effort to exclude the public from the beach. Consequently, nearby residents had long since become accustomed to crossing the dry sand area of the club's beach to reach the wet sand portion of the beach, the land between the mean high tide and water, which is owned by the state. In 1996, the club began attempting to bar nonmembers from crossing its property, eventually erecting a gate at its entrance. Local residents

---

[6] See *Uston v. Grand Resorts, Inc.*, 564 F.2d 1217, 1218 (9th Cir. 1977).

[7] See Kevin Gray and Susan Francis Gray, "Civil Rights, Civil Wrongs, and Quasi-Public Space," EUR. HUM. RTS. L. REV. 4 (1999): 46, 85–9; Joseph William Singer, "No Right to Exclude: Public Accommodations and Private Property," NW. U.L. REV. 90 (1996): 1283, 1292, 1303–48.

[8] See *Uston v. Resorts Int'l Hotel, Inc.*, 445 A.2d 370 (N.J. 1982).

[9] See *Raleigh Avenue Beach Association v. Atlantis Beach Club*, 879 A.2d 112 (N.J. 2005).

who were not club members went to court claiming that they were entitled to access the beach via the club's land under the public trust doctrine.[10]

Historically, public access to privately owned beaches was quite limited. The public was permitted to enter only the wet sand areas. And the purposes for which the public was permitted to access this land were themselves limited to activities like fishing and navigation. In recent years, several courts, including the New Jersey Supreme Court, have expanded the purposes for which the public is entitled to use the wet sand portion of the beach to encompass recreation.[11] They have also expanded the spatial reach of public rights of access to include portions of the so-called dry sand areas landward of the mean high tide line.

Addressing the claim brought by the local residents against the beach club, the New Jersey Supreme Court concluded that, in light of the specific history of public access to the club's parcel and the lack of public beaches in the area, the club was required to make its upland sand area, though privately owned, available for use by the general public to the extent necessary to provide the public with "reasonable access" to the wet sand beach. The court stated:

> [R]ecognizing the increasing demand for our State's beaches and the dynamic nature of the public trust doctrine, we find that the public must be given both access to and use of privately-owned dry sand areas as reasonably necessary. While the public's rights in private beaches are not coextensive with the rights enjoyed in municipal beaches, private landowners may not in all instances prevent the public from exercising its rights under the public trust doctrine. The public must be afforded reasonable access to the foreshore as well as a suitable area for recreation on the dry sand.[12]

The club would, however, be permitted to charge nonmembers a reasonable fee (approved by the state) to cover expenses like lifeguarding and trash removal.

As these disparate examples suggest, the contours of the right to exclude are both more complex and interesting than the homeowner's or the deli owner's claim of an unqualified right to exclude allows. In the remaining sections of this chapter, we will discuss these (and other) examples through the lenses of the

---

[10] Although courts have provided for public access to beaches on various doctrinal grounds, the most important of these has been the public trust doctrine. That doctrine provides that navigable waters, tidal wetlands, beds of navigable waters, and the wet sand portion of beaches are held by the sovereign in trust for use by the public in connection with commerce, navigation, and fishing. When the sovereign conveys such property to private owners, the property remains encumbered by the public trust, restricting the private owner's right to exclude the public.

[11] See, for example, *Borough of Neptune City v. Borough of Avon-by-the-Sea*, 294 A.2d 47 (N.J. 1972); *State* ex rel. *Thornton v. Hay*, 462 P.2d 671 (Or. 1969); *Hixon v. Public Service Comm'n*, 146 N.W.2d 577 (Wis. 1966). But see *Bell v. Town of Wells*, 557 A.2d 168 (Me. 1989) (refusing to extend public trust doctrine to recreational uses); *Opinion of the Justices*, 313 N.E.2d 561 (Mass. 1974) (same).

[12] *Raleigh Avenue Beach Association v. Atlantis Beach Club*, 879 A.2d at 121.

various theories of property we introduced in Part I of the book. The choice of one theory or another may not always translate into specific positions on these examples. But, as we will see, each theory addresses the question of the right to exclude in different ways.

THE RIGHT TO EXCLUDE IN UTILITARIAN PERSPECTIVE

As we observed in the first chapter of this book, one of the notable features of traditional utilitarian property theorizing, particularly when its practitioners have been attentive to rigorous empirical methods, is its great sensitivity to context. Rather than supporting Blackstonian private ownership rights across the board, utilitarians can favor a robust right to exclude in some situations while recommending extensive rights of access in others. John Stuart Mill, for example, thought it obvious that depriving agricultural landowners of the right to exclude – except as necessary to protect their crops or livestock – would enhance overall utility by increasing everyone else's enjoyment of access rights. "The pretension of two Dukes to shut up a part of the Highlands," he said, "and exclude the rest of mankind from many square miles of mountain scenery...is an abuse; it exceeds the legitimate bounds of the right of landed property."[13]

But utilitarianism's potential for contextual sensitivity concerning the scope of the right to exclude generates its own concerns. In fact, this has been the subject of one of the most fertile areas of utilitarian property theorizing in recent years. On one side of this debate is traditional utilitarian-economic analysis of property rights, which explores different claims of ownership to determine whether some particular change in property rules, large or small, would be utility enhancing. The agnostic and somewhat irreverent attitude toward the right to exclude that Mill exhibited in his discussion of enclosure in the Highlands exemplifies a tendency in utilitarian theory to treat property as a so-called bundle of sticks, that is, as a discrete and ultimately

---

[13] John Stuart Mill, *Principles of Political Economy*, Bk. 2, (2004) (1848), ch. 2, § 6. Harold Demsetz, in his classic article on property rights discussed how the Algonquin Indians in Labrador developed a system of private ownership in response to the changing economic value of beaver pelts. Where economic pressures to hunt pelts for an export market threatened the beaver population with extinction, Demsetz argued, what had been a functional commons became a potential tragedy, resulting ultimately in the Indians' adoption of a private property in land. Demsetz's article has been subjected to a great deal of criticism concerning both its explanatory completeness and its descriptive accuracy. See, for example, James E. Krier, Evolutionary Theory and the Origin of Property Rights, 95 CORNELL L. REV. 139 (2009); Eric T. Freyfogle, "Land Use and the Study of Early American History," YALE L. J. 94 (1985): 717, 740 n73. However, his telling of the story suggests that – in contrast with libertarian, rights-based property theories – utilitarian property theory is in principle capable of being significantly more sensitive to context.

flexible set of specific use rights with respect to things, the precise content of which is largely indeterminate and subject to constant (re)evaluation.[14]

As we discussed in Chapter 6, contemporary utilitarian property theorists typically favor voluntary market transactions to reallocate property rights toward those who will derive the greatest utility from them. But the possibility that high transaction costs or some other impediment might stand in the way of such transactions means that utilitarian theorists are open to the need for governmental reallocation or redefinition in situations of market failure. For any given assertion of a right to exclude, the bundle-of-sticks approach treats it as, at least initially, an open question whether the law should honor the owner's desire to exclude or the nonowner's desire for access.

Opposed to the bundle-of-sticks approach is a more recent strain of utilitarian property scholarship expressing the worry that the claim-by-claim evaluation risks undermining the core logic of property institutions, which allocate in rem rights in things.[15] Crucial to that logic, these scholars argue, is the right to exclude.[16] "Exclusion" theorists such as Thomas Merrill and Henry Smith focus on the way in which property institutions employ what they characterize as an architecture of boundaries, which economizes on information costs by delegating most decision making about the exercise of those rights to owners. By establishing boundaries and by granting to owners the broad power to control access to (and therefore uses of) an object within those boundaries, the institution of private property, they argue, rewards people who successfully gather information about the most productive use for the things they own. According to Merrill and Smith, maintaining a robust and relatively simple law of trespass is crucial to property's boundary logic and its attendant information cost savings:

> The right to exclude allows the owner to control, plan, and invest, and permits this to happen with a minimum of information costs to others. People generally do not need to consult lists of use-conflict resolutions (or specific right-duty pairs) when they approach a piece of property they do not own. Instead, they know that, unless special regulations or private contracts carve out some specific use rights, the bright-line rules of trespass apply.[17]

---

[14] See Thomas W. Merrill and Henry E. Smith, "What Happened to Property in Law and Economics," YALE L. J. 111 (2001): 357, 360–83 (describing the bundle-of-sticks approach in contemporary economic analysis of property).

[15] See ibid.; see also Michael A. Heller, "The Dynamic Analytics of Property Law," THEORETICAL INQUIRIES L. 2 (2001): 79 (criticizing the bundle-of-rights approach for failing to account adequately for the "thingness" of property).

[16] See Thomas W. Merrill, "Property and the Right to Exclude," NEB. L. REV. 77 (1998): 730; Henry E. Smith, "Exclusion Versus Governance," J. LEGAL STUD. 31 (2002): 453.

[17] Merrill and Smith, "What Happened to Property?" 389.

To sum up, the legal recognition of a robust right to exclude – according to exclusion theorists – has the effect of creating an open-ended set of in rem rights that grants owners broad freedom to deploy the information they have gathered in choosing how to exploit the object without seeking the permission of others. And, because they can exclude others from their property, those who gather the best information about the most productive uses of that property will reap the rewards of their efforts. In addition, these theorists argue, by creating a relatively simple set of duties (e.g., "keep out"), trespass law's exclusion logic makes respecting the rights of others less demanding for nonowners.[18] For the exclusion theorist, then, the sheer importance of the power of physical exclusion – and the utilitarian benefits it generates – constitutes a further reason for honoring the owners' exclusion claims, even in the presence of evidence of some degree of market failure.

Some decisions by owners will so obviously undermine utility that deviation from this core logic of exclusion is occasionally justified. In these circumstances – for example, when the law of nuisance limits owners' freedom to engage in actions that impose significant harm on neighboring owners – the law may opt for modes of decision making that rely more heavily on use-by-use evaluations of utility ("governance," as Smith has put it).[19] But, although governance strategies are sometimes necessary, exclusion theorists argue that excessive reliance on them will end up being counterproductive because the governance calculation is so costly to carry out and because creating too many exceptions to the logic of exclusion undermines the open-ended reward structure it establishes. Case-by-case allocation associated with governance also generates increased information costs for nonowners.

At the outset, it is worth emphasizing that these two utilitarian camps are not as far apart in practice as this stark description suggests. Bundle theorists are indeed comfortable with case-by-case tinkering. But, at least among legal theorists, their analysis typically starts with existing property institutions, whose basic outlines they tend to take for granted, rather than with a call for wholesale stick-by-stick reevaluation of property entitlements from the ground up. This observation does not detract from the importance of Merrill's and Smith's contribution, which helps to illuminate utilitarian implications of the modularity of existing property institutions. But it does mean that the differences between exclusion and bundle-of-rights theorists operate more at the level of emphasis and presumption.

Exclusion theorists are no doubt correct that relentless right-by-right, case-by-case allocation of property interests, with no standardization of bundles of rights, would place enormous informational demands on owners and nonowners

---

[18]   Henry E. Smith, "Property and Property Rules," *N.Y.U. L. Rev.* 79 (2004): 1719, 1729–31.
[19]   See Smith, "Exclusion Versus Governance"; Henry E. Smith, "Exclusion and Property Rules in the Law of Nuisance," *Va. L. Rev.* 90 (2004): 965, 973–4.

alike.[20] But what seems insufficiently defended is the exclusion theorists' claim that there is a specific connection between information costs and the right to exclude as such. Containing information costs is arguably just as consistent with understanding property as the delegation to owners of broad, spatially defined, standardized bundles of affirmative use rights as it is with understanding property as the residuum of negative liberty created by protecting a robust right to exclude. This is particularly true if the contours of the more qualified right to exclude conform to an intelligible pattern that permits us to form generalizations and (tentative) predictions about the likely outcome of cases of first impression.

The conceptual gap between the right to exclude and the information costs story told by exclusion theorists is most apparent with property onto which the owner has invited the general public. For these kinds of property, it is far from clear that unfettered exclusion rights make the world an easier place to navigate for nonowners. For private property that is open to the public, such as a department store, the message sent by the legal ratification of private control of property boundaries is, in practice, far more complex than "keep off." In the pre-civil-rights-era South, that message might have been: If you are white, come in and browse, shop, sit down, and eat; if you are African American, come in, shop, order food at our lunch counter, but do not sit down to eat or interact with white customers. In the modern shopping center, the message might be: Come in, browse, walk around, sit down, eat, perhaps even participate in an aerobics class or watch school children put on a show, but do not engage in political speech, no matter how orderly. Particularly in the case of land, which can sustain multiple nonconflicting uses at the same time, a system that permits owners to create intricately qualified invitations to the general public may generate higher information costs than a system in which owners of commercial property must choose from a limited menu of exclusion options.[21] Moreover, this latter regime is consistent with a coherent conception of private ownership, since, although owners would enjoy a more limited right to exclude, nonowners would still be obligated not to interfere with the use decisions that owners have made.[22]

Another complication for exclusion theories results from their uncertain fit with existing structures of property lawmaking and enforcement. We can think of exclusion accounts of property as analogous to the rule-utilitarian position within moral theory. While some utilitarians (so-called act-utilitarians) apply their calculus to individual actions or decisions, others (rule-utilitarians) argue that the utility-enhancing strategy is not to subject each decision to thoroughgoing utilitarian

[20] Smith, "Property and Property Rules," 1753.

[21] See Thomas W. Merrill and Henry E. Smith, "Optimal Standardization in the Law of Property," YALE L. J. 110 (2000): 1.

[22] See Larissa Katz, "Exclusion and Exclusivity in Property Law," U. TORONTO L. J. 58 (2008): 1710; Eric R. Claeys, "Exclusion and Exclusivity in Gridlock," ARIZ. L. REV. 53 (2011): 9–49.

analysis, but instead to cabin utilitarian decision making to certain limited rule making contexts. Outside those contexts, the best strategy is simply to follow the rules laid out in advance. A rule-utilitarian might argue, for example, that it is utility enhancing if people always keep their promises, even in those (presumably exceptional) situations in which not to keep the promise would be utility enhancing. The loss of utility in the exceptional case is outweighed, the argument goes, by the costs of having to constantly weigh whether keeping a promise in a particular situation would be utility enhancing as well as by the gains made possible by being able to rely on other people always keeping their promises.

The exclusion theory of property works in roughly the same way: It argues that an exclusion strategy is utility enhancing even though in individual instances it might seem better (in the short term) to deviate from it, because adhering to the relatively simple core structure of exclusion over the long run economizes on the need to constantly engage in utilitarian calculation and avoids the costs arising from uncertainty (among owners and nonowners alike) about the scope of property rights. But exclusion theory also confronts some of the same kinds of objections that have been leveled against rule-utilitarianism. Most important among these is the difficulty of preventing rule-utilitarianism from collapsing back into act-utilitarianism. For every rule that is supposedly utility enhancing, it would at least arguably be even more utility enhancing to craft a rule that is nearly as simple but that also builds in an exception to the rule for certain situations in which it is clearly not utility enhancing to follow it. The problem is that, if we make too many exceptions, the rule simply disappears and we are left with act-utilitarianism.[23]

Something similar seems true of the exclusion theories of property. As exclusion theorists recognize, in some situations exclusion is so costly that it is worth paying the price of governance. In evaluating the various exceptions to the right to exclude discussed at the beginning of this chapter, an exclusion theorist might well endorse one or more of them on this ground. The problem, from the perspective of exclusion theory, is that too many exceptions will undermine the informational efficiencies asserted on behalf of the open-ended right to exclude. But this raises a difficult question for the exclusion theorist. Apart from being able to rule out the extremes (unlimited exclusion power without exception and universal case-by-case utilitarian [re]calculation of each and every claimed right of access), how can we know what mode of decision making to employ in any given situation? How are we to know whether the costs of considering this particular exception to the core exclusion structure of property outweigh the benefits unless we actually carry out a full utilitarian calculus? Perhaps more importantly, how are we to evaluate the actual substantive

---

[23] See David Lyons, *The Forms and Limits of Utilitarianism* (1965), chap. 4; R. M. Hare, *Freedom and Reason* (1963), 130–6.

question whether making a new, seemingly utility-enhancing exception to the core structure is utility enhancing (even over the long run) or, instead, a bridge too far? We cannot make the just-so move of simply assuming that the existing state of the common law of property (or the common law as it existed prior to the rise of the regulatory state) is the optimal one.

Thus, the apparent lack of fit between the exclusion theory and the existing law concerning the right to exclude, pock-marked as it is with exceptions, is something of an embarrassment for this approach. The exclusion theory struggles to offer a genuine explanation for the many qualifications to the right to exclude already built into the law of property (and not just in New Jersey). These include (among others) Title II; the law of adverse possession and prescription, which places a time limit on owners' rights to exclude; the numerous doctrines of implied easements; the law of airplane overflights;[24] the doctrine of necessity, which requires owners to allow those in extreme situations of need onto their property; the law governing innocent improvers; and the conflagration doctrine we mentioned at the beginning of the chapter. Each of these doctrines is, from the exclusion standpoint, a departure from property's core logic of exclusion that must be justified to the same extent as proposed new exceptions, such as beach access, that exclusion theorists tend to oppose.

One response to this problem of fit might be to shift our focus toward considerations of institutional competence. Legislatures, the argument might go, are well equipped to engage in a comprehensive utilitarian calculus that evaluates the costs and benefits of prospectively incorporating into property law exceptions to the right to exclude. Courts, on the other hand, have limited investigatory tools, and must approach decision making through the lens of the disputes parties bring before them. On this view, a legislatively enacted exception to property's exclusion logic, such as Title II, might be entitled to more deference than judge-made exceptions, such as the New Jersey Supreme Court's apparent solicitude for novel claims of access rights to beaches or commercial establishments.

As we noted in our discussion of Uston's unsuccessful claims against Las Vegas casinos, however, prior to the mid-nineteenth century, the common law of property recognized broad rights of access to commercial establishments. Judges then changed the law to narrow those access rights to inns and common carriers. This sort of judge-made change has been the rule rather than the exception in property law. If judge-made law were suspect, a great deal of *existing* trespass doctrine would be called into question. Since part of the exclusion theory's project is to describe how property law actually operates, this is not a result that they can accept lightly.

---

[24] See Stuart Banner, *Who Owns the Sky? The Struggle to Control Airspace from the Wright Brothers On* (2008).

On the other hand, if we try to incorporate judge-made rules into the exclusion model, maintaining the stability of its two-tiered (exclusion/governance) structure becomes even more challenging. How is a court to know whether a particular case is the proper vehicle for introducing an exception to the logic of exclusion or whether instead it is an occasion merely to enforce the baseline boundary principle? And if the court opts for the former, how is it to gather the vast amount of data necessary to answer the second-order question? Again, besides ruling out the corner solutions of no exclusion and an unlimited power to exclude, the empirical burden seems daunting.

A broader question for the utilitarian approach to the right to exclude, one that affects both the exclusion and bundle-of-sticks camps equally, concerns the nature of the interests at stake. These interests frequently resist the common utilitarian characterization of the value to be maximized as preference satisfaction or wealth maximization. For example, in determining the utilitarian implications of a provision like Title II, it seems morally questionable to evaluate the strength of African Americans entitlement not to be excluded from places of public accommodation in terms of which rule would satisfy more (or more intense) preferences. It is easy to imagine situations in which the calculus would come out against rights to be free from racial discrimination – for example, where intense racist sentiment is widespread among the majority of the population and the excluded minority is small in number. But most people reject the notion that, under such conditions, legally sanctioned racial discrimination would become morally acceptable (or even obligatory). This observation about the utilitarian misconceptions of the moral foundations of civil rights, while commonplace, is still an important one. Its salience in the context of civil rights statutes is an example of a broader challenge for utilitarian theory that we first mentioned in Chapter 1 – its willingness, in principle, to trade off on the well-being of individuals. As we will discuss later in this chapter, Aristotelian property theories seem to offer a way to capture many of the benefits of utilitarian theories' contextual flexibility without losing the ability to account for the kinds of robust individual moral entitlements implicated by laws like Title II.

It is worth noting that New Jersey's sliding scale approach to the right to exclude, much criticized by exclusion theorists for its alleged ad hocery and indeterminacy, offers a relatively elegant explanation of the complex pattern of discrete access and exclusion rights operating within the law of property.

Figure 7.1 plots the outcomes of various exclusion cases and hypotheticals along two axes. The horizontal axis reflects the degree to which the owner has invited the public onto her property. Using the New Jersey approach to trespass, we can view this variable as inversely related to the objective weight of the owner's interest in being able to exclude those seeking entry to the property against the owner's will.

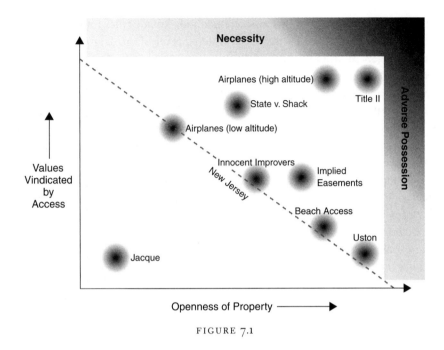

FIGURE 7.1

The vertical axis represents the importance of the values (which is not the same as the intensity of the preferences) that would be vindicated by granting the entrant access to the property. The circles represent the approximate location of the various doctrines on the two axes. They have indistinct edges to represent the room for reasonable disagreement over their proper placement. The doctrines of adverse possession and necessity are depicted as bars because they operate across the entire range of their correseponding axes. That is, necessity is usually understood to operate without regard to the nature of the needed property, and adverse possession operates without regard to the claimant's need. In a sense, these two doctrines form the outer frontiers of all owners' rights to exclude.

Cases falling in the upper right corner of the graph should constitute relatively uncontroversial cases for protecting access rights, and cases falling in the lower left corner should be uncontroversial cases for protecting rights of exclusion.[25] Cases close to the line running across the chart are "hard cases" and likely to be more controversial. So, for instance, while the necessity doctrine does not itself change based on the type of property at issue, the gap between the claimant's need and the owner's interest in exclusion narrows the more "private" the property to which the person in need

---

[25] Although the *Jacque* case came from Wisconsin, there is no reason to think the New Jersey courts would have decided it differently.

seeks access. We should expect, then, that the doctrine's application will be more controversial the less the owner has opened up her property to the public. Similarly, while there is no "necessity" requirement for adverse possession, we should expect the doctrine to generate more discomfort the more frivolous the claimant's interest in the disputed property. This pattern, although not based on the mechanical application of any single rule, is consistent with the use of subsidiary rules at the corners. And the resulting mix of rules and standards interacting in an intelligible way helps to avoid the high information costs that exclusion theorists predict will result from embracing this sort of qualified conception of the right to exclude.

The defender of the New Jersey approach to trespass can go even further, though. Arguably, Figure 7.1 suggests that the charge of ad hocery is more appropriately leveled against the approach to trespass used by the federal district court in Uston's Las Vegas case, the one which happens to be the same approach used in most other jurisdictions and that is embraced by exclusion theorists. This approach insists that owners enjoy a robust interest in exclusion across the board. Consequently, it treats each of the many widely recognized exceptions to the right to exclude as an anomalous intrusion on owner's rights that stands in need of explanation. The problem for this latter approach is that there are so many exceptions to the right to exclude built into the common law of property that justifying the status quo requires a great deal of special pleading.

THE RIGHT TO EXCLUDE IN HEGELIAN PERSPECTIVE

A limited version of the right to exclude is integral to Georg W. F. Hegel's theory of property. Recall from the discussion in Chapter 3 that Hegel identified three essential components of property: possession, enjoyment, and alienation. Each of these three elements is simultaneously individualistic and relational. Precisely for this reason, each requires that the individual be entitled to exclude others, at least to some degree. Hegel wants us to understand possession in terms of the possessor's exclusion of others from the same object.[26] The right to exclude others grows out of the purpose of possession itself, namely, to objectify the normative claim that the self is "an absolute end commanding respect."[27] Similarly, for Hegel, enjoyment entails some degree of exclusion. However, although Hegel recognizes a right to exclude, this right is not absolute. It is defeasible and necessarily so because of its relational character.

Hegel recognized that the rights of exclusive possession and enjoyment are relational and, as far as they go, contradictory. They are contradictory *because* they

---

[26] See: Jeanne L. Schroeder, *The Vestal and the Fasces: Hegel, Lacan, Property, and the Feminine* (1998), 42.

[27] See Alan Brudner, *The Unity of the Common Law* (1995), 46.

are relational: The possessor's or user's right requires recognition of this right by others, and such recognition comes only through reciprocal recognition of their rights of exclusive possession and use. But that reciprocal recognition means denying the person's right to infinite appropriation. As Alan Brudner puts it, "I cannot consistently with my right recognize the other's possession; yet I cannot consistently with my right avoid recognizing it."[28]

For Hegel, the path to reconciling this contradiction is the third element of property, the right of exchange, or alienation. The reconciliation occurs as a result of the reciprocal nature of the transaction. In Brudner's words, "In exchange, I recognize the other's property by awaiting his decision to alienate and by giving him an equal value in return; yet I do not thereby foreclose my opportunities for unlimited acquisition, for I recognize his right to the thing only insofar as it becomes available to me (only insofar as he ceases to be the owner), while he recognizes mine under the same proviso."[29]

It is one thing to recognize the right to exclude; it is quite another to place that right at the conceptual core of ownership. Does the Hegelian personality theory place the right to exclude at the core of property, as modern exclusion theorists do? This does not seem to be a plausible reading of Hegel. First, it is worth reemphasizing that the point of Hegel's personality theory was not maximizing social welfare but rather self-actualization. For Hegel, freedom, and so, property, is always situated in human society. The self as embodied free will certainly requires some degree of exclusionary power over objects, but the right to exclude is epiphenomenal rather than fundamental.

Second, as we observed in Chapter 3, the whole point of the self becoming realized is movement toward high stages of ethical development that lead to membership in ethical communities. As the free will becomes realized in property, others are then able to relate to the self. Property is not the basis for withdrawal from others but precisely the opposite: It is the foundation for socialization with others. As Jeremy Waldron has observed, this relationship between property and self-development within Hegel's theory pushes it toward recognizing affirmative entitlements to access property, although Hegel himself may not have fully appreciated this implication.[30] Thus, Hegel was comfortable with the doctrine of private necessity, which we mentioned at the beginning of this chapter:

> If for example it is only by stealing bread that the wolf can be kept from the door, the action is of course an encroachment on someone's property, but it would be wrong to treat this action as an ordinary theft. To refuse to allow a man in jeopardy

---

[28] Ibid., 56.
[29] Ibid.
[30] See Jeremy Waldron, *The Right to Private Property* (1988), 377–89.

for his life to take such steps of self-preservation would be to stigmatize him as without rights, and since he would be deprived of his life, his freedom would be annulled altogether.[31]

The doctrine of necessity can be justified in Hegelian terms on the ground that, because self-realization is the end of property, in cases where self-realization and property conflict, the interests of the self must be given priority.[32] But what if necessity is not involved? On the one hand, the Hegelian basis of the right to exclude likely supports a broad scope of the right to exclude for homeowners like the Jacques. After all, if, as Waldron points out, "property protects the development of will by erecting normative fences around the objects in which will have become embodied,"[33] presumably one's home is in the class of objects in which one's will becomes embodied. On the other hand, a business open to the public is arguably more removed from the process of self-development, seen in relation to the consequences of exclusion for self-development of patrons, especially if the basis for exclusion is a historical form of discrimination. On this view, Title II of the Civil Rights Act seems entirely consistent with the Hegelian perspective of the right to exclude.

Hegelian arguments could also be constructed in favor of access to unique resources, such as the beach. Although it is true that normally the private home should receive strong protection from the Hegelian perspective, the beach access disputes implicate competing considerations that matter a great deal to Hegel. A strong version of the right to exclude, expressed by the saying that "a man's home is his castle," is, in Hegelian terms, an assertion of property as a strictly *formal* right, held by a formal self. But this formal right cannot exist as an absolute right without undermining its very end – self-determination. This is why in the cases of necessity Hegel says that a person in jeopardy of her life must be permitted to take steps of self-preservation even if that involves encroaching upon another's private property. To refuse to do so would be to deprive her of her self-development, indeed her very freedom. Hegel treats such cases as matters of equity, but he does not view equity as external to the law or inconsistent with it. To the contrary equity is part of the law itself.[34] All individuals have a positive right to self-determination, and at its broadest, that right includes "a right to the material and cultural preconditions of autonomous action."[35]

Applied to the context of beach access disputes, the right to self-determination arguably includes a right of reasonable access to those privately owned material resources that are aspects of self-determination beyond mere survival. These aspects include health – both physical and mental – and recreation and relaxation are important

---

[31]   Georg W. F. Hegel, *Hegel's Philosophy of Right*, trans. T. M. Knox (1952), § 127.
[32]   See Brudner, *Unity of the Common Law*, 62.
[33]   Waldron, *Private Property*, 377.
[34]   See Brudner, *Unity of the Common Law*, 74.
[35]   Ibid., 73.

contributors of both forms of health. To the extent, then, that recreation and relaxation are essential to self-realization and to the extent that access to the beach is otherwise not reasonably available, there is reason to think that the right of reasonable access recognized in the beach access cases is consistent with Hegelian property theory.

THE RIGHT TO EXCLUDE IN LOCKEAN
AND LIBERTARIAN PERSPECTIVE

As we discussed in Chapter 2, Locke's theory of property is far more flexible than its contemporary libertarian proponents make it out to be. The theory's indeterminacy results from its vagueness about the precise contours of the moral entitlements that follow from Locke's makers' right argument. Locke's argument establishes that, in the state of nature, people who labor on common resources possess some individual entitlement to the product of that labor. But, as we discussed, the property rights that follow from this argument are necessarily indeterminate and limited by the rights everyone else holds to the raw materials on which the laborer works. Moreover, once the state of nature gives way to civil society, Locke's theory of consent seems to leave a great deal of room for (and, indeed, very much depends on) democratic governments defining and refining the precise content of property rights.

The consequence of these observations is that Lockean property theory, especially when read in light of Lockean political theory, leaves fairly open-ended the question of how to understand the right to exclude. The notion of makers' rights on which Locke builds his theory of property is consistent with numerous – and highly qualified – conceptions of the right to exclude. Attempts to buttress the maker's private rights by emphasizing the limited contribution of the value of the raw materials to the final product are unconvincing. This is particularly true of land, where the productivity of human labor depends very heavily on raw materials that are given by nature. Thus, it is not surprising that, where Locke's theory does provide concrete guidance about the content of property rights, it seems to point as much in the direction of rights of access as the right to exclude. For example, in his discussion of charity, Locke stresses the entitlement of those unable to provide for themselves to take what they need from the surplus of others, trumping the rights of owners to exclude them.

These qualifications on the right to exclude generated by Locke's theory have largely fallen by the wayside among contemporary self-described Lockeans. For these theorists, the property rights established in the state of nature are both more determinate in their content and less susceptible to political rearrangement once the civil government forms. Chief among the rights they have identified as established within the state of nature is the right to exclude. As Richard Epstein put it in his 1985 book, *Takings*, the very idea of property "embraces the absolute right to exclude." Only those to whose presence the owner consents may enter private property, and "[n]othing therefore allows the state to place conditions upon the owners' right to admit or exclude, or to insist that if A is admitted to the property, then B must be admitted as well."[36]

Despite the apparent consensus among libertarians against access rights, the correct libertarian approach to the right to exclude is, at least at first glance, not immediately obvious. As Joseph Singer and Eric Freyfogle have independently noted, and as Mill's objection to enclosure illustrates, the liberty to exclude impairs the liberty to move about freely (or the "right to roam," as it is called in the United Kingdom).[37] Freyfogle, echoing Mill, observes that:

> [I]t is on the issue of public wandering rights, where access would cause no harm, that one sees perhaps the greatest incongruity in contemporary libertarian thought. According to libertarians, expansive property rights foster liberty, and the more expansive the rights, the greater the liberty. But what about the liberty of citizens generally?...When landowners close off their lands, using state power to do so, they limit the liberties of citizens to wander at will.[38]

It is hardly self-evident that the correct liberty-focused position is to favor robust rights of exclusion over rights of access. Nevertheless, contemporary libertarians have uniformly privileged the right to exclude. The conception of exclusion rights favored by libertarians leaves little room for the kinds of limitations we discussed at the beginning of this chapter.

In more recent writings, Epstein has carved out room for the enactment of civil rights statutes on the grounds that it is justified for the state to combat the private violence and anticompetitive coordination that, as a historic matter, accompanied racial exclusion from places of public accommodation.[39] But he believes that, even if civil rights laws like Title II may at one time have been justified on this basis, the circumstances permitting that qualification of the right to exclude no longer exist. If Title II's guarantee of access to public accommodations is as exceptional (and anachronistic) as Epstein believes, then it seems clear that the state would not – in his view – be justified in forcing private owners to permit access to casinos (or other nonmonopoly businesses) and private beaches in the service of less apparently compelling interests.[40] On the other hand, if the right to exclude is more qualified

---

[36] Richard A. Epstein, *Takings* (1985), 65.

[37] See, for example, Joseph W. Singer, "After the Flood: Equality and Humanity in Property Regimes," *LOY. L. REV.* 52 (2006): 271–2.

[38] Eric T. Freyfogle, *The Land We Share* (2003), 251.

[39] See, for example, Richard A. Epstein, "Standing Firm, On Forbidden Grounds," *SAN DIEGO L. REV.* 31 (1994): 26–9.

[40] Epstein, *Takings*, 64–6 (discussing with disapproval the California Supreme Court's decision to require access to private shopping centers for political speech and the U.S. Supreme Court's determination that requiring such access does not "take" property from the owner of the shopping center).

(as in New Jersey), Title II becomes, not an anomaly, but merely a specification of limitations already inherent in the owner's right to exclude. The Lockean-libertarian critic of Title II needs a convincing argument for why acts of appropriation in the state of nature require the Nevada approach to exclusion rather than the New Jersey approach.

Even working within the broad outlines of a libertarian reading of Lockean property theory, we can construct a case for limiting exclusion rights somewhat, at least when it comes to unique natural places such as the waterfront. As we discussed in Chapter 2, Locke is careful to limit private appropriation to situations in which private ownership of a resource would not make others worse off. When land is abundant, as it is in the Lockean state of nature, individual acts of appropriation are likely to satisfy this proviso. But certain categories of land might be sufficiently unique that their appropriation, even amidst the relative abundance of the state of nature, harms nonappropriators and triggers the "enough, and as good" limitation from the outset. For example, as Robert Nozick admits, "a person may not appropriate the only water hole in a desert" without violating Lockean principles.[41] This is true, Nozick argues, even if the scarcity arises at some point after a valid act of appropriation.[42]

The waterfront has long been viewed as a scarce natural resource, and its scarcity has only been enhanced as populations have grown and waterfront living has become more socially desirable. This scarcity value is reflected in the traditional public trust doctrine, by which the common law has long recognized special rights of access to the water and adjacent lands subject to occasional tidal flooding. That doctrine is itself rooted in Roman law, which regarded the seashore as *res communes*, a resource owned and used by all in common.[43] In most common law jurisdictions, the boundary between privately owned waterfront land and the state's waters (from which, under the public trust doctrine, the public may not be excluded) is formed by the mean high tide line.[44]

The most significant innovation among courts in recent years has been to extend the spatial reach of the public's right of access landward of the mean high tide line, as the New Jersey case we discussed at the beginning of the chapter illustrates. Courts in other states have made similar moves. Although the purpose of the public trust doctrine was to protect public access to engage in obviously valuable economic

---

[41] Robert Nozick, *Anarchy, State, and Utopia* (1974), 180.

[42] Ibid.

[43] Mary Christina Wood, "Advancing the Sovereign Trust of Government to Safeguard the Environment for Present and Future Generations (Part 1)," ENVTL. L. 39 (2009): 43, 80 & n. 202.

[44] High tide lines fluctuate as a result of a number of variables, such the position of the sun and the moon, as well as weather and the earth's rotation. Consequently, jurisdictions usually take the average high tide over a period of several years to determine the location of the boundary between the state's waters and the private owner's land.

activities, particularly navigation and fishing, Lockean theory seems perfectly capable – at least in principle – of recognizing the unique suitability of waterfront land for particular recreational uses such that its privatization makes those excluded from access to it worse off in a significant way.

The contemporary Lockean libertarian might try to resist this extension of the public trust doctrine by denigrating the moral significance of recreation or by deploying Nozick's highly constrained version of the "enough, and as good" proviso. For Nozick, the point of the proviso is not to ask whether nonowners are worse off *in any respect* than they would be without appropriation, but rather whether, on the whole, they are better off than they would be in a world in which private property did not exist. That all-things-considered inquiry, however, depends on a refusal to take seriously the breadth and complexity of human well-being. In effect, it forces people to accept the improved economic opportunity possible within a regime of private ownership in exchange for constraints on access to unique natural or recreational resources like the waterfront.[45] Insofar as Nozick thinks monetary compensation is adequate to ensure that loss of access to unique natural spaces does not trigger the "enough, and as good" proviso, he assumes a unitary conception of human well-being in which – through the medium of wealth – every form of well-being can be reduced to (or substituted for) every other form. This move is not available to theorists who adhere to a pluralist account of human well-being such as the one offered within Aristotelian property theory.

THE RIGHT TO EXCLUDE AND HUMAN FLOURISHING

Because they aim to foster an objective conception of human flourishing, the Aristotelian theories of property we introduced in Chapter 5 are not as preoccupied as utilitarian property theory with satisfying individual preferences. Preferences are relevant to human flourishing theories, but they are not decisive measures of value or individual well-being. As a consequence, this property theory assigns less significance to the possibility that market transactions will reallocate the right to exclude on the basis of the preferences of the parties involved. In addition, while it shares the libertarian concern with individual autonomy, it regards that autonomy as just one dimension of flourishing, subject to qualification in pursuit of other components of well-being. Consequently, it is compatible with the kinds of legal qualifications on the right to exclude discussed at the beginning of this chapter. But, as we will see, while structuring property law so as to facilitate the pursuit of human flourishing can justify significant limitations on the right to exclude, Aristotelian theories still retain conceptual tools for recognizing the

---

[45] See Gopal Sreenivasan, *The Limits of Lockean Rights in Property* (1995), 135.

kinds of strong moral entitlements with which Lockeans and libertarians have traditionally been concerned.

In terms of their impact on human flourishing, the case for access is easiest to make for the kinds of status-based exclusions addressed by Title II. Excluding people from places of public accommodation on the basis of morally irrelevant character- istics – particularly characteristics over which they have little control – has obvious implications for their ability to participate fully in the social life of the community. And, as we discussed in Chapter 5, such social exclusion inhibits the capacity to flourish. When legal enforcement can be effective, and when countervailing inter- ests in the owner's right to exclude are not overriding, Aristotelian property theories offer support for using the law to prevent private owners from exercising the right to exclude in ways that undermine the ability of others to flourish.

While by no means always easy, enforcing antidiscrimination norms against deliberate racial discrimination in privately owned (but publicly accessible) spaces is relatively straightforward. Enforcement is arguably made easier, however, if the exercise of exclusion rights in places of public accommodation is an exception that needs to be justified, rather than the norm. There is a connection, then, between the grave interests protected by Title II and the seemingly frivolous case of Kenneth Uston's conflict with the casinos. As the New Jersey Supreme Court suggested in its *Uston* decision, the extension of rights of access to all users – including card counters – makes some sense if it is understood as an indirect means of protecting against more morally troubling forms of exclusion.[46] Creating an open-ended right of reasonable access to places of public accommodation also helps to economize on information costs.

As Lior Strahilevitz has argued, even where the law deprives owners of the right to exclude (by limiting what he calls owners' "Bouncer's Rights"), owners retain a great deal of power over who will enter their premises.[47] Through the use of indirect means (what he calls "Exclusionary Vibes" and "Exclusionary Amenities"), owners can deter many people from even seeking entry. For example, after being told by the New Jersey Supreme Court that they could not exclude card counters from their tables, Atlantic City casinos employed other means to accomplish their goals. If they suspected a patron of counting cards, they might lower the bet limit at the table or slow the game down, both of which would reduce the return the card counter could hope to earn. Relatedly, owners can manipulate their use of the Bouncer's Right in ways that evade enforcement of antidiscrimination norms, through the use of such ostensibly race neutral mechanisms as price and dress code. One bar in

---

[46] 445 A.2d at 374 n.4.
[47] See Lior Jacob Strahilevitz, "Information Asymmetries and the Rights to Exclude," MICH. L. REV. 104 (2006): 1835, 1843.

New York City, for example, has been investigated by the New York Human Rights Commission for enforcing a "no baggy jeans, no bling" dress code that many potential patrons perceive to be racially coded.[48] Once in place, these indirect uses of the Bouncer's Right create their own Exclusionary Vibe.

Such indirect means of exclusion are often, as Strahilevitz observes, imperfect substitutes for the direct use of the Bouncer's Right to exclude the targeted group. Proxies for race will allow some unwanted people in while excluding some of the desired group. Lowering bet limits and slowing down the dealer cost the casino money. Because they are often more costly and less effective for owners, the possibility that owners will resort to these less direct means of excluding does not make it unreasonable for the law to focus on trespass law as a strategy for combating racial discrimination more broadly. In addition, there is a difference, from the agent-focused Aristotelian perspective, between legally sanctioned racial exclusion (as in the pre-Title II South) and exclusion achieved through informal means, without the law's affirmative cooperation. The former invokes the law's agency on its behalf (e.g., when police cleared out sit-in protesters from private lunch counters at the owner's request) while the latter does not.

Moreover, punishing unwanted acts of exclusion is just one way that a legal prohibition, such as Title II, changes behavior. In addition to forcing some owners to resort to more costly means of satisfying their preference to exclude, such a legal prohibition not only penalizes those preferences but may also, over time, change owners' (and customers') preferences for the better. There is some evidence of such a cultural shift against preferences for racially segregated places of public accommodation in response to Title II. Indeed, Epstein's argument that Title II is no longer necessary depends very strongly on the notion that just such a shift has occurred. His argument, however, ignores the continuing expressive (preference-forming) value of a law like Title II, even where it does not coerce. His argument also depends on the notion that Title II is an intrusive rule that deprives owners of common law exclusion rights they would otherwise have – a view that in turn depends on a conception of the right to exclude that, as we hope this chapter has shown, is highly contestable on descriptive grounds.

A property theory focused on human flourishing can recognize that the limits of legal enforcement of antidiscrimination norms do not reach the outer boundaries of owners' moral obligations not to discriminate. This is because countervailing interests of owners, such as personal security and expressive or associational freedom, are implicated by owners' ability to exclude others from property, even when they will predictably exercise that ability immorally. Certainly, when no comparable human

---

[48] See Douglas Quenqua, "Dress Codes in New York Clubs: Will This Get Me In?," in *N.Y. Times*, July 27, 2011, E1.

capabilities are at stake on the other side, owners should be entitled to exclude unwanted intruders or users, and so the result in *Jacque v. Steenberg Homes*, which we discussed at the beginning of this chapter, is consistent with this approach.

Even when there are weighty interests in favor of access, however, those access interests must sometimes give way if there is a powerful connection between the right to exclude and the owner's own capability for flourishing. As the New Jersey Supreme Court has repeatedly observed (and as the U.S. Supreme Court has occasionally acknowledged), owners of places of public accommodation have attenuated associational interests in picking and choosing among those who can enter their property.[49] On the other hand, the common law has historically (and properly) attached great weight to the interests of privacy and associational autonomy by recognizing a robust right to exclude in the residential context. Tellingly, from the standpoint of human flourishing, the rights of tenants to receive visitors have traditionally trumped the rights of landlords to control access to their land.[50] Although the right to exclude, even in residential contexts, has long been subject to certain limited exceptions, such as the privilege of firefighters to enter for purposes of protecting the home, it has always been regarded as strongest with respect to the home.

This emphasis on the value of residential privacy makes sense from the point of view of Aristotelian property theory. Developing the capability of sociability, for example, depends upon one's having a significant degree of control over those with whom she will socialize, a sense that many, perhaps most, people experience most strongly in their own homes. A willingness to protect a zone of autonomy, however, does not require a commitment to the view that the choices people make within that zone are a matter of moral indifference. It is no less immoral to refuse to invite people into your home because of their race than it is to refuse to serve them in your restaurant. But the impact for the excluded person's ability to flourish is usually greater in the public accommodations context, and, in addition, concerns with residential owners' and occupants' interests in privacy, security, and associational autonomy justify protecting the power to exclude in certain contexts even when doing so will predictably result in forms of discrimination that are nonetheless immoral. Thus, antidiscrimination law generally – and not just Title II – carves out space for such private associational decisions.[51] Viewed from the perspective of human

---

[49] See *New Jersey Coalition Against War in the Middle East v. J.M.B. Realty Corp.*, 650 A.2d 757 (N.J. 1994); see also *Amalgamated Food Employees Union Local 590 v. Logan Valley Plaza, Inc.*, 391 U.S. 308 (1968), overruled by *Hudgens v. National Labor Relations Board*, 424 U.S. 507 (1976). But see *PruneYard Shopping Center v. Robbins*, 447 U.S. 74 (1980) (employing the distinction between commercial and noncommercial property within a takings challenge to a state law decision requiring access to shopping centers for certain expressive activities).

[50] See *State v. Shack*, 277 A.2d 369 (N.J. 1971).

[51] The same considerations would seem to explain the so-called Mrs. Murphy exception in the federal Fair Housing Act's ban on racial and other forms of discrimination by landlords in the selection of

flourishing, the point of these exceptions is not that such intimate discrimination is morally justifiable or harmless. It is, instead, that competing dimensions of human flourishing – combined with the difficulty of enforcement – render the direct legal prohibition of such discrimination unworkable and inappropriate.

The comfort of Aristotelian theory with this kind of balancing differs in a crucial way, however, from the flexibility and contextual sensitivity we observe in utilitarian property theory. Protecting a zone of private choice in order to safeguard the affirmative value of intimate association is not the same as carving out the same space in order to maximize the satisfaction of preferences. Weak entitlements (from the standpoint of flourishing) can be coupled with intense preferences, and vice versa.

The Aristotelian focus on the dimensions of flourishing, rather than on preferences and their intensity, means that it is consistent with the recognition of a strong moral entitlement to (for example) access without regard to race – irrespective of the balance of preferences – even when it declines for any number of reasons to enforce that entitlement through law.[52] Moreover, when confronted with such strong entitlements, the human flourishing position can justify legal efforts to combat immoral preferences (e.g., for racial exclusion even in intimate contexts) in ways that do not impinge as heavily on owner autonomy, whereas the traditional utilitarian calculus, which tends to take preferences as they are, finds it difficult to explain the point in trying to shape preferences in this way.

Thus, the human flourishing theory offers a distinctive view on why, for example, the Fair Housing Act (FHA) permits discrimination in certain private housing markets (e.g., small-scale rental by owner occupants) but prohibits even those exempted property owners from advertising their (legally permissible) discriminatory preferences.[53] This explanation for FHA's prohibition on advertisements goes beyond the standard utilitarian explanations of the advertising prohibition in terms of externalities. Those

---

tenants 42 U.S.C. § 3603(b)(2), 3604(a). Although the statute bars landlords from refusing to rent to otherwise qualified applicants on the basis of race, religion, gender, national origin, and familial status, it permits them to do so when the unit in question is part of a dwelling intended for occupancy by no more than four families living separately if the owner actually occupies one of the units. This exception and other statutorily permitted forms of discrimination in housing can be understood as reflecting the same concern with protecting the associational interests of owners in the privacy of their homes. It is in that context that a robust right to exclude is most easily justified on the basis of nurturing the capabilities necessary for human flourishing.

[52] This is not to say that utilitarian theories cannot also acknowledge a gap between first-order utilitarian analysis and the indirect pursuit of utility through law. See Henry E. Smith, "Mind the Gap: The Indirect Relation Between Ends and Means in American Property Law," *Cornell L. Rev.* 94 (2009): 959.

[53] See Rigel C. Oliveri, "Discriminatory Housing Advertisements Online," *Ind. L. Rev.* 43 (2010): 1125. After the FHA was enacted in 1968, the U.S. Supreme Court decided *Jones v. Alfred H. Mayer, Co.*, 392 U.S. 409 (1968), which held that the Civil Rights Act of 1866 (Section 1982) prohibited *racial* (but not other forms of) discrimination in housing markets. That law includes none of the exemptions contained within the FHA.

explanations, while plausible, are incomplete, even in utilitarian terms. Identifying an externality is only the first step in the utilitarian determination whether to prohibit a particular behavior. That determination ultimately rests on an empirical question about the cost of the externality relative to the costs (in terms of frustrated preferences) of prohibiting the conduct. Unlike utilitarian theory, however, the Aristotelian analysis assigns no weight to the racist preference frustrated by FHA's restrictions on advertising those preferences, even while it declines to prohibit some owners from acting on them.[54]

Aristotelian property theories can also shed light on the beach access cases. From the point of view of human flourishing, recreation is not a luxury but a necessity. It is important to maintaining mental and physical health, themselves vital dimensions of well-being. Recreation also supports sociability. And sociability in turn encompasses subsidiary goods such as friendship and compassion.[55] It includes the ability "to recognize and show concern for other human beings, to engage in various forms of social interaction; [and] to be able to imagine the situation of another."[56] Moreover, through recreation, people of varied backgrounds mingle together and learn how to treat one another civilly, with respect and courtesy. Thus, creating focal points for such indiscriminate recreational mingling may well help indirectly to combat the sorts of intimate associational discrimination the law wisely declines to prohibit directly.[57] The opportunities for these educative experiences are greatest in spaces that are open to all, or reasonably so. Strictly private spaces inhibit the process of socialization that result from serendipitous interactions with strangers, through which we learn how to be concerned for those who are very different from us, how to show that concern, and how to place ourselves in their shoes.

Access to the resources needed to engage in recreation and to escape social isolation is a particularly acute challenge for the poor. Aristotelian property theory recognizes owners' obligations to contribute to the vitality of the community's material infrastructure in order to enable others, particularly the poor, to cultivate capabilities like sociability. For private beach owners, particularly those who have opened their beaches up to the (paying) public, this obligation may sometimes include providing a broader segment of the general public with reasonable access to portions of their beach. Of course, this obligation cannot be open-ended. A challenge for

---

54 As we noted above in chapter 1, some utilitarians would favor disregarding certain preferences, such as preferences for racial exclusion, within their utilitarian calculus. Such a move makes their theories less purely consequentialist and brings their approach closer to the kind of objective account of well being favored within Aristotelian property theory.

55 See Martha C. Nussbaum, *Women and Human Development* (2000), 82–3, 92.

56 Martha C. Nussbaum, "Human Rights and Human Capabilities," HARV. HUM. RTS. J. 20 (2007): 1, 23.

57 Cf. Elizabeth F. Emens, "Intimate Discrimination," HARV. L. REV. 122 (2009): 1307; Carol Rose, "The Comedy of the Commons," U. CHI. L. REV. 53 (1986): 711.

a human flourishing approach to the beach access cases is to offer useful ways to generalize about whether and when the landowner's obligation to contribute to the vitality of capabilities nurturing aspects of her community includes sharing with members of the general public access to her land. When the public has reasonable means of access to the beach elsewhere, its interest in access to any particular private waterfront parcel is reduced. Moreover, as in the antidiscrimination context, the community's interest in access to unique recreational resources, like beaches, even where strong (because of, say, the lack of publically accessible alternatives) must be weighed against owners' legitimate interests in privacy and freedom of intimate association, interests that decline the more an owner (as in the New Jersey beach club case) has opened up his property to all those willing to pay the price. Although by no means uniquely mandated by a concern with human flourishing, the outcome in the New Jersey beach access case (and, indeed, the New Jersey Supreme Court's treatment of the right to exclude more generally) is broadly consistent with that approach to property theory.

The point of the foregoing discussion is not to argue that a focus on human flourishing in property theory decisively demonstrates the propriety of the New Jersey Supreme Court's treatment of beach access or of the civil rights laws' precise mixture of prohibitions and exceptions. Nor is it to argue that no other theory can offer a competing explanation of the complex mix of exclusion and access within existing property law. Like the other approaches to exclusion we have explored in this chapter, a focus on human flourishing is arguably consistent with a number of different ways of structuring owners' rights to exclude. And a number of different theories are consistent with the existing law. What is genuinely distinctive about Aristotelian theories, however, is that their pluralistic approach to the values implicated by exclusion more faithfully describes the complexity of the moral landscape. Such fidelity helpfully structures deliberation about the value judgments and tradeoffs that property systems necessarily need to make when they decide how to weigh owners' rights to exclude against the interests of others in access and inclusion.

8

Eminent Domain and Regulatory Takings

One of the most controversial aspects of American property law, and the subject of this chapter, is the government's authority to expropriate private property through eminent domain. Although the origins of collective expropriations of land for the public good are quite old,[1] in the United States, the eminent domain power originates from the Fifth Amendment of the U.S. Constitution, which provides, in relevant part, "nor shall private property be taken for public use, without just compensation."[2] This is the so-called takings clause of the federal constitution. It permits government at all levels, federal, state, and local, to expropriate (or condemn) land and other forms of property on two conditions – the expropriation must be for public use and the government must pay just compensation. Although the meaning of *just compensation* is now well-settled, the precise meanings of *take* and *public use* remain the subject of much debate.

The takings clause is also implicated when the government, rather than condemning land, regulates the use of land under police power but does so to an extent that seems tantamount to a confiscation. These so-called regulatory takings have been at the center of some of the most intractable controversies involving the takings clause. As we will see, rival views on these controversies reflect competing underlying theories of the nature of and reasons for private property.

UTILITARIANISM

Utilitarian Theory and Government Takings

Assume that a highway will increase overall utility but that the government needs the highway to run in a more or less straight line. To accomplish this, the government

---

[1] See Susan Reynolds, *Before Eminent Domain: Toward a History of Expropriation of Land for the Common Good* (2010).

[2] U.S. Constitution, amend. 5. Technically, the Fifth Amendment does not grant the eminent domain power; it only confirms it. It is, as the U.S. Supreme Court has said, "a tacit recognition of a pre-existing power." *United States v. Carmack*, 329 U.S. 230, 241–2 (1946).

must assemble a large number of contiguous parcels. As it begins to acquire parcels, the owners of the remaining parcels can easily perceive that refusing to sell their parcel could significantly increase the government's construction costs. Suppose that an owner's parcel is worth ten thousand dollars for any other use, but rerouting the highway around the owner's parcel would cost the government one hundred thousand dollars in additional construction costs. A rational actor would try to capture as much of the one hundred thousand dollars in avoided costs as possible. The consequence of a large number of owners engaging in this sort of strategic behavior is a higher cost for the government of assembling large parcels of land, perhaps even to the point of destroying the utility gains that the project (absent those transaction costs) would generate.

Transaction Costs and the Holdout

As we discussed in Chapter 6, utilitarian property theorists generally favor the use of consensual market transactions to transfer property from one user to another. When transaction costs are high, however, consensual transfers may not succeed in moving property from its current owner to a user who would derive more utility from it. As Thomas Merrill has observed, the classic examples of eminent domain involve situations where transaction costs are likely to be very high.[3] On the utilitarian view, this makes good sense. Utilitarians view the government's power of eminent domain as a mechanism for overcoming high transaction costs associated with holdout behavior. To use the terminology of Guido Calabresi and A. Douglas Melamed, which we introduced in Chapter 1, eminent domain reduces transaction costs by changing the protection of a property owner's entitlements (as against the government) from a property rule to a liability rule. Instead of a property owner's power to unilaterally – and for any reason – veto the sale of her property (a property rule), when the state is acquiring land, the owner's right to block a sale is extinguished upon the state's payment of compensation (a liability rule).

Just Compensation

Under the federal constitution, a taking of property under the eminent domain power must be accompanied by just compensation. Courts have long interpreted *just compensation* to mean the fair market value of the property.[4] That is, an owner is entitled to receive the amount a hypothetical willing buyer would pay a willing seller for the parcel in an arm's length transaction.[5] This measure of damages does not include any subjective value the present owner may place on the property over

---

[3]   See generally Thomas W. Merrill, "The Economics of Public Use," CORNELL L. REV. 72 (1986): 61.
[4]   See, for example, *United States v. 50 Acres of Land*, 469 U.S. 24, 25–6 (1984).
[5]   See ibid., 25 n. 1.

and above its market value. Nor does it include costs that the owner may incur as a result of the condemnation, such as relocation costs, lost business goodwill, or even the costs of procuring a replacement property.

From a utilitarian standpoint, this suggests that just compensation usually under-compensates expropriated property owners. The reason is that, if expropriated owners valued their property at nothing more than fair market value, they would likely have already put the property up for sale. The fact that they have not suggests that keeping ownership of the property brings them some utility above and beyond what a willing buyer would pay for the property. This possibility of high subjective valuations puts holdouts in a different light from a utilitarian perspective. Although some holdouts may simply be behaving strategically in order to extract concessions from land assemblers, it is likely that some holdouts simply place a high valuation on retaining the property in question, relative to its market value.

Most commentators agree that, because of (among other things) high subject-ive valuations, just compensation amounts to systematic undercompensation.[6] But most also acknowledge that the difficulties of reliably determining the subjective value an owner places on a property preclude courts from adopting any other stand-ard.[7] As Lee Anne Fennell has explained, "people cannot be counted on to volun-teer honest and accurate valuations of entitlements that they own or might wish to own. Because it is usually evident whether a higher or lower valuation will better serve the self-interest of the person asked to do the valuation, there is a temptation to lie or unconsciously shade one's answer in a self-serving direction."[8]

In a series of articles and a recent book, Fennell has proposed a number of innovative techniques for eliciting accurate self-valuations from owners or putative owners. Most relevant for the problem of undercompensation of subjective value in eminent domain is the so-called Entitlement Subject to a Self-Made Option or ESSMO. The ESSMO, Fennell explains, "requires one party to package her sub-jective valuation in the form of an option, while allowing the other party to act uni-laterally on that option."[9] The government's power to act on the option creates the incentive for owners to claim high values for their property. In order to ensure that owners do not simply specify unrealistically high valuations, the ESSMO mech-anism would need to be coupled with the requirement that owners pay for their valuation (for example, by basing property tax assessments on the claimed value). Although the ESSMO device holds great promise for encouraging owners to

---

6   See Lee Anne Fennell, "Taking Eminent Domain Apart," *Mich. St. L. Rev.* 4 (2004):957, 960–1; James
    E. Krier and Christopher Serkin, "Public Ruses," *Mich. St. L. Rev.* 4 (2004): 859, 865; Christopher
    Serkin, "The Meaning of Value," *Nw. U. L. Rev.* 99 (2005): 679.
7   See *United States v. 564.54 Acres of Land*, 441 U.S. 506, 511 (1979).
8   Lee Anne Fennell, *The Unbounded Home* (2009), 106.
9   Ibid., 105; see also Lee Anne Fennell, "Revealing Options," *Harv. L. Rev.* 118 (2005): 1339, 1442–3.

reveal high (and low) subjective valuations, in societies characterized by economic inequality, self-reported valuations may be subject to significant wealth effects that could lead to continued undercompensation of those owners for whom reporting a higher valuation constitutes more of a financial sacrifice.

Public Use

The utilitarian, transaction costs account of eminent domain raises a number of interesting questions. Among them is that – at first glance – the power of eminent domain, as it has traditionally been understood, appears to be both underinclusive and overinclusive. The potential overinclusiveness derives from the fact that many uses for which the government must acquire land do not require the assembly of large parcels for which transaction costs would be exceptionally high. Clearly the highway land assembly involves high transaction costs, but the construction of a small police station or a post office would not present the same problems. The government could simply buy an appropriately sized parcel on the open market and proceed with construction. If the owner tried to hold out, the government could just move on to another owner. And yet, at least as a matter of federal constitutional law, the government enjoys the power of eminent domain even when the project for which it is acquiring the property does not involve the presence of high transaction costs.

Many states require governments to negotiate in good faith with owners before initiating a condemnation proceeding. Of course, this negotiation will occur in the shadow of the government's power to condemn. As a consequence, the government will likely not offer much more than the fair market value of the property, and an owner who places a high subjective value on the property will not find much protection in the bargaining requirement. Similarly, although many states require condemners to demonstrate that the exercise of condemnation is somehow necessary to achieve a public benefit, the necessity inquiry typically focuses on the benefits to be derived from the ultimate use to which the property is put and not on the availability of alternative means of acquiring a parcel for the project in question.[10] This problem of overinclusiveness may be more apparent than real. As Merrill has argued, government actors perceive the eminent domain process to be cumbersome, time consuming, and politically costly, and so seem to prefer, when possible, to acquire land through consensual market transactions.[11]

The potential underinclusiveness of eminent domain power stems from the situations in which high transaction costs stand in the way of successful (and let us assume utility enhancing) land assembly by actors other than government bodies.

[10] See, for example, Appeal of City of Keene, 141 N.H. 797, 802 (1997).
[11] See Merrill, "Economics of Public Use," 80.

Any land assembler, public or private, faces potential holdouts who can drive up transaction costs to such an extent that a utility-enhancing project becomes unfeasible. Why does the government enjoy the power of eminent domain while private land assemblers, for the most part, do not? To begin with, private land assemblers are not identically situated with state actors. Private actors have tools at their disposal for overcoming holdouts that would be either legally or politically unworkable in public hands. For example, a private land assembler can employ agents to surreptitiously assemble large parcels without alerting potential holdouts that land assembly is occurring.[12] But because the government cannot normally – and for good reasons – acquire land secretly, this is a mechanism not available to it.[13]

Private land assemblers' ability to use tools, such as secret purchases, not available to the government can reduce the high transaction costs associated with land assembly, but it may not eliminate them. Perhaps for this reason, in many jurisdictions, private actors who face persistent land assembly problems, such as railroads and utilities, have traditionally been given the power of eminent domain. In addition, though more controversially, state actors may occasionally use the power of eminent domain on behalf of private land assemblers. This is, in a nutshell, what happens in so-called private-to-private expropriations, which today most commonly (though by no means exclusively) occur in the context of urban redevelopment. In the infamous *Poletown* case, the city of Detroit used its power of eminent domain to assemble a large parcel on behalf of General Motors so the automaker could build a factory in the city.[14] More recently, as described in the U.S. Supreme Court's 2005 decision in *Kelo v. New London*, the New London Development Corporation (NLDC) used its power of eminent domain (in combination with negotiated purchases) to assemble large parcels in the Fort Trumbull neighborhood of New London. Part of the land the NLDC acquired was to be leased to private developers for construction of residential and commercial projects.[15] In both the *Poletown* and *New London* cases, the stated goal of the land assembly was not primarily to benefit favored private parties, but instead to increase municipal tax revenues and to create jobs.

The use of eminent domain on behalf of private land assemblers has sparked considerable public outrage.[16] Although the court has traditionally read the "for

---

[12] See Peter Hellman, "How They Assembled the Most Expensive Block in New York's History," in *New York*, Feb. 25, 1974, 31 (excerpted in Robert C. Ellickson and Vicki L. Been, *Land Use Controls*, 3rd ed. (2005), 846–53).

[13] See Daniel B. Kelly, "The Public Use Requirement in Eminent Domain Law," CORNELL L. REV. 92 (2006): 1, 18–25.

[14] See *Poletown Neighborhood Council v. City of Detroit*, 410 Mich. 616 (1981), overturned by *County of Wayne v. Hathcock*, 471 Mich. 445 (2004).

[15] See *Kelo v. City of New London*, 545 U.S. 469 (2005).

[16] See Janice Nadler and Shari Seidman Diamond, "Government Takings of Private Property: *Kelo* and the Perfect Storm," in *Public Opinion and Constitutional Controversy*, ed. Nathaniel Persily et al., (2008), 287.

public use" language in the takings clause as constituting an outer limit on the scope of the eminent domain power (private property may only be taken for public use), in a series of cases, it has held that *any* legitimate "public purpose" qualifies as a public use.[17] In other words, any goal the government can legitimately pursue through some other policy tool, it can pursue using the power of eminent domain. And the Supreme Court has consistently deferred to state actors in its determination that an act of condemnation is in the public interest. The court reaffirmed this position in *Kelo,* but seemed to add the clarification that the government acts unconstitutionally if its actual motive in undertaking an act of eminent domain is not to provide a public benefit but merely to benefit the private beneficiary of the expropriation.[18]

From a strictly utilitarian standpoint, the court's traditionally broad interpretation of public use as a public purpose might seem puzzling. After all, the test does not directly ask courts to determine whether the project at issue enhances aggregate utility. Instead, it asks courts to defer to political actors (executives or legislatures) and to their determination that a project is in the public interest. But this institutional deference may itself be defensible on utilitarian grounds. Courts are not particularly well suited to engage in a wide-ranging cost-benefit analysis of what are often highly localized land use decisions. In addition, political actors will be more easily held to account for gross errors in their cost-benefit calculus. The *Kelo* court's emphasis on intent is somewhat harder to explain in utilitarian terms, but even that might make sense. Although courts are generally not as well situated to engage in the kind of cost-benefit analysis utilitarians think should underlie a determination whether to use the power of eminent domain, evidence that a political actor has used a legitimate public purpose as a mere pretext to confer a private benefit on a well-connected developer might suggest that, in this particular instance, the political body has been corrupted or has abdicated its duty to conduct a careful cost-benefit analysis before using the power of eminent domain. And, in those circumstances, the normal institutional advantage of political bodies may be sufficiently vitiated that courts are justified in intervening.

Utilitarian Theory and Regulatory Takings

Although there is widespread (though not universal) agreement that compensating property owners is utility enhancing when the government expressly seizes land (or other property) for a public project, there is far less utilitarian consensus about whether (if ever) the government should compensate property owners when it merely regulates the use to which they may put their property. This latter question

---

[17] See *Berman v. Parker,* 348 U.S. 26 (1954); *Hawaii Housing Authority v. Midkiff,* 467 U.S. 229 (1984).
[18] See *Kelo,* 545 U.S. 478.

is typically discussed under the rubric of so-called regulatory takings. The modern law of regulatory takings originated with the Supreme Court's 1922 decision in *Pennsylvania Coal Co. v. Mahon*.[19] In that case, the court confronted a challenge to a Pennsylvania law that prohibited coal companies from mining in a way that caused the surface of land to collapse when there was a house on the surface. The case was complicated by the fact that, in Pennsylvania, unlike in other states, the owners of the surface property were empowered to sell their rights to have their land supported from below. The homeowners' deed in the *Mahon* case had done just that. In finding the Pennsylvania law to have taken the coal company's property in violation of the Fifth Amendment, the Supreme Court (in an opinion by Justice Oliver Wendell Holmes) noted that "[g]overnment hardly could go on if to some extent values incident to property could not be diminished without pay for every such change in the general law."[20] But "while property may be regulated to a certain extent, if regulation goes too far it will be recognized as a taking."[21] The case did not provide a great deal of guidance about how to make that determination.

A theory's approach to the question whether a regulation "goes too far" and requires compensation depends in part on the theory's reasons for compensating owners for losses caused by state action. As it turns out, justifying the payment of compensation even for explicit exercise of the eminent domain power is a complex undertaking within utilitarian property theory. After all, assuming that the project for which the government will be taking property is utility enhancing, why, as a utilitarian matter, must it pay compensation to the original landowner, whether measured by fair market value or some other formula? Although, as we will see, there are a number of nonutilitarian arguments for a compensation requirement, utilitarian theorists' focus on aggregate welfare makes the case for compensating individual landowners somewhat more complicated. If a government project generates more benefits than costs, compensating the expropriated landowners does not (without additional assumptions) make the project more efficient. It simply reallocates some of the gains from the project back to the original landowner. An important question is why, in utilitarian terms, society should care how the costs and benefits of a utility-enhancing project are allocated. The difficulty of justifying compensation in utilitarian terms also results from the fact that administering a system of compensation is, in itself, a significant expense that, if sufficiently costly, can eat away at the utility gains we are assuming the government's project will generate.

A number of utilitarian justifications for compensation for takings have been proposed. These share the feature of asserting a connection between the failure to

---

[19]   260 U.S. 393 (1922).
[20]   Ibid., 413.
[21]   Ibid., 415.

compensate landowners and the generation of some quantum of disutility that would not exist upon the payment of compensation. Under the right circumstances, paying compensation therefore reduces disutility associated with a particular government policy and, consequently, from a utilitarian standpoint, can enhance overall utility. Utilitarian theorists differ, however, in how they describe the utility costs of non-compensation. Some theories focus on the costs of noncompensation on affected owners, which we – borrowing from Frank Michelman's classic article – will call "demoralization."[22] Others focus on the impact of noncompensation on government incentives to regulate or expropriate property. And yet others, which we will group under the rubric of "public choice theories," focus on the interaction between the compensation requirement and interest group politicking. It is important to acknowledge that we are presenting discussions of these approaches in a stylized way that does not do justice to their subtlety. Moreover, these approaches are in many ways complementary. Thus, sophisticated utilitarian theories of compensation for government takings frequently draw on several of them at once.

Owner Demoralization

Demoralization theories of compensation argue that if owners are not compensated when their property is regulated or expropriated, they will suffer disutility from their uncompensated losses. In addition to owners' own feelings of mistreatment and loss, citizens in general may suffer from some demoralization by observing others losing their property without just compensation. This may lead them to feel more insecure in ownership of their own property, which in turn may result in an unwillingness to engage in productive investment.

Any disutility caused by uncompensated takings of property can be offset by compensating owners only if it is the case that the disutility caused by owners' losses is asymmetric with the loss others would suffer in having to pay (e.g., through the tax system) to compensate them. Otherwise, compensation will simply move disutility from one person to another, generating no net utility gain but imposing significant administrative costs. Michelman hypothesizes such an asymmetry, noting that owners will treat concentrated losses at the hands of the human agents (such as government actors) differently than other sorts of uncompensated losses. In addition, deeply rooted conceptions of fairness are likely to cause owners to be more demoralized by what Michelman calls "capricious redistribution" than the more predictable and fairly allocated (even if equally redistributive) systems of taxation used to generate the funds for payment of compensation to expropriated owners.

---

[22] Frank I. Michelman, "Property, Utility and Fairness: Comments on the Ethical Foundations of 'Just Compensation' Law," *HARV. L. REV.* 80 (1967): 1165.

Michelman does not argue that government should always seek to avoid demoralization costs. Instead, his position is that government should pursue projects that increase aggregate utility, but should pay the compensation necessary to reduce or eliminate demoralization costs when doing so would be less expensive than merely accepting the demoralization that would result from uncompensated takings. Michelman argues that his theory robustly justifies the practice of compensation for explicit exercise of the government's eminent domain power and predicts that it will call for compensation of regulations that narrowly single out particular categories of property owners for significant losses. In these situations, affected owners are relatively easy to identify and so the costs of administering a system of compensation will be manageable.

While Michelman's powerful theory is helpful in providing a utilitarian explanation for the practice of compensation in eminent domain, it is worth noting that some property owners seem much more likely than others to suffer demoralization costs when confronted with an uncompensated loss, whether due to eminent domain or regulatory takings. As Lawrence Blume and Daniel Rubinfeld have suggested, for example, the subjective state of owners who are risk averse – such as those for whom the property in question is a large part of their net worth – will be more dramatically affected by the risk of uncompensated expropriation than owners for whom any particular parcel of land is a small portion of a larger investment portfolio.[23] The possibility that different owners will experience different amounts of demoralization from uncompensated losses resulting from government actions means that careful utilitarian analysis of compensation in terms of demoralization costs is likely to be extremely sensitive to context. It may even be open to treating different types of owners (and even different types of property) differently for takings purposes.

Government Incentives

Another category of utilitarian compensation theory focuses broadly on the impact that the compensation requirement has on government actors' incentives in conducting their own cost-benefit analysis concerning which policies to undertake. In the absence of a compensation requirement, the argument goes, rational government actors are likely to treat private property like a commons. Consequently, they will tend to overregulate and overexpropriate, undertaking projects that are not necessarily utility enhancing because one of the principal inputs (regulated and expropriated land) is free.[24] As Justice Antonin Scalia put it in his opinion in *Pennell v. City of*

---

[23] See Lawrence Blume and Daniel L. Rubinfeld, "Compensation for Takings: An Economic Analysis," CAL. L. REV. 72 (1984): 603–8.

[24] See Richard A. Posner, *Economic Analysis of Law*, 6th ed. (2003), 57; Blume and Rubinfeld, "Compensation for Takings," 571; Michael A. Heller and James E. Krier, "Deterrence and Distribution

San Jose, "[t]he politically attractive feature of regulation is not that it permits wealth transfers to be achieved, but rather that it permits them to be achieved 'off budget,' with relative invisibility...."[25]

The biggest problem with these so-called fiscal illusion theories lies in the assumption that government actors are rational in the sense of responding to price incentives as would a wealth maximizing private firm. As Daryl Levinson has persuasively argued, the actual behavior of government actors does not appear to respond to price incentives in this way.[26] If, as Levinson suggests, government actors are not profit maximizers but political maximizers, requiring government to pay compensation may not do much to ensure that government power will be used in utility-enhancing projects.

Public Choice

The final category of compensation theory – which we will refer to as *public choice theories* – focuses on interest group politicking. The political implications of compensation are complex. Many public choice theorists share the utilitarian view that the goal of the compensation requirement should be to ensure that the political process pursues utility-enhancing policies at the lowest cost. But there is no general agreement among these theorists about the implications of interest group analysis for the compensation requirement. For example, in a kind of inversion of the fiscal illusion theory, some argue that compensating those whose property is burdened by regulation might discourage those who lose from government action from resisting it.[27] This political consequence may in turn lead political actors to underestimate the costs of their decisions. On the other hand, in the absence of compensation, those who stand to lose might fight excessively against efficient policies or projects, driving up political transaction costs and, in the process, deterring many utility enhancing government decisions.

A related application looks to the status of groups affected by government action. Groups likely to be cut off from the political process are often less likely to have their interests taken into account by decision makers. On one view, groups who are persistently disadvantaged in the political process should receive compensation for property losses at government hands.[28] Even here, however, theorists disagree about whether diffuse majorities or discrete minorities are at a greater political

---

in the Law of Takings," *Harv. L. Rev.* 112 (1999): 997, 999; Michael H. Schill, "Intergovernmental Takings and Just Compensation: A Question of Federalism," *U. Pa. L. Rev.* 137 (1989): 859–60.

[25] 485 U.S. 1, 21–2 (1988) (Scalia, J., concurring in part and dissenting in part).

[26] See Daryl J. Levinson, "Making Government Pay," *U. Chi. L. Rev.* 67 (2000): 345, 357.

[27] See Saul Levmore, "Just Compensation and Just Politics," *Conn. L. Rev.* 22 (1990): 309–10.

[28] See, for example, William Michael Treanor, "The Original Understanding of the Takings Clause and the Political Process," *Colum. L. Rev.* 95 (1995): 782, 875.

disadvantage and therefore more in need of compensation.[29] For those who hold the view that small minorities are relatively disadvantaged in the political process, regulations that single out small groups of property owners for exceptional losses should trigger a compensation requirement. For those who hold the view that small minorities are more likely to organize themselves for effective political action, however, imposing a compensation requirement for regulation that concentrates its costs on small groups may make utility-enhancing regulation too difficult to enact.

Conclusion

In light of the complexity and uncertainty we have identified in utilitarian analysis of government takings and the scope of the compensation requirement, it would be misleading to assert that there is one utilitarian position on any of these questions. As with other property questions, however, utilitarian property theory provides a rich set of tools for thinking about these issues. Although commentators often make an easy move from utilitarian concerns with aggregate utility to robust protection of individual property entitlements, the utilitarian commitment to maximizing utility complicates that relationship such that there is no reason to think that utilitarian considerations will inevitably recommend the protection of private property rights in any given case. Utilitarian theory only favors those rights as a means to the larger end of enhancing overall utility. As we will see in the next section, libertarian property theorists approach the question of government takings from precisely the opposite direction.

LIBERTARIANISM AND GOVERNMENT TAKINGS

Libertarian approaches to eminent domain and regulatory takings begin with the premise that property rights and allocations are rooted in natural rights that preexist the political community. On the libertarian view, individuals enter the political community with property entitlements already in place, and, consequently, their use and enjoyment of private property can only be restricted in extremely circumscribed ways necessary for the protection of correlative property rights in others. Libertarians often endorse John Locke's general statement that the government "cannot take from any Man any part of his Property without his own consent."[30] As we discussed in Chapter 2, however, contemporary libertarians do not typically subscribe to Locke's

---

[29] Compare Daniel A. Farber and Philip P. Frickey, *Law and Public Choice* (1991), 72 (diffuse majorities disadvantaged in the political process), with Treanor, "Original Understanding of the Takings Clause," 875 (discrete and insular minorities disadvantaged); Levmore, "Just Compensation," 310 (same).

[30] John Locke, *Two Treatises of Government*, ed. Mark Goldie, Everyman's Library (1993), 138.

expansive conception of consent as encompassing, for example, the tax burdens allocated by a democratically elected legislature.[31] Although they differ with one another on the details, they agree that the power of the modern democratic state is strictly limited by existing property entitlements.[32]

It is not clear, even having jettisoned Locke's notion of consent, that Locke's conception of property is up to the task that contemporary libertarians want to assign to it. As we observed in Chapter 2, Locke never describes precisely what rights an appropriator acquires in items she takes out of the commons. Nor does his labor theory of appropriation successfully support the sort of robust natural private rights contemporary libertarians would like to entrench. If the natural rights of property are highly qualified or extremely indeterminate, they cannot serve as much of a check on the power of government through the takings clause. Since the clause only requires the government to compensate you for taking something you in fact own, we need a more determinate way to ascertain the content of natural property rights than Locke's theory seems to provide.

Eminent Domain

The absence of powerful philosophical arguments for robust and specific natural rights of property has not stopped libertarians from treating putatively natural property rights as stringent limitations on the power of government. This general statement, however, masks a significant diversity of opinion among thinkers frequently classified as libertarian.

At one extreme, for example, is Ayn Rand. As we discussed in Chapter 6, Rand argues that, although government has an essential role to play in the protection of property rights, it may not fund its activities through coercively enforced schemes of taxation.[33] By extension, Randian libertarians oppose any exercise of the government's inherently coercive eminent domain power as inconsistent with private property rights. And, since their position is based on a nonconsequentialist account of individual rights, Randians reject the significance of the transactions costs analysis that drives the utilitarian case for both coercive taxation and eminent domain. They do not seem troubled by the enormous utility losses that would be sustained in carrying out public projects without the power to tax or to use eminent domain to overcome holdout problems. They imagine a fee-for-service government, but they have no solution to the problem posed by public goods, such as national defense or crime prevention, from whose non-fee-payers cannot be (completely) excluded. Seemingly oblivious to the

---

[31] Ibid., 140.
[32] See Richard A. Epstein, *Takings* (1985), 162.
[33] See Ayn Rand, "Government Financing in a Free Society," in *The Virtue of Selfishness* (1964), 157.

problems of free riding and moral hazard, Rand says that "[s]ince the proper services of a government – the police, the armed forces, and the law courts – are demonstrably needed by individual citizens and affect their interests directly, the citizens would (and should) be willing to pay for such services, as they pay for insurance."[34]

More sophisticated property rights conservatives, such as Richard Epstein, take into account the enormous social losses associated with ignoring altogether the problem of transaction costs. Epstein, for example, permits the introduction of utilitarian considerations through his theory of forced exchanges, whereby the state can compel individuals to submit to utility-enhancing modifications of their natural rights as long as it pays them just compensation in exchange.[35] Although, for reasons we have already discussed, this Pareto requirement does not fully protect individual preferences, it does protect them more than more permissive aggregation standards such as Kaldor-Hicks.[36] At the same time, Epstein's theory of forced exchanges substantially softens the indifference of libertarian theories to transaction costs.

The question is whether Epstein can keep his theory of forced exchanges within the boundaries he would like to set for it. We have already discussed how the issue of baselines complicates Epstein's theory.[37] In the context of eminent domain, the problem is particularly acute. Epstein does not want to create open-ended power for the state to force private owners to convey their property upon payment of just compensation. To this end, he argues that the public use requirement should be read narrowly to prevent the state from becoming an agent of private parties who want to use the power of eminent domain to keep for themselves the lion's share of whatever surplus may be gained from a particular transaction. Epstein would therefore limit the power of eminent domain to projects that will generate public goods or in which the ultimate recipient of the property acquired by eminent domain will be, in effect, a common carrier, meaning the recipient must make the property open to all who are willing to abide by a uniform set of rules governing access.[38] He therefore shares the broad libertarian objection to the Supreme Court's traditional interpretation of "public use" as "public purpose," and has taken particular exception to its decision in *Kelo v. New London*, discussed previously.[39]

It is not clear, however, that, once he has unleashed the concept of forced exchanges, Epstein can successfully keep them within the boundaries he would like to set. As Thomas Merrill has observed, the notion of public good is sufficiently broad that it can be made to fit almost any collective action problem.[40] It might

[34] Ibid.
[35] See Epstein, *Takings*, chap. 14.
[36] See Chapter 1, supra.
[37] See Chapter 2, supra.
[38] See Epstein, *Takings*, chap. 12.
[39] See, for example, Richard A. Epstein, "Kelo: An American Original," *Green Bag* 8 (2005): 355.
[40] See Merrill, "Economics of Public Use," 74.

plausibly be thought to encompass the ability to overcome the kinds of holdout and collective action, transaction-costs challenges that impede utility enhancing private land assembly. But this is exactly the sort of broad justification for the use of eminent domain that Epstein would like to rule out. If the public derives a benefit, even if only indirectly, from overcoming transaction costs and fully compensates the original owner, however, the requirements of Pareto would seem to be satisfied, irrespective of the use to which the property is ultimately put. From the libertarian perspective, then, Epstein's efforts to make concessions to the goals of utility enhancement are hard to cabin and seem to give up too much.

Regulatory Takings

The question of regulation presents even more of a conceptual problem for libertarians. Because regulation of the exercise of property rights is often undertaken in order to protect the rights of neighboring property owners, the same categorical opposition that characterizes the strict libertarian opposition to eminent domain is not an attractive position. After all, as Rand observes, one of the principal purposes of government is to protect property owners from nonconsensual losses at the hands of others.[41] As scholars like Joseph Singer, Eric Freyfogle, and Laura Underkuffler have argued, however, this libertarian commitment to protect owners from one another creates a seemingly intractable conflict between the rights of owners to do what they want with their property and the rights of other owners to be left alone on their property, free from the consequences of others owners' property decisions.[42] The concept of property rights as protecting negative liberty, without a great deal more, simply cannot adjudicate between these two sets of claims.

Some libertarians, notably Epstein and Randy Barnett, avoid this indeterminacy by treating common law property rights as a baseline for their takings analysis.[43] Property owners are entitled to the rights they had – whether to use or to be free from the consequences of others' uses – at common law. Government action that intrudes on that set of rights – either through direct regulation or reallocation – takes property from owners and therefore gives rise to a duty to compensate. As Epstein puts it, "[l]et the government remove any incidents of ownership, let it diminish the rights of an owner in any fashion, then it has prima facie brought itself within the scope of the eminent domain clause, no matter how small the alteration and no matter how general its application."[44] The Supreme Court, in its decision in *Lucas v. South*

---

[41] See Ayn Rand, "The Nature of Government," in *Capitalism: The Unknown Ideal* (1966), 295, 300.
[42] See Laura S. Underkuffler, *The Idea of Property* (2003); Eric T. Freyfogle, *The Land We Share* (2003); Joseph William Singer, "After the Flood," LOY. L. REV. 52 (2006): 243, 257–8.
[43] See Randy E. Barnett, *Restoring the Lost Constitution* (2004), 264–6; Epstein, *Takings*, 58–9.
[44] See Epstein, *Takings*, 57.

Carolina Coastal Council, expressed some sympathy with this common law baseline approach to regulatory takings, though perhaps only indirectly. In that case, it held that, when an owner has suffered a complete wipeout as a result of government regulation, the government could avoid paying compensation only if it could show that the restrictions on use imposed by the government were merely codifications of restrictions already inherent in the owner's title, through, for example, the common law of nuisance.[45]

But the common law baseline approach introduces its own complications. Perhaps the most basic of these is the challenge of determining what the "common law" actually says on any given issue.[46] In addition, however, there is the problem of determining the normative significance of the common law baseline. One answer, suggested by Epstein, appeals to positive constitutional law. "There is no reason to think," he says, "that private property, as an undefined term in the Constitution, should be understood in a way completely at variance with the accepted usages of the time...."[47] But, from the standpoint of natural rights, it is not clear why one community's body of positive law (the common law as it existed at the time the Constitution was enacted) should be frozen into place when it may well already represent substantial deviations from the requirements of natural rights, as theorists like Robert Nozick and Epstein have spelled them out. Absent some assurance that the late eighteenth-century common law was itself a just system of property rights that conformed to, say, Nozick's theory of acquisition and historical distributive justice, it seems fairly arbitrary to treat it as the baseline for contemporary takings analysis. The treatment of slaves, women, and Native Americans within the eighteenth-century American property system, to raise just a few obvious examples, points toward significant concerns in this regard.[48]

Relatedly, the baseline approach leads to the question of the status of limitations on property rights that, though long-standing, nonetheless diverge from the common law baseline. Consider, for example, a zoning law first enacted shortly after the turn of the twentieth century. As long as at least some of the uses it excludes are not nuisances, it constitutes a state-imposed restriction on common law use rights. But it has now existed for nearly 100 years. The property subject to it has changed hands a dozen times since the law's enactment. The law would seem to amount to a taking

---

[45] See *Lucas v. S.C. Coastal Council*, 505 U.S. 1003 (1992).

[46] Compare Lior Jacob Strahilevitz, "The Right to Abandon," *U. PA. L. REV.* 158 (2010): 355 (affirming a robust common law right to abandon chattels), with Eduardo M. Peñalver, "The Illusory Right to Abandon," *MICH. L. REV.* 109 (2010): 191 (questioning the existence of a robust common law right to abandon chattels).

[47] See Epstein, *Takings*, 58.

[48] Cf. Robert Nozick, *Anarchy, State, and Utopia* (1974), 231 ("For example, lacking much historical information, and assuming (1) that victims of injustice generally do worse than they otherwise would and (2) that those from the least well-off group in the society have the highest probabilities of being

on the baseline approach. But who, if anyone, is entitled to just compensation for the taking? The original owner? The current owner?

This is a variant on the question the Supreme Court struggled with in *Pallazzolo v. Rhode Island*.[49] In that case, the property owner, who had acquired his land after wetlands regulations had gone into effect, argued that the application of the regulations to his land constituted a regulatory taking. In rejecting his claim, the Rhode Island Supreme Court created a bright-line rule requiring regulatory takings claimants to have acquired their property *before* the imposition of the regulation they were challenging. The U.S. Supreme Court rejected this categorical approach, holding that the mere fact that property was acquired after a regulation went into effect did not rule out the possibility of a successful regulatory takings claim. In a concurring opinion, Justice Scalia argued that the timing of the acquisition of the property relative to the regulation was irrelevant to the regulatory takings inquiry.[50]

The timing question points toward a tension within the project of attempting to use the Constitution's takings clause – and the common law baseline – as a means of protecting what libertarians take to be natural rights inherent in ownership. If property rights are natural rights, then why can they be infringed, even upon payment of just compensation? One answer is that it is the uncompensated loss of ownership rights, and not distortion of some conception of ownership founded in natural law, that is the wrong identified by the baseline version of libertarian regulatory takings doctrine. But, if that is the case, then – contra Scalia – timing seems crucial to the regulatory takings inquiry, since the more time that has passed between the regulatory adjustment of property rights and the acquisition of property by the claimant, the more likely it is that the impact of the regulation on ownership rights has been incorporated into the price the claimant paid for the property such that compensation to the claimant would be unnecessary.

Another answer is that a robust compensation requirement will deter governments from enacting new regulations. On this view, regulatory takings doctrine is not a first-best manifestation of moral entitlement, but instead a pragmatic tool for discouraging governments from violating private property rights. There is some evidence to back up the prediction that requiring compensation deters regulation, particularly from jurisdictions that have adopted expansive regulatory takings

---

the (descendants of) victims of the most serious injustice who are owed compensation by those who benefitted from the injustices (assumed to be those better off, though sometimes the perpetrators will be others in the worst-off group), then a rough rule of thumb for rectifying injustices might seem to be the following: organize a society so as to maximize the position of whatever group ends up least well-off in the society.").

[49] 533 U.S. 606 (2001).

[50] 533 U.S. at 636 (Scalia, J., concurring). In her own concurring opinion, Justice O'Connor argued the opposite. See 533 U.S. at 632–3.

statutes.[51] This chilling effect argument only underscores the importance of the need to justify privileging the common law of property as it existed at a specific moment in time in the past. Doing so remains an ongoing challenge for libertarian theorists.

THE PERSONALITY AND PERSONHOOD THEORIES

Hegel rejected the notion of absolute private ownership of property. Moreover, his theory of the state is hardly libertarian. As we saw in Chapter 6, the atomistic self is an inadequate foundation for embodied freedom because it is insecure and, ultimately, self-defeating. Individual freedom that is truly secure requires acceptance of the common will, that is, mutual recognition between the self and the other as ends. Part of the content of the common will, we also saw, is a collective obligation to alleviate poverty, and this obligation has implications for the shape of the negative right of freedom. Specifically, an owner's negative right is internally limited by the equal right of all persons to the material preconditions of their own self-determination.[52]

This limitation has important consequences for the state's powers to expropriate property with compensation and to regulate property without compensation. To undertake a Hegelian approach to distinguishing compensable from noncompensable state actions, we need to understand how Hegel strives to overcome the basic tension between the atomistic self and the community, which is reflected in the positive freedom of the socially situated self. Hegel does not treat these as opposed ends, constantly warring with each other for supremacy, but rather as interdependent aspects of the other. Each contains the other within itself.[53] Personal autonomy presupposes community, and the good of the community just is the freedom of the self. One makes no sense without the other. Their mutual need constitutes a totality that Alan Brudner calls "dialogic community."[54] The self is unstable when isolated and seeks stability through recognition of other selves. As the self enters into these relationships, it implicitly undermines the claim to self-sufficiency of the atomistic person. The community in turn defers to the self's actions insofar as these reflect the community's own status as the individual's end. Legal institutions, including property, reflect this process of mutual recognition by self and community. Indeed, the

[51] Governments subject to a strict compensation requirement do not, as predicted by fiscal illusion theorists, pick and choose in favor of the most efficient regulations. Instead, they tend to simply cease regulating in order to avoid paying compensation. See Bethany R. Berger, "What Owners Want and Governments Do," FORDHAM L. REV. 78 (2009): 1290. Of course, this is precisely what libertarians – in contrast to utilitarians – want to see happen.

[52] See Alan Brudner, *The Unity of the Common Law: Studies in Hegelian Jurisprudence* (1995), 74.

[53] See ibid., 78.

[54] Ibid.

idea of dialogic community can be said to be the foundation of the entire system of property law.[55]

We need to recall that, for Hegel, the state, the political expression of the community, emphatically does not represent the dominant economic interests of society.[56] Nor does it represent a mere aggregation of individual wills or the coercive antithesis of individual wills. Rather, the Hegelian state represents a universality, a genuinely "general will."[57] This is the point at which the metaphor of the dialogic community becomes useful.

Dialogic community constitutes the whole, of which both private property and the common good are mutually reinforcing constituent parts. But neither part is absolute because it is only an element of the whole, rather than the whole itself. Specifically with respect to property, private property certainly exists, but it is not absolute. It is subordinate to the principle of moral autonomy, which reflects inter-action between the self and the community and provides a means for coping with the tension between them.

What exactly is the character of this subordinated property right? More specific-ally, does it have any stiffness against actions of the state? The short answer is that, within the Hegelian framework, it does and it must because property is logically necessary for the individual's essential freedom.[58] Concretely, this means that in property disputes, courts should evaluate property rights without regard to commu-nity concerns. They should "treat each right [possession, use, and alienation] as an integral component of a conceptual whole rather than as an isolated stick one may remove from a bundle without destroying the bundle itself."[59]

At the same time, this property right is not absolute. Consequently, the formal property right is subject to the state's power to modify it so long as such modifi-cation is done for the common good. Modification may occur either legislatively or judicially. Legislative modification amounts to external override of property rights and is appropriate when legislatures choose to subordinate formal prop-erty rights in the interest of some distributive principle. Judicial modification, by contrast, is an internal suspension of the formal property right rather than an

---

[55] See ibid., 81.
[56] See Shlomo Avineri, *Hegel's Theory of the Modern State* (1972), 99.
[57] Ibid.
[58] See Jeanne L. Schroeder, *The Vestal and the Fasces: Hegel, Lacan, Property, and the Feminine* (1998), 294.
[59] Brudner, *Unity of the Common Law*, 83. In referring to "bundles" and "sticks," Brudner has in mind the bundle of sticks metaphor, which we introduced in Part I. Brudner rightly interprets Hegel as implicitly rejecting such a fragmented understanding of ownership in favor of a unified conception. See also Schroeder, *The Vestal and the Fasces*, 4–7, 185–93.

override.[60] It is justified when enforcement of the formal property right would result in oppression, thereby undermining the rule of law ideal itself. Within the Hegelian system, internal suspensions of property rights in the interest of distributive principles are not legitimate, for that would amount to subsuming property to the supreme common good. The common good is not supreme in Hegel's theory; only the unity represented by both formal property rights and the community, in a dialogic relationship, is supreme.

When the legislature overrides property rights in pursuit of distributive justice, the override is valid so long as the legislature acted for a public good and, further, so long as it pays compensation to the property owner. A compensation requirement is warranted by recognition of the existence of the formal property right prior to considerations of distributive justice.[61] But if the override is done for the sake of some private gain or benefit, the legislative action is invalid. Even if the legislative override is undertaken for a public benefit, however, compensation may not be due to the property owner. Compensation is then required only if the property owner would otherwise be singled out as a contributor to the common good. Under those circumstances, and only under those circumstances, redistribution amounts to coerced contribution to the community, thereby infringing on the owner's property right.[62]

When courts suspend or legislatures regulate property rights because the exercise of those rights would lead to interpersonal oppression, no compensation is due. Such an exercise of a property right is beyond its legitimate scope insofar as it amounts to an assertion of the supremacy of the autonomous self over the common good. As Brudner explains, "no property is taken if its enforcement would pervert law into a private power...."[63] By the same token, within the Hegelian framework, a judicial decision that amounts to a taking for a distributive purpose violates the affected property right whether compensation is paid to the owner or not.[64] Payment of compensation does not save the judicial action because it effectively relegates property rights to a secondary and subordinate position behind the interest of the common good, destroying the dialogue between the self and the community.

To illustrate these distinctions, consider the case of *Andrus v. Allard*.[65] In that case, a federal statute, the Eagle Protection Act, prohibited commercial transactions in eagle parts or any artifacts made with parts of eagles legally killed prior to enactment of the statute. The purpose of the act was to prevent the destruction of certain species of eagles. The owners of businesses engaging in the trade of Indian artifacts, many

---

[60] See Brudner, *Unity of the Common Law*, 83.
[61] Ibid.
[62] Ibid.
[63] Ibid., 84.
[64] Ibid.
[65] 444 U.S. 51 (1979).

of which were made with eagle feathers, challenged the act as an unconstitutional taking of their property under the takings clause of the U.S. Constitution's Fifth Amendment. The U.S. Supreme Court held that the statute did not effect a taking. The statute destroyed the owners' right to commercially exploit their property, but it left the remaining sticks in the bundle of rights, including the rights of possession, use, and gift, intact. From a Hegelian perspective, this decision is arguably wrong.[66] This is a legislative override of the right of commercial alienation that disrupts the unity of ownership. Although it was done for a public good, compensation is due because otherwise the eagle part owners would be singled out as contributors to the common good. Such disproportionate burdening amounts to subordination of property rights to the interests of the community, destroying the delicate Hegelian balance.

The analysis of the takings question in terms of Margaret Jane Radin's personhood theory is more straightforward. In her view, both the limits of the eminent domain power and the determination of whether a regulatory taking has occurred should be guided by the type of property interest involved. *Personal property*, that is, property connected with "the proper development and flourishing of persons,"[67] has greater moral weight and deserves more constitutional protection, she believes,[68] than *fungible property*, that is, property that "represent[s] interchangeable units of exchange value."[69]

With respect to the scope of the power of eminent domain, Radin suggests that some types of assets should not be subject to the state's power at all, compensation or no compensation. For there are some assets for which no compensation can be "just," she argues. Such assets would be those closely associated with personhood, "or at least inalienable involuntarily to the government."[70] For example, can the state legitimately condemn body parts, say, a kidney? Radin recognizes that the personhood perspective is not expressed in the actual law of eminent domain. If it were, then one might expect to find, for example, distinctions drawn between government condemnation of commercial buildings and personal residences.[71]

The distinction between personal and fungible property is not binary; rather, it creates a continuum of types of property interests. The personal/fungible continuum involves complications in applying any of the extant legal tests for determining when a property use regulation has "go[ne] too far," becoming a de facto taking.[72]

---

[66] See Brudner, *Unity of the Common Law*, 310–311 n. 124.
[67] See Margaret Jane Radin, *Reinterpreting Property* (1993), 153.
[68] See ibid., 154.
[69] Ibid.
[70] Ibid., 156.
[71] Radin concedes that various considerations might count against drawing such a simple distinction. The administrative costs of applying this approach, for example, might be high. Moreover, not all personal residences are so intimately connected with personhood. Some people buy second or even third residences for mixed motives, including investment purposes. See ibid., 66.
[72] *Pennsylvania Coal Co. v. Mahon*, 260 U.S. 393 (1922).

For example, one such test is the permanent physical occupation rule: If the effect of a regulation is to enable the government or someone acting under the authority of the government to physically and permanently occupy a landowner's property, no matter how trivial the occupation, the regulation is per se a taking, as the Court held in *Loretto v. Teleprompter Manhattan CATV Corp.*[73] At first blush, the rule might appear to vindicate the owner's personhood interest. On closer inspection, however, the personhood perspective does not justify such an inflexible rule. Many affected owners will be business firms, not individuals, and Radin tends to treat property owned by businesses as fungible rather than personal.[74] Moreover, even if the owner is an individual, the building may still be fungible to her, if, for example, it is investment property. Even if we assume that the building is personal property, de minimis physical encroachments, such as the cable television equipment at issue in the Supreme Court's decision in *Loretto*, might not constitute significant intrusions on personal identity. The point is that the personal/fungible continuum creates too many complexities to make such a binary rule feasible. More generally, it makes alignment with any of the existing tests for takings only partial.

Radin considers the regulatory taking problem "intractable."[75] Its intractability ultimately stems from "our inability to specify in any general way when we should be governed by the ideal and when we should pay attention instead primarily to the nonideal."[76] Working out a general solution from the ideal perspective would require a completely developed normative theory of property, and that in turn would require a complete theory of politics and the person. The contested nature of any and every theory of property holdings renders such an ideal itself tenuous. Radin concludes, "It seems that if theories of property are contested, because theories of politics and the person are contested, then the takings issue must remain contested."[77] All that we can do is to "work more consciously within the framework of the dilemmas of transition, in the tension between ideal and nonideal worlds."[78]

ARISTOTELIAN PROPERTY THEORY AND GOVERNMENT TAKINGS

Eminent Domain

One of the strengths of the Aristotelian human flourishing theory is its ability to take seriously both utility and nonutilitarian values such as human dignity and fairness.

---

[73] U.S. 419 (1982) (New York City regulation required residential landlords to permit cable television operators to attach cable boxes and cables to the exterior of their buildings).

[74] See Radin, *Reinterpreting Property*, 155.

[75] Ibid., 162.

[76] Ibid.

[77] Ibid., 163.

[78] Ibid., 165.

In the context of eminent domain, the theory explains why the state may legitimately demand some sacrifice from individuals (and, hence, is comfortable with the standard compensation practice of paying fair market value, which sometimes provides less than full compensation) while not totally subordinating individual interests in the pursuit of aggregate social utility. In its focus on human flourishing through development of requisite capabilities, the theory also provides room for accommodating nonfungible attachments to certain assets worthy of respect and legal recognition. As we discussed in Chapter 5, the pluralist character of human flourishing, incorporating as it does multiple values, provides the theory with greater adaptability and sensitivity to nonreductive factors, such as nonfungible attachments, than do theories like utilitarianism.

Like utilitarianism, the human flourishing theory explains the government's power of eminent domain in terms of the common good, but it understands the common good as more complex than aggregate utility or preference satisfaction. It is the social infrastructure necessary for individuals to develop human capabilities. To develop the capacities necessary to flourish as autonomous moral agents, individuals depend on the existence of social networks within which they can carry out the activities that enable them to experience freedom. This includes what Charles Taylor calls "the mundane elements of infrastructure without which we could not carry on these higher activities. . . ."[79] These elements of infrastructure include just the sorts of public projects for which the power of eminent domain is routinely exercised: roads, airports, utility lines, public buildings, communication systems, and the like. Each of us depends upon the continued effectiveness of this infrastructure, and that dependence requires that we bear some responsibility for maintaining it, even at some personal cost that is not equally shared with others.

Eminent domain is a legal and political process for determining just what that responsibility is. Although eminent domain has a component of shared sacrifice, it also includes an element of irreducible individual loss. Its effects are necessarily concentrated on those whose property is expropriated. Because just compensation is, under current American judicial doctrine, fair market value, those who lose their property through eminent domain really do lose something that the rest of us (who are paying our taxes in part to fund their compensation) do not.

Not every social structure or political institution and not every social activity is necessary to foster the goods that are required for a well-lived life. From the perspective of developing these essential goods, some social structures or activities are more important than others. A tighter nexus between the institution whose activity is under challenge and the goods necessary to a well-lived life is required before

---

[79] Charles Taylor, "Atomism," in Charles Taylor, *Philosophy and the Human Sciences*, vol. 2 of *Philosophical Papers* (1985), 205.

the political community can legitimately demand that an owner sacrifice property entitlement. This is especially true when the affected property interest is the owner's personal residence. The Supreme Court's controversial decision in *Kelo v. City of New London* illustrates the point.[80]

The *Kelo* decision aroused considerable public outrage.[81] From the perspective of the human flourishing theory, the reaction to *Kelo* is understandable. The plaintiffs had strong flourishing-related reasons for resisting the forced sale. The common law historically, and properly, has attached great weight to protecting the privacy and autonomy interests of homeowners by recognizing a strong right to exclude the public from entering their property without permission. As we discussed in Chapter 7, although this right has long been subject to certain limited exceptions, the right to exclude has generally been strongest with respect to the home. From the perspective of the human flourishing theory, with its focus on human capabilities necessary for the well-lived life, this emphasis on privacy within the home makes sense. The home is a central locus for developing and experiencing many of the capabilities necessary for human flourishing. Moreover, the home is example par excellence of an asset to which most owners have nonfungible attachments.[82] As Radin states, the home "is the scene of one's history and future, one's life and growth.... [O]ne embodies or constitutes oneself there."[83] The home is a place where, above all other places, most people experience a sense of belonging. This sense of belonging grows stronger for most people as they remain in the same place longer. This is one reason why moving, even if just to a new house or a different apartment in the same city or town, is an emotionally challenging experience for many individuals. Homes are not fungible: Most of us do not discard one and acquire a new one lightly, like an article of clothing. We invest much more of our personality in them. The human flourishing theory gives considerable weight to that sense of attachment and the reasons behind it. In the context of *Kelo*, it might have led the court to be far more sensitive to the concerns that the *Kelo* plaintiffs raised.

On the other side of the ledger, the importance of jobs to members of the New London community is not to be underestimated from the standpoint of human flourishing. But the linkage between the jobs the city hoped to produce through its redevelopment project and the land acquired from the *Kelo* plaintiffs was more attenuated than the impact the use of eminent domain had on the plaintiffs' sense of security and personal autonomy. Taking into account all of the relevant values at

---

[80]   545 U.S. 460 (2005).

[81]   See Nadler and Diamond, "Government Takings," 287.

[82]   For some contrary evidence, see Stephanie M. Stern, "Residential Protectionism and the Legal Mythology of Home," MICH. L. REV. 107 (2009): 1093. But see Lorna Fox, *Conceptualising Home: Theories, Laws, and Policies* (2007).

[83]   Margaret Jane Radin, "Property and Personhood," STAN. L. REV. 34 (1982): 957, 992.

stake rather than just aggregate utility, human flourishing seems best advanced by protecting the homeowner's interests here. For this reason, as a first-order question, the exercise of eminent domain in *Kelo* was probably inconsistent with the human flourishing theory.[84]

To say that the exercise of eminent domain was not wise, however, is not the same as saying that the Supreme Court was necessarily wrong to avoid intervening on behalf of the *Kelo* plaintiffs. Although it views property as a morally laden institution, Aristotelian property theory does not reduce questions of property doctrine to a simple moralistic analysis. Rather, it distinguishes between the first-order moral question and the second-order question of how best to respond to the demands of morality through the law and legal institutions. The court's opinion in *Kelo* focused a great deal on these sorts of second-order questions, such as federalism and institutional competence. The moral complexity and contextual sensitivity of the implications of any particular exercise of eminent domain may counsel in favor of delegating decisions about its propriety to local officials, who are closest to the situation, reserving (federal) judicial intervention for situations in which those officials appear to have abdicated their responsibility to act on behalf of the public welfare. That did not appear to have been the case in New London, as the Supreme Court noted in emphasizing that the use of eminent domain in *Kelo* was the product of a lengthy and comprehensive planning process. And so it is possible to affirm from within the flourishing theory both that the use of eminent domain in New London was likely wrong and that *Kelo* was nonetheless correctly decided.

Regulatory Takings

The value pluralism of human flourishing theory also provides a rich moral vocabulary for discussing the problem of regulatory takings. As is evident from our discussion of *Kelo*, the value of this vocabulary lies not in its tendency to generate a single legal outcome across all cases. No theory of regulatory takings has been able to accomplish that. But the human flourishing approach excels in its ability to structure deliberation about how much the state can fairly demand from property owners without triggering a compensation requirement. As with its treatment of eminent domain, this theory of regulatory takings is sensitive to context, distinguishing both among categories of property owners and types of regulatory burdens in an effort to determine whether the state has exceeded the boundaries of fairness by concentrating the costs of a regulatory burden on particular owners.

---

[84] Cf. Laura S. Underkuffler, "*Kelo's* Moral Failure," WM. & MARY BILL RTS. J. 15 (2004): 377; Andre van der Walt, "Housing Rights and the Intersection Between Expropriation and Eviction Law," in *The Idea of the Home in Law* (Lorna Fox and James A. Sweeny eds. 2011), 55.

The Supreme Court's decision in *Penn Central Transportation Co. v. New York City* is in many ways emblematic of this sort of contextualized approach,[85] which stands in marked contrast to the more rule-based approaches in *Lucas* and *Loretto* that we discussed earlier. In *Penn Central*, the New York City Landmark Commission had previously designated the famous Grand Central Terminal, which Penn Central owned, as an historical landmark because of the building's incomparable nineteenth-century beaux-arts façade. Penn Central wished to erect a multistory commercial building atop the terminal, and the commission disapproved two submitted plans, claiming that both plans would do serious damage to unique aspects of the terminal. Penn Central went to court, claiming that the commission's denial of its plans to develop the airspace above the terminal amounted to an unconstitutional taking of its private property.

The court upheld the commission's actions. In the process, it laid out a three-part regulatory takings inquiry that constitutes the default framework for regulatory takings cases, the test that courts will employ if other rules – such as those set out in *Lucas* and *Loretto* – do not apply. The *Penn Central* inquiry, which is more open-ended and equitable in nature than the per se *Lucas* and *Loretto* rules, is a comfortable fit with Aristotelian property theory. It directs courts considering regulatory takings claims to look to (1) the extent of the economic burden the regulation imposes on owners; (2) the degree to which the regulation interferes with owners' "investment backed expectations;" and (3) the character of the government action. In considering these three factors, the court first concluded that the financial burden that historic preservation imposed on Penn Central was not overwhelming, since the law only required the company to continue to operate its terminal as it had for decades and because Penn Central was still able to earn a reasonable return from those operations. Moreover, the court said, the commission's development denial did not eliminate all of the owner's possible uses of its preexisting rights in the airspace above the terminal. The owner had been granted transferable development rights (TDRs) in the airspace, and it could use those rights to develop the airspace above other buildings that it owned in the vicinity. Writing for the majority, Justice William Brennan stated: "While these [TDR] rights may well not have constituted 'just compensation' if a 'taking' had occurred, the rights nevertheless undoubtedly mitigate whatever financial burdens the law has imposed on [the owner] and, for that reason, are to be taken into account in considering the impact of the regulation."[86] The court concluded next that the commission's action did not interfere with any investment-backed expectation of the owner because the company had not yet invested any money in the development project. Indeed, the law

[85] 438 U.S. 104 (1978).
[86] Ibid., 137.

simply required Penn Central to continue using the terminal as it had voluntarily chosen to do for decades, and it provided a means for Penn Central to request regulatory relief in the event that use became unprofitable in the future.

One might justify the decision on the basis of long-term reciprocity. According to one version of a reciprocity theory, the state is not required to pay compensation:

> [i]f...the disproportionate burden of the public action in question is not overly extreme and is offset, or is likely in all probability to be offset, by benefits of similar magnitude to the landowner's current injury that she gains from other – past, present, or future – public actions (which harm neighboring properties).[87]

Applying that test, one might argue, as Hanoch Dagan has, that the owners of Grand Central Terminal "will benefit directly and proportionately in the long-term from the aggregated benefits of the city's public actions, despite the transient disproportionate burden."[88] This is especially the case when the private owner is a corporate entity like Penn Central. Its predecessors, the Pennsylvania Railroad and the New York Central Railroad, had deep and mutually beneficial relationships with the local, state, and federal governments. Its power and access suggest that, considered over the long term, the relationship between Penn Central and New York City was likely characterized by a high degree of reciprocity, even taking into account the disproportionate costs imposed by landmark designation.

The human flourishing theory does not ignore the issue of reciprocity, with its strong implications for fairness, but it also asks an additional set of questions: What sacrifices may the state legitimately ask these private landowners to make concerning the use of their land? What obligations do these landowners owe to their communities with respect to the use, condition, or care of their property? The human flourishing theory recognizes that, because individuals can develop as free and fully rational moral agents only within a particular type of culture, all individuals owe their communities some obligation to support in appropriate ways the institutions and infrastructure that are part of the foundation of that culture. The support that government requires may sometimes involve sacrificing the otherwise most profitable uses of a piece of property.

The implications of the designation of Grand Central Terminal for human flourishing were particularly lopsided. Although individual human beings (shareholders) ultimately owned Grand Central Terminal, the impact of the terminal's designation as an historic landmark on shareholders' ability to flourish was extremely attenuated. The regulations only marginally affected their wealth and autonomy as individuals. In contrast, buildings like Grand Central Terminal play an extremely important

---

[87] Hanoch Dagan, "Takings and Distributive Justice," VA. L. REV. 85 (1999): 769–70 (footnote omitted).

[88] Ibid., 798.

and nonfungible role in the cities of which they are a part. Distinctive architectural sites are integral to an urban community's identity and the identities of its inhabitants. Historical landmarks create collective urban memory; destruction or radical alteration of such landmarks erases collective historical memory. Erasure of historical memory destabilizes a society and its culture. Were New York City to lose all of its historic architectural patrimony, its culture would be not merely different but civically impoverished.

Special obligations accompany private ownership of those aspects of a society's infrastructure upon which the civic culture depends. Those obligations may require that an owner forego compensation if an urban authority legitimately invokes its power to protect private property from being altered in ways that would permanently destroy its civically unique and supportive aspects. The development of Grand Central Terminal contemplated in *Penn Central* would have inflicted on the community of New York a significant loss of cultural meaning and identity. And, in contrast, the burden imposed on Penn Central was to forego additional profits it would have obtained by altering the long-standing use to which it had chosen to put its terminal.

The Landmark Preservation Commission's designation of Grand Central Terminal as an historical landmark was a legal recognition that Penn Central, as owner of an obviously unique building that had long benefitted from public largesse, owed the community an obligation not to use it in ways that would irrevocably destroy its unique architectural status. Viewed from the perspective of human flourishing, some historic designations might well raise serious concerns of fairness. And alternative approaches to landmark designation might have different impacts on landowner incentives, which are also relevant to Aristotelian property theory insofar as it views legal rules as indirect mechanisms for fostering human flourishing. But, in light of the circumstances surrounding Grand Central Terminal and its distinctive owner, *Penn Central* was not a particularly hard case.

9

Intellectual Property

INTRODUCTION

In the academic world, the law of intellectual property and tangible property are two separate fields that frequently fail to engage with one another. But the theories that have been used to justify ownership of tangible property apply without too much difficulty to the ownership of ideas. Indeed, the ease of discussing intellectual property using several of the theories we have been exploring in this book suggests that the legal protection of at least some intellectual property is normatively sound. As we will discuss in this chapter, however, the main theories of property suggest that rights of intellectual property, like those of tangible property, must be highly qualified in order to accommodate the many competing values they implicate. Given the massive breadth of this topic, we can barely scratch the surface. Our principal focus in this chapter will be on the domains of copyright and patent, though we will make brief references to other forms of intellectual property.

ENCOURAGING INVENTION: UTILITARIAN THEORIES OF INTELLECTUAL PROPERTY

In Chapter 1, we introduced the Tragedy of the Commons and the problem of free riding. Within the commons tragedy, the rational actor model predicts that, if all of its underlying assumptions hold, the inability to exclude people from using a resource leads to its eventual overconsumption and degradation. With regard to free riders, the model predicts that, if rational individuals are unable to capture the full benefits generated by their productive efforts, they will tend to underinvest in production, because they can simply capture some of the benefits of others' labor without doing the hard work. The result will be levels of productivity that fail to maximize aggregate utility. Of course, as we will discuss in more detail later in this chapter, human motivations are far more complex than either of these simple discussions assumes. But for the moment we will hew closely to the predictions of the rational actor model.

As we saw in Chapter 1, one of the assumptions necessary to drive the Tragedy of the Commons is that consumption of the commons degrades it – that is, consumption must be rivalrous. But information, unlike tangible resources, is not consumed rivalrously. To say that consumption is nonrivalrous means that one person's consumption of a piece of information leaves just as much information behind for others to consume – and in as good a condition – as was there before. As Thomas Jefferson observed, information simply cannot be overconsumed: "He who receives an idea from me, receives instruction himself without lessening mine; as he who lights his taper at mine, receives light without darkening me."[1] Because information consumption is nonrivalrous, the utilitarian case for intellectual property cannot be based on the risk of overconsumption embodied in the Tragedy of the Commons.

Indeed, the utilitarian case for intellectual property depends solely on the concern that excessive free riding will discourage investment in the production of new information. To see why this is the case, consider the fictional example of a new antibiotic, Novamycin, able to fight drug-resistant bacteria. Novamycin's developer, Pharma Inc., has been trying to develop a new antibiotic for nearly a decade. Before finally synthesizing Novamycin, it spent years (and hundreds of millions of dollars) working with several other compounds, none of which yielded a safe and effective antibiotic. Once it discovered Novamycin, Pharma spent five years testing the drug, a process that brought its total production costs to well over billion dollars. Despite the difficulty in discovering and testing the compound, Novamycin is very easy to mass produce. Pharma estimates that it can manufacture enough Novamycin to meet market demand at a cost of approximately one dollar per dose. If it sells Novamycin for eleven dollars per dose, Pharma estimates that it will recoup its total investment in the drug in just a few years. But Pharma is not the only company interested in selling Novamycin. One of its competitors, Generico Inc., has been able to reverse engineer Novamycin for a trivial cost. Like Pharma, it can manufacture the drug at a cost of one dollar per dose. If it can sell the drug for anything more than one dollar per dose, Generico estimates that it can reap huge profits based on the volume of expected sales as older antibiotics become less effective due to drug resistance in bacteria.

The story of Pharma and Novamycin presents the classic utilitarian case for intellectual property protection. If Generico can cheaply reverse engineer Novamycin and develop a manufacturing process that allows it to produce the drug at something close to Pharma's marginal costs, it can drive the market price down toward that marginal cost and still make a profit. But if Pharma is forced to sell its product for

---

[1]   Thomas Jefferson, letter to Isaac McPherson, August 13, 1813.

one dollar per dose, it will not be able to recover the costs it has sunk into developing Novamycin. If Pharma is a rational actor and knows in advance of the likelihood that it will not be able to make a healthy return on its overall investment in Novamycin, it will refuse to invest its resources trying to develop the drug in the first place.

The standard model predicts this deterrent effect of free riding whenever an innovator has to invest resources into the development of a new product such that its average cost of production (the combined cost of development and production per total number of units produced) is higher than the marginal cost of production (the cost of producing each additional unit, disregarding costs that have already been incurred), and when there is no way to exclude competitors from using the innovation to produce the product at less than the innovator's average cost. If a competitor can cheaply copy the product, it can drive the market price of the product down toward that marginal cost, which for certain products may be close to zero. When these assumptions hold, the innovator will conclude that it will not be able to earn a profit on its initial investment. Under these circumstances, an innovator who is also a rational actor will simply decline to make the initial investment.

But innovation may be socially valuable, even when it would not be profitable for an individual inventor. So the inventor's (rational) decision not to invest in the creation of new inventions may constitute a net loss of utility to society as a whole. From a utilitarian perspective, the purpose of intellectual property rights, in a nutshell, is to encourage individual investment in innovation by protecting the ability of innovators to recapture the cost of inventing new products. Intellectual property law does this by granting innovators a legal monopoly over their creations for a limited period of time, which permits them to charge prices higher than they would be able to obtain in a competitive market.

But the monopoly created by intellectual property law does not come without costs. The creation of intellectual property rights means higher prices for consumers. In the case of our fictional drug Novamycin, for example, it means that consumers will have to pay more for a potentially life-saving drug. In the absence of mechanisms to ensure access to needed medicines, the difference between making the dose available for one dollar and eleven dollars may be the difference between life and death for those who cannot afford to pay the higher price.

In addition to higher prices for consumers, the intellectual property monopoly yields higher prices for future innovators. New inventions always depend to some extent on existing knowledge. The fictional researchers who invented Novamycin, for example, would have relied on existing biological knowledge, including knowledge about antibiotics generated by the creators of earlier drugs. The protection of that prior knowledge with intellectual property rights would have made it more expensive to invent Novamycin. On the other hand, if Pharma did not have the prospect of charging consumers more than the marginal costs of producing its antibiotic, it might not have developed Novamycin at all. From a utilitarian perspective, the law should aim to balance these various considerations – the need to encourage innovation, the inevitability of reduced consumption due to higher prices, the importance of access to prior inventions in the creation of new inventions – in a way that maximizes overall utility over the long run. The existing law of intellectual property does seem to reflect an attempt to accomplish this kind of rough balancing in two key ways: first, by limiting the circumstances under which it will grant a monopoly; second, once a monopoly has been granted, by limiting its scope and duration.

Requirements for Protection

Both patent and copyright impose limitations on the creation of intellectual property rights. But each does so somewhat differently. Patent law requires inventors seeking patent protection to show that their invention is actually "novel" (i.e., new) and, relatedly, that it is "nonobvious" (i.e., that its development was not a trivial accomplishment in light of the existing state of knowledge).[2] Both of these requirements make good sense from the standpoint of utilitarian theory. If the goal of intellectual property law is to encourage costly innovation that might not otherwise occur, its scope should be limited to inventions that require some significant effort. As Richard Posner put it, "[t]he lower the cost of discovery, the less necessary patent protection is to induce the discovery to be made."[3] If it were otherwise, patent protection would generate only the costs of monopoly without its benefits. Copyright law limits its protections to "original works of authorship,"[4] a requirement significantly less onerous than patent law's requirements of novelty and nonobviousness. Copyright also limits its protection to discrete categories of subject matter: literary, musical, dramatic, and choreographic works; visual artistic works; motion pictures and other audiovisual works; sound recordings; and architectural works.[5] These subject matter limitations may represent a judgment that these areas of creative endeavor are particularly valuable and worthy of legal encouragement or, perhaps, particularly susceptible to free riding problems. (Alternatively, they may simply represent the interest groups who have, historically, been most successful in getting lawmakers to grant them legal monopolies.)

Intellectual property law also attempts to maintain a sphere of intellectual commons that is not subject to appropriation by innovators. Thus, copyright makes a distinction between ideas, which are not subject to copyright protection, and particular

---

[2]   See 35 U.S.C. §§ 102, 103.
[3]   Richard A. Posner, *The Economic Analysis of Law*, 6th ed. (2003), § 3.3, at 38.
[4]   17 U.S.C. § 102.
[5]   See ibid.

expressions of ideas, which may be.[6] Patent law makes a similar distinction in its prohibition on granting patent protection for ideas that are too fundamental. For example, laws of nature – such as Einstein's theory of relativity – may not be patented.[7] The principal purpose of these distinctions, from a utilitarian perspective, seems to be to avoid unduly burdening subsequent innovators.

Limits on Protection

Once intellectual property rights are created, the law restricts them in a number of ways. Most obviously, it does this by limiting the duration of copyright and patent protection. This limitation is more significant in the case of patents, which expire after twenty years. Copyright, though time limited, currently survives for seventy years after the death of the author or, in the case of works produced for hire, ninety-five years after the work is produced. But copyright law limits the reach of intellectual property rights in other ways. Copyright, for example, protects those who create similar works without relying on protected content; patent law does not.[8] And copyright provides a broad doctrine of fair use, which protects the unauthorized use of protected works "for purposes such as criticism, comment, news reporting, teaching (including multiple copies for classroom use), scholarship, or research."[9] Although patent law lacks a formal fair use exception, in the past it was understood to permit use for the purposes of pure scientific research.[10]

As with the requirements for the creation of intellectual property, these limits on rights (once they have been created) can be understood as efforts to balance the need to create incentives for innovation with a recognition of the costs of intellectual property rights, both for consumers and for subsequent innovators. To illustrate the point, consider the fair use doctrine in copyright law. From within utilitarian theory, the doctrine of fair use can be viewed as a sort of in-kind redistribution. Although, as we discussed in Chapter 6, utilitarians typically prefer to use the market to distribute goods to their highest value users, they make room for state-sponsored redistribution when transaction costs or some other kind of market failure would otherwise prevent consensual transfers.[11] Parody and criticism, for example, are core examples of fair use, and they fit well with these market failure theories of fair use. Intellectual

---

[6] See 17 U.S.C. § 102(b).

[7] See, for example, *Diamond v. Chakrabarty*, 447 U.S. 303 (1980).

[8] See Robert P. Merges et al., *Intellectual Property in the New Technological Age*, 3rd ed. (2003), 493.

[9] 17 U.S.C. § 107.

[10] See *Whittemore v. Cutter*, 29 F. Cas. 1120 (C.C.D. Mass. 1813) (Story, J.); see also Rebecca S. Eisenberg, "Patents and the Progress of Science," *U. CHI. L. REV.* 56 (1989): 1017; but see *Madey v. Duke*, 307 F.3d 1351 (Fed. Cir. 2002).

[11] See generally William M. Landes and Richard A. Posner, *The Economic Structure of Intellectual Property* (2003); Wendy J. Gordon, "Fair Use as Market Failure," *COLUM. L. REV.* 82 (1982): 1600.

property owners are likely to resist consensually transferring use rights to those who wish to mock them, even when doing so would create net gains in utility, and so, through the doctrine of fair use, the law reassigns the right to the user.[12] From the standpoint of this very basic exploration of the power of utilitarian property theory in the domain of intellectual property, the important points to recognize are that utilitarian theory can easily support both the creation of intellectual property rights and their dramatic limitation, and a great deal of the existing structure of intellectual property law makes good sense in broadly utilitarian terms.

Qualifying the Utilitarian Case for Intellectual Property

Although the utilitarian case for at least some intellectual property protection is strong, it is important to keep in mind two significant complications. First, inventors can often find – and indeed have found – ways other than legal monopolies to recover the costs of their investments in innovation. And, second, as we discussed in Chapter 1, the utilitarian discussion of free riding, and therefore its prescription of intellectual property, depends on the critical assumption of a rational, self-interested motivation. Relaxing that assumption will undermine the degree to which utilitarian theory supports the creation of strong intellectual property rights.

Recovering the Costs of Innovation without Intellectual Property
The utilitarian case for intellectual property depends on the assumption that the inventor's competitors can swoop in after an invention and distribute it to the public at something approaching the inventor's marginal costs. But many kinds of inventions are hard to copy. For example, if the invention is a new, cheaper process for making an existing product, it may be difficult to reverse engineer the invention merely by looking at the final product itself. In such cases, the inventor can recoup costs merely by keeping the process secret and taking advantage of the increased profit margin that it offers. Even when the invention is the final product (as opposed to a process), the inventor may still take steps to inhibit cheap copying. For example, the inventor may distribute the product in a form that makes it expensive for competitors to replicate. Distributing motion pictures on film stock or encrypting data are examples of this strategy at work.

---

[12] See Posner, *Economic Analysis of Law*, § 3.3, at 42–4. Another source of market failure may stem from a kind of "endowment effect" that afflicts the creators of intellectual property. As Christopher Sprigman and Christopher Buccafusco have argued, innovators appear to place unrealistically high valuations on their creations. See Christopher Buccafusco and Christopher Jon Sprigman, "The Creativity Effect," *U. Chi. L. Rev.* 78 (2011): 31–52. Such high valuations may impede consensual transfers. Doctrines permitting nonconsensual transfers, such as fair use or compulsory licensing, may help to overcome this "creativity effect" by paving the way for utility-enhancing transactions that otherwise would not occur.

Even when the possibility of cheap copying looms large, however, the particular dynamics of a business may make it possible for innovators to recover the costs of their investment without intellectual property protection. When, for example, a business thrives on a nearly constant cycle of innovation, nimble inventors can exploit a first-mover advantage that will allow them to reap large rewards that copiers cannot capture, or at least not capture so much as to make the initial investment in innovation unprofitable. Two important industries that some have argued share this dynamic are news and fashion.

The life cycle of news, for example, is so short that it leaves little time for copying to work as a strategy. Yochai Benkler argues that "[n]o daily newspaper would survive if it depended for its business on waiting until a competitor came out with an edition, then copied the stories and reproduced them in a competing edition."[13] Benkler therefore concludes that abolishing copyright law would not have a significant impact on newspaper revenues. Pushing in the other direction is the Supreme Court's famous decision in *International News Service v. Associated Press.*[14] In that case, International News Service (INS), an early competitor of the Associated Press (AP), was trying to compete with the AP by copying some of the AP's stories and reselling them to INS's own member publications. The court held that, while (under the law at the time) news stories were not protected by copyright, the AP enjoyed a short-term "quasi-property" right protection in hot news it gathers, one that is good only against its competitors in the news business. As a consequence, it concluded, INS's copying was a form of unfair competition.[15] The decision can be explained within the utilitarian framework. The difficulty lies in knowing whether to credit AP's claims about the impact of INS's copying on the viability of the news-gathering business.

In the fashion industry, rapidly changing styles give successful innovators an edge in the marketplace that copiers can only partially dull. Indeed, as Chris Sprigman and Kal Raustiala have argued, copying actually spurs greater investment in fashion innovation, as high-end designers constantly update their looks to stay one step ahead of the knockoffs.[16] These innovators are able to sell their work for high prices to affluent consumers who place a premium on being perceived as trendsetters and who are eager to distinguish themselves from those willing to wear copies of

---

[13] Yochai Benkler, *The Wealth of Networks* (2006), 40.

[14] 248 U.S. 215 (1918).

[15] For discussions of *INS v. AP*, and the "hot news" doctrine, see Shyamkrishna Balganesh, "'Hot News': The Enduring Myth of Property in News," COLUM. L. REV. 111 (2011): 419, and Richard Epstein, "*International News Service v. Associated Press*: Custom and Law as Sources of Property Rights in News," VA. L. REV. 78 (1992): 85.

[16] Kal Raustiala and Christopher Sprigman, "The Piracy Paradox," VA. L. REV. 92 (2006): 1687. For an alternative analysis of the "virtues" of copying for fashion innovation, see C. Scott Hemphill and Jeannie Suk, "The Law, Culture, and Economics of Fashion," STAN. L. REV. 61 (2009): 1147.

successful designs that hit the market a little later than the original item. The U.S. fashion industry does not enjoy the protection of copyright in clothing designs, but it appears to be both profitable and innovative, despite widespread copying.[17] Within the fashion industry, then, copying appears to be a utilitarian win-win. Without undermining investment in innovation, copying spreads the enjoyment of successful designs to people who cannot afford to pay top dollar.

Relaxing the Assumption of Rationality: Nonmarket Production

The utilitarian case for intellectual property also relies on the assumption that innovators are rational, self-interested actors who will be deterred by excessive free riding. In many contexts, this assumption of rationality will be plausible. This is particularly true when successful innovation by private actors is dependent upon the ability to concentrate large amounts of capital. Thus, as Benkler observes, "[t]here are no non-commercial automobile manufacturers. There are no volunteer steel foundries."[18] But, when the technology of production makes it effective for individuals to engage in inventive activity, the assumption of narrow self-interested behavior becomes less reliable and the salience of other motivations increases dramatically. In these contexts, the inability to prevent copying may have little detrimental effect (and will often have positive impacts) on incentives to invent.[19]

In his important book *The Wealth of Networks*, Benkler explores the impact of the networked society on the utilitarian case for intellectual property. The rise of the Internet, he argues, has dramatically reduced the costs of producing and disseminating many cultural and informational products. As recently as twenty years ago, an individual, nonprofessional author or composer could only reach a relatively small, local audience without access to expensive printing or recording technology and distributional networks. Today, that individual can produce a high-quality product on a few hundred dollars worth of equipment in her own home and, using the Internet, access an audience that (at least potentially) includes a significant percentage of the planet's population. "The economics of production in a digital environment," Benkler says, "should lead us to expect an increase in the relative salience of nonmarket production models in the overall mix of our information production system, and it is efficient for this to happen – more information will be produced, and much of it will be available for users at its marginal cost."[20]

---

[17] This has not, of course, stopped the industry from lobbying for the extension of copyright protection to fashion designs. See Raustiala and Sprigman, at 1715–16.

[18] Benkler, *Wealth of Networks*, 35. Presumably, Benkler is limiting his claims here to private industry. State-owned industries might well seek to produce, say, automobiles for reasons other than profit.

[19] See ibid., chap. 2.

[20] See ibid., 56.

Benkler points to phenomena like Wikipedia and the free software movement to demonstrate the potential commercial importance of nonmarket motives in this new, networked world.

Within Benkler's utilitarian model of nonmarket, often social, production, intellectual property rights can easily become counterproductive from a utilitarian standpoint. They can inhibit nonmarket actors by raising the costs of information. And they protect incumbent producers eager to maintain a market share that is itself the artifact of outdated production and distribution techniques based on the centralized, capital-intensive technologies.

Whether one agrees or disagrees with Benkler's description of the networked world, it is important to recognize that his discussion remains firmly rooted within utilitarian property theory. If his account of the increasing importance of nonmarket motives is correct, then his diagnosis of the possible harms of excessive intellectual property protection on the production of culture and information follow. Benkler's argument therefore serves as another example of the flexibility and empirical sensitivity of utilitarian property analysis.

LOCKEAN AND NATURAL RIGHTS THEORIES
OF INTELLECTUAL PROPERTY

As numerous commentators have observed, Locke's theory of appropriation seems at first glance easier to defend in the context of intellectual property than it is in the domain of tangible property.[21] Thus, Lockean property theory might seem to provide an even more solid foundation than utilitarian theory for extremely robust and unqualified intellectual property rights. The argument for strong Lockean intellectual property rights would be a straightforward application of Locke's theory of appropriation to the domain of ideas: (1) the inventor/creator owns herself; (2) she therefore owns her own labor; (3) invention and intellectual creation are the products of labor; and (4) consequently, she owns the inventions/creations generated through her intellectual labor.[22]

---

[21] See Justin Hughes, "The Philosophy of Intellectual Property," GEO. L. J. 77 (1988): 287, 296–7 (arguing that Locke's theory "can be used to justify intellectual property without many of the problems that attend its application to physical property"); Lawrence C. Becker, "Deserving to Own Intellectual Property," CHI.-KENT L. REV. 68 (1993): 609 (observing that desert arguments "seem especially powerful for intellectual property"); Seana Valentine Shiffrin, "Lockean Arguments for Private Intellectual Property," in *New Essays in the Legal and Political Theory of Property*, ed. Stephen R. Munzer (2001), 138, 139 (noting but not endorsing the view that "it seems easier to satisfy Lockean conditions on appropriation for intellectual property than for real property").

[22] See Tom W. Bell, "Indelicate Imbalancing in Copyright and Patent Law," in *Copy Fights: The Future of Intellectual Property in the Information Age*, ed. Adam Thierer and Wayne Crews (2002), 1, 3 (describing the argument for extending the Lockean theory of appropriation to intellectual property).

This perceived affinity between intellectual property rights and Lockean theory derives from three sources.[23] First, at least superficially, intellectual creation seems more like creation ex nihilo than the creation of tangible products from resources appropriated out of an initial commons. Consequently, it does not seem to suffer from the complications that arise in trying to separate out the relative contributions of the individual laborer and the material on which she labors.[24] Second, as long as intellectual property protects only new inventions or expressions that did not exist before, the inventor/creator does not actually take anything out of the commons, and so granting her ownership of her invention or creation leaves as much and as good for others. Indeed, if intellectual property rights are time limited, the inventor actually *increases* the common stock.[25] Finally, Locke's spoilation condition is less of an obstacle in the context of intellectual property. Because ideas are intangible, they cannot spoil in the possession of their appropriator.[26]

In light of these preliminary observations, it should perhaps come as no surprise that a number of prominent property rights libertarians have embraced the strong protection of intellectual property as an important dimension of property rights more generally. Ayn Rand, for example, argues that, even more than rights in tangible property, intellectual property rights exist independent of government, and that the government is morally obligated to protect them. "Patents and copyrights," she says, "are the legal implementation of the base of all property rights: a man's right to the product of his mind."[27] And Robert Nozick thought that time-limited patents followed from his Locke-inspired theory of appropriation.[28]

Despite support for intellectual property rights among leading property rights figures like Rand and Nozick, however, there is a significant, dissenting strain of libertarian discomfort with intellectual property as an infringement on liberty and, in particular, on tangible property rights. Tom Bell lays out this libertarian anxiety when he notes with concern that, "by invoking state power, a copyright or patent owner can impose prior restraint, fines, imprisonment, and confiscation on those engaged in peaceful expression and the quiet enjoyment of their tangible property. Because it thus gags our voices, ties our hands, and demolishes our presses, the law of copyrights and patents violates the very rights that Locke defended."[29]

---

[23] Shiffrin, "Lockean Arguments," 139–40.
[24] Becker, "Deserving to Own Intellectual Property," 611.
[25] See ibid., 616; Hughes, "Philosophy of Intellectual Property," 315.
[26] See Hughes, "Philosophy of Intellectual Property," 328. But see John Perry Barlow, "The Economy of Ideas," *Wired*, March 1994 ("Information is perishable.").
[27] Ayn Rand, "Patents and Copyrights," in *Capitalism: The Unknown Ideal* (1966), 125.
[28] See Robert Nozick, *Anarchy, State, and Utopia* (1974), 181–2; see also Richard A. Epstein, "Liberty v. Property? Cracks in the Foundations of Copyright Law," *San Diego L. Rev.* 42 (2005): 1, 24–6 (arguing that libertarian commitments are consistent with limited, though still robust, intellectual property rights).
[29] Bell, "Indelicate Imbalancing," 4.

Freidrich Hayek worried that the "forced scarcity" generated by intellectual property monopolies might not be "the most effective way to stimulate the human creative process."[30] In light of this libertarian discomfort with intellectual property, it should probably not be too surprising that vaguely Lockean-libertarian commitments are very common among proponents of the movement of intellectual property skepticism sometimes called the "copyleft."[31]

Digging a little bit deeper into the relationship between Lockean theory and intellectual property reveals some potential complications that may justify this suspicion. Seana Shiffrin's reading of Locke's property theory (like Jeremy Waldron's) treats the "paradox of plenty," which we discussed in Chapter 2, as a limitation on the proper domain of private appropriation. The paradox is the result of the assumption that God granted the world to human beings in common in order to sustain us. This intent would be frustrated if at least some private appropriation were not possible, since no one could benefit from the commons (e.g., by eating an acorn) without some right of appropriation.[32] Shiffrin argues for reading Locke's theory of property as permitting appropriation only when private ownership is necessary for the effective use of the commons.[33] Because ideas are consumed nonrivalrously, they do not give rise to the same paradox of plenty. Unlike tangible property, Shiffrin argues, "[t]he fully effective use of an idea, proposition, concept, expression, method, invention, melody, picture or sculpture generally does not require, by its nature, prolonged exclusive use or control."[34]

In Chapter 2, we favored treating the paradox of plenty more as a rhetorical device for communicating the importance of finding a valid theory of appropriation consistent with the situation of original common ownership. On our reading, the paradox does not operate for Locke as a limitation on appropriation. But we agree with Shiffrin that the inapplicability of the paradox in the context of ideas suggests that – for Locke – the problem of developing a system of private ownership is significantly less urgent for intellectual property than for tangible property. It is perhaps for this reason that Locke did not discuss the subject of intellectual property in the *Two Treatises*, and only mentioned it in passing in other writings.

Recall that, on our reading of Locke, the case for private appropriation rests on Locke's theory of makers' rights. From this point of view, a disanalogy between invention or generation of a new idea and creation ex nihilo would pose a significant

---

[30] Friederch A. Hayek, *The Fatal Conceit* (1988), 35.
[31] See Benkler, *Wealth of Networks*, 21 (referring to his position as "libertarian"); John Perry Barlow, "A Declaration of Independence of Cyberspace," EFF: Electronic Frontier Foundation website, February 8, 1996, available at https://projects.eff.org/~barlow/Declaration-Final.html.
[32] John Locke, *Two Treatises of Government*, ed. Mark Goldie, Everyman's Library (1993), II, 28.
[33] See Shiffrin, "Lockean Arguments," 144–54.
[34] Ibid., 156.

problem for attempts to craft a Lockean theory of intellectual property rights. Although highly romanticized accounts of the creative process treat the invention or new idea as a wholly individualized act emerging out of nothing that came before,[35] a more sophisticated and accurate description of intellectual creation will admit that, in virtually every case, the inventor or creator builds to some extent on the intellectual accomplishments of her predecessors.[36]

Henry Ford once said, "I invented nothing new. I simply assembled the discoveries of other men behind whom were centuries of work. Had I worked fifty or ten or even five years before, I would have failed. So it is with every new thing. Progress happens when all the factors that make for it are ready and then it is inevitable. To teach that a comparatively few men are responsible for the greatest forward steps of mankind is the worst sort of nonsense."[37] At the most basic level, any intellectual activity depends upon the existence of communicative systems, such as language or mathematics, developed over thousands of years by countless human beings. No one person who employs those systems to create a new idea or product can claim total credit for her creations. And once we admit that all intellectual creation draws at least to some extent on the prior intellectual labor of others, the Lockean case for intellectual property finds itself in the same murky domain of shared credit as the Lockean case for ownership of tangible property.

Moreover, focusing on the creation of value does not clarify things in the intellectual property context any more than it does in the context of tangible property. To assert that human labor – as opposed to the constituent raw materials – accounts for the bulk of the value in useful things seems more plausible in the case of intellectual and cultural goods than in the case of tangible property. But when it comes to isolating the value of any individual innovator's labor in these cultural products, we confront an analogous problem to the one we discussed in Chapter 2.

To see why, let us return to Nozick's famous Wilt Chamberlain example, which we first discussed in Chapter 6. Although not strictly addressing intellectual property, it nonetheless provides a useful example of the difficulties in isolating an individual's contribution to cultural production:

> [Wilt Chamberlain] signs the following sort of contract with a team: In each home game, twenty-five cents from the price of each ticket of admission goes to him....

---

[35] Rand, "Patents and Copyrights," 125 (calling intellectual property "the property right of mind to that which it has brought into existence").

[36] See James Boyle, Shamans, Software and Spleens (1996); Peter Jaszi, "Toward a Theory of Copyright," Duke L.J. (1991): 455.

[37] Quoted in Kirby Ferguson, "Everything is a Remix, Part 3," available at http://vimeo.com/25380454. In a similar spirit, Isaac Newton is said to have observed that "[i]f I have seen farther, it is because I have stood on the shoulders of giants." Quoted in Benkler, *Wealth of Networks*, 37, 39; see also Shiffrin, "Lockean Arguments," 159–66.

The season starts and people cheerfully attend his team's games; they buy their tickets, each time dropping a separate twenty-five cents of their admission price into a special box with Chamberlain's name on it.... Is he entitled to this income?[38]

Nozick thinks it is obvious that, if Chamberlain is good at basketball, he deserves to own the resources people are willing to pay him to enjoy watching him perform, as long as they in turn were entitled to the money they paid him. But why is this necessarily the case? In the same way that we have difficulty isolating the value that individual labor (as opposed to raw materials) contributes to a productive cornfield, how can we separate the value contributed by Chamberlain's skill at playing basketball from the use value of a host of conditions necessary for the realization of that value, conditions which Chamberlain had nothing to do with creating? These include, for example, the existence of the game of basketball itself, whose arbitrary rules favor Chamberlain's unique physical characteristics and talents; institutions like the NBA and youth basketball leagues, which help popularize the game; and, perhaps most importantly, communications technologies like television, radio, and (after Chamberlain's time) the Internet, which expand the potential audience for professional basketball. These conditions even extend to the existence of a stable, affluent society with enough resources to permit people to spend money on leisure activities like watching basketball.

We could go through a similar analysis for virtually any intellectual achievement with economic value. The economic value of every invention or creation will be found to depend to some extent on a social context for which the inventor can claim no credit but from which she benefits enormously. Thus, even assuming that a person is entitled to own the increment of value she creates through her intellectual work – an assumption that is not on its face implausible – isolating the precise boundaries of that increment may be an impossible task. As a general matter, then, we can say with confidence that a Lockean theory of intellectual property offers support for only qualified property rights in the product of intellectual labor.

Limitations on Intellectual Property Rights

On the Lockean view, the imposition of preconditions on the creation of (natural) intellectual property rights may be easier to justify than qualifications on the extent of those rights, once created.[39] Doctrines like the subject matter restrictions in patent and copyright, the idea/expression distinction, and patent's prohibition on owning laws of nature make some sense as efforts to restrict monopoly rights to the domain of the individual's actual creative contribution. Copyright's protection of independent

---

[38] Nozick, *Anarchy, State, and Utopia*, 161.
[39] See Chapter 2, *supra*.

invention is also consistent with this desire. Indeed, on the Lockean view, patent's *failure* to protect independent invention is something of a puzzle, though one might argue – as Nozick suggested – that the relatively short period of protection for patent constitutes an effort to protect independent invention indirectly.[40]

Limitations on intellectual property rights, once they exist, however, are somewhat harder to explain in narrowly Lockean terms. Time limitations, for example, seem to make more sense when understood as rooted in other considerations. Of course, because of Locke's political theory, with its majoritarian conception of consent, the scope of intellectual property rights justified within the state of nature would be subject to a great deal of revision within civil society, for a variety of reasons (including utilitarian concerns). But Lockean property theory itself does not readily supply its own reasons for adopting those limitations.

Justifying a doctrine like fair use in strictly Lockean terms is also something of a challenge. For the Lockean, the transaction costs and market failure theory of fair use would not provide independent reasons for limiting intellectual property rights. Over the last decade or so, some commentators have detected a shift in courts' interpretations of the fair use doctrine that may bring it closer to Lockean property theory. According to Neil Netanel, prior to about 2005, courts' discussions of fair use focused on the sorts of transaction-costs considerations that fit comfortably with the market failure theory of fair use.[41] But, in more recent years, courts have increasingly focused on the transformative nature of the use in determining whether it qualifies as a fair use.[42] "Under this [transformative use] paradigm, the key question in fair use analysis is whether the defendant's use is 'transformative,' not whether the defendant might have obtained a license or the copyright owner would have reasonably consented to the use."[43] Netanel credits Pierre Leval with first devising the transformative use conception of fair use in an influential 1990 *Harvard Law Review* article.[44] According to Leval, a use is transformative when it creates "new information, new aesthetics, [or] new insights and understandings."[45] The transformative use paradigm fits more comfortably with Lockean theories of intellectual property than the earlier, market failure approach. To a Lockean theorist, the considerations that would justify the conclusion that a use is transformative would also justify treating the

---

[40] Nozick, *Anarchy, State, and Utopia*, 182.

[41] See Neil Weinstock Netanel, "Making Sense of Fair Use," LEWIS & CLARK L. REV. 15 (2011): 715, 734; see also Barton Beebe, ""An Empirical Study of U.S. Copyright Fair Use Opinions, 1978–2005," U. PA. L. REV. 156 (2008): 549.

[42] See Netanel, at 734.

[43] Ibid. at 736.

[44] See Pierre N. Leval, "Toward a Fair Use Standard," HARV. L. REV. 103 (1990): 1105. The Supreme Court endorsed the standard in *Campbell v. Acuff-Rose Music, Inc.*, 510 U.S. 569, 579 (1994), but, according to Netanel, it did not begin to be widely applied in the lower courts until approximately 2005.

[45] Leval, 1111.

(fair) use as a new creation of the sort that would give rise to (qualified) intellectual property rights for its own creator.[46]

The Duty of Charity in Lockean Intellectual Property

Even in Locke's expansive theory of legislative power, the state cannot abrogate an owner's duty of charity, since the beneficiaries of the duty cannot waive their own obligation of self-preservation. Because an individual cannot escape that duty, which is owed to God, the legislature cannot eliminate it on her behalf. Strangely, however, the duty of charity comes in for very little discussion in Lockean theories of intellectual property. But the inescapability of the duty of charity is clearly relevant for owners of intellectual property governing products necessary for human survival. The most obvious of these would be patents for life-saving medicines. But the principle might also apply to other sorts of intellectual products, such as patents governing genetically modified crops that could alleviate starvation. A straightforward application of Locke's principle of charity would seem to obligate owners of these sorts of life-saving patented inventions to make them available to those who cannot afford to purchase them at monopoly prices. And, when individual owners appear inclined to shirk this duty, it is – for Locke – well within the legitimate power of civil government to enforce it through coercive mechanisms like compulsory licensing.

HEGELIAN/PERSONHOOD INTELLECTUAL PROPERTY THEORY

Intellectual Property and Personhood

As a source justifying at least some forms of intellectual property rights, Hegel's personality theory provides a strong alternative (or supplement) to both utilitarianism and Lockean theory.[47] The core idea behind a Hegelian conception of intellectual property rights is that "an idea belongs to its creator because the idea is a manifestation of the creator's personality or self."[48] As we saw in Chapter 3, from Hegel's perspective, property's role is to realize that aspect of the self that is the necessary predicate for political citizenship, what Jeanne Schroeder calls "legal subjectivity"[49]

---

[46] The affinity between "transformative use" and Lockean theory is more true of the "transformative use" as Leval described it than as courts have actually implemented it. Commentators have observed that the notion of transformativeness is ambiguous between new purposes and new content. See Netanel, 746. The latter has more normative bite within Lockean theory, but, Netanel argues, courts have tended to focus on the former in assessing whether uses are fair. Ibid.

[47] See Hughes, "Philosophy of Intellectual Property," 330.

[48] Ibid.

[49] Jeanne L. Schroeder, "Unnatural Rights: Hegel and Intellectual Property," *U. Miami L. Rev.* 60 (2006): 455.

(i.e., subjection to the rule of law). Hegel refers to the self who has this capacity as the self whose subjectivity is created by "abstract" right.[50] The subjectivity that this abstract right creates is purely formal. Hence, only the *form* of property, not its content, matters to Hegel. This is why there is no special injunction that the legal system create intellectual property rights or any other particular type of property.

Arguably, intellectual property, because of its intangibility, serves the function of creating subjectivity better than tangible forms of property. So, Hegel states:

> Mental aptitudes, erudition, artistic skill, even things ecclesiastical (like sermons, masses, prayers, and consecration of votive objects), inventions, and so forth, become objects of contract, brought on to a parity, through being bought and sold, with things recognized as things. It may be asked whether the artist, scholar, &c., is from the legal point of view in possession of his art, erudition, ability to preach a sermon, sing a mass, &c., that is, whether such attainments are "things." We may hesitate to call such abilities, attainments, aptitudes, &c., "things," for while possession of these may be the subject of business dealings and contracts, as if they were things, there is also something inward and mental about it, and for this reason the Understanding may be in perplexity about how to describe such possession in legal terms, because its field of vision is as limited to the dilemma that this is "either a thing or not a thing" as to the dilemma "either finite or infinite." Attainments, erudition, talents, and so forth, are, of course, owned by free mind and are something internal and not external to it, but even so, by expressing them it may embody them…and in this way they are put into the category of "things."[51]

Precisely because intellectual property is "inward and mental," it aptly suits abstract property right's role to create pure subjectivity, that is, a personality that is formal only, lacking content. (Morality and ethics, not law, are the realms that add content to the personality.)

Paradoxically, perhaps the best example of Hegelian property theory's application to intellectual property concerns the right of publicity. A relatively new right, the right of publicity, protects a person's interest in the commercial exploitation of her name, likeness, and identity.[52] It gives the individual the economic value that derives directly from one's persona. What makes the application of Hegelian theory to the right of publicity paradoxical is the fact that the right asserted seems to be anything but purely formal. After all, it is its content – the claimant's likeness or identity – which is unique to each claimant. Still, the right is formal and abstract in the sense that Hegel described. It is "inward and mental" and nonexternal. Each person's persona may be unique, but the idea of persona itself is purely abstract.

---

[50] Georg W. F. Hegel, *Hegel's Philosophy of Right*, trans. T. M. Knox (1952), par. 38.
[51] Ibid., par. 43.
[52] See Restatement of the Law of Unfair Competition § 46 (1995).

Some commentators have noted apparent problems with Hegel's account of alienation of intellectual property.[53] One commentator, for example, observes that alienation ends the owner's personal connection to the object that is the expression of her personality. This is especially true, he believes, of copyright because the objects of copyright, as creations of the author or composer, would seem to be inextricably connected with the author's personality. Thus an owner's present desire to alienate an object does not fit with the justification for property.[54] But, as Schroeder has pointed out, this account mistakenly supposes that the legal property right relates to creation of the fully formed person in its own personal network of relationships. As we have seen, this is not the case. In Hegel's theory, property rights relate only to the creation of abstract legal subjects, which are strictly formal and relate to other legal subjects only in the same capacity. (For the same reason, Hegel would have had no truck with the image of writers, inventors, and the like, as "romantic" creators.) As we discussed in Chapter 3, the only assets that are inalienable according to Hegel are those that are essential to concrete personality such that their alienation would effectively alienate personality itself.[55]

In short, there is nothing unique or even special about intellectual property in Hegel's account. Hegel treats intellectual property like other species of property and renders it strictly formal and abstract. So presented, it lacks any of the special creative, even romantic, allure that surrounds it in much of today's literature.

Limits on Hegelian Intellectual Property

However appealing Hegel's theory may be as a justification for intellectual rights, its support for a regime of legal protection is limited. As Schroeder points out, Hegel's theory has nothing to say about whether a legal system *should* adopt a regime of protection for intellectual property. It only suggests that *if* a society decides to adopt such a legal regime, then it is logically coherent to formulate such a regime in terms of true property rather than some sui generis form of property.[56] Thus, intellectual property has no special place in Hegel's theory; in his view any form of property right can fulfill the personality function.[57] Moreover, while Hegelian theory may serve as

---

[53] See, for example, Hughes, "Philosophy of Intellectual Property," 339, 345–50 (characterizing the theory as "incoherent").

[54] Ibid., 345.

[55] Jeremy Waldron believes that for Hegel, the case for alienation is not rights-based. Rather, Hegel accepts the relationship of alienation to property as historically given and hence, contingent. In the society in which he happened to live, property was alienable, so Hegel undertook to explain that characteristic. See Jeremy Waldron, *The Right to Private Property* (1988), 368.

[56] See Jeanne L. Schroeder, "Unnatural Rights: Hegel and Intellectual Property," U. MIAMI L. REV. 60 (2006): 453.

[57] Ibid.

a justification for legal protection of use and enjoyment of property, it does not fully explain intellectual property's alienability.

INTELLECTUAL PROPERTY IN ARISTOTELIAN PROPERTY THEORY

A human flourishing approach to intellectual property differs from other approaches primarily in terms of the range of interests it deems relevant to decisions about how to structure intellectual property. For instance, it is capable of accepting the predictions (and even many of the prescriptions) of utilitarian intellectual property theory. It may be true that, as Benkler has persuasively argued, in a world with no intellectual property rights, many people would continue to create and invent. But many would not, particularly where innovation requires large capital outlays. Thus, in a great many contexts, the utilitarian argument that excessive free riding will discourage investment in the production of new information seems correct. Since a commitment to human flourishing includes a concern with aggregate social wealth, Aristotelian theory takes seriously utilitarian arguments about the need to reward (and thereby encourage) productive intellectual labor. What the Aristotelian approach rejects is the strong utilitarian claim that utility (or wealth or pleasure or preference satisfaction) is the sole end to be maximized by an intellectual property regime. In contrast, Aristotelian theory regards wealth or preference satisfaction (or some other such subjective account of well-being) as a relevant, but not decisive, consideration in deciding how to structure a system of intellectual property rights.[58]

Similarly, and unlike Lockean intellectual property theory (or, more precisely, its contemporary libertarian form), the human flourishing approach does not view intellectual labor as creating unqualified moral entitlements to control the products of that labor. Although useful labor – including useful intellectual labor – is virtuous and worthy of reward and encouragement, the entitlements it creates must always (within Aristotelian property theory) be balanced against other human goods, such as the need to ensure that human beings have access to resources necessary to sustain life. Intellectual property rights may therefore be overridden in order to ensure adequate access. But it does take inventors' moral entitlements seriously.

Aristotelian theory accepts many of the claims on behalf of intellectual property rights made within utilitarian, Lockean, and even Hegelian theory. But it embraces them in a qualified way and brings them into dialogue with one another by acknowledging the plurality of goods that intellectual property rights implicate. In some cases, these goods point toward convergent conclusions. Access to life-sustaining intellectual property (for example, medicines) is relatively easy to justify in utilitarian, Lockean, and Aristotelian terms. For the utilitarian, the obligation to provide

[58] See Richard Kraut, *Aristotle* (2002), 72.

access to those who cannot afford life-saving medication operates as an example of justified redistribution to overcome wealth effects or market failure. For the Lockean who is faithful to the limits Locke's theory sets on property rights, it arises under the owner's duty of charity, which operates as an original constraint on the owner's rights. And for the Aristotelian, the duty to provide access arises both as a matter of the individual owner's obligations to share the necessities of life, which the state may be justified in enforcing, and the state's own duty to secure access to the resources its citizens need in order to flourish.

Aristotelian capabilities theory also provides a helpful framework for weighing the many tangled considerations raised by intellectual property law where the answers seem less clear cut. Aristotelian intellectual property theory contributes an account of the human values at stake that is more capacious than the traditional utilitarian analysis in terms of wealth or preference satisfaction, the libertarian focus on freedom, or the Hegelian focus on personal development. Although it reaches beyond them, however, Aristotelian intellectual property theory remains able to give weight to each of these important values.

For example, Aristotelian theory recognizes a connection between intellectual property law and the creation of a particular type of cultural framework helpful for fostering human flourishing. Several, perhaps all, of the human capabilities that are necessary prerequisites for the well-lived life demand a certain kind of culture that enables humans to develop those capabilities and then, once developed, sustain them.[59] Charles Taylor explains how individual freedom itself depends upon the existence of a culture that enables a person to develop as one "capable of conceiving alternatives and arriving at a definition of what [she or he] really want[s] ...."[60] As Taylor further explains, individuals are not born with the ability to conceive of and discern among alternative choices available to them. They must develop that ability, and they can develop the ability to conceive of an array of alternatives only within the kind of culture that nurtures such a capability.[61] Taylor's discussion points toward the value of fostering a cultural environment that encourages innovation, for a key task of the culture is to encourage human flourishing by enabling individuals to conceive of ever-broadening horizons.

Closely related to culture's role in fostering the good of individual autonomy is the contribution that it makes to the development of practical reason. Developing

---

[59] In saying that development of the requisite capabilities demands a certain kind of culture, we do not mean to suggest that one and only specific type or form of culture will do. There are, of course, myriad cultures throughout the world, and many (though not all) of them can and do enable individuals to develop the human capabilities necessary for human flourishing.

[60] Charles Taylor, "Atomism," in *Philosophy and the Human Sciences*, vol. 2 of *Philosophical Papers*, (1985), 204.

[61] See ibid., 205.

the capability of practical reason is a prerequisite for conceiving of and discerning among alternative choices available to individuals as they pass through life. An environment in which innovation flourishes cultivates our ability wisely and deeply to discern among possible options and then to act. Such an environment enables us to understand that fresh choices are available to us.

A culture that fosters creativity and innovation can also encourage sociability. Terry Fisher captures the core of the relationship between sociability and a robust innovative culture when he points out that "[a]n attractive society is one rich in 'communities of memory.' Persons' capacity to construct rewarding lives will be enhanced if they have access to a variety of 'constitutive' groups – in 'real' space and 'virtual' space."[62] In referring to "virtual" communities, of course, Fisher has in mind groups that constitute themselves through the Internet, but the point is more general than that. Consider the other ways in which individuals socialize with one another with respect to shared interests, whether music, art, theatre, or whatever, whose existence requires a richly creative cultural environment.

Despite the many undeniable contributions that innovation makes to a culture that values autonomy, practical reason, and sociability, excessive rewards for innovation can lead to the valorization of a kind of empty frivolity, in which innovation is valued for its own sake. Excessive innovation can (at best) be harmless. But it may also undermine important human goods, both by breaking down social bonds nurtured by traditional standards of excellence and by drawing effort away from more worthwhile pursuits.[63] The legal recognition of intellectual property rights has an important part to play in modulating this culture of vibrant intellectual and cultural production.

In addition, all of these reasons for wanting to encourage the development of human capabilities by rewarding innovation through the grant of intellectual property rights are also reasons for wanting to limit those rights to ensure that human beings enjoy adequate access to the products of that innovation, both cultural and material. Brett Frischmann and Mark Lemley, for example, have argued that part of the reason why copyright law creates a fair use doctrine is to facilitate positive externalities, or "spillovers."[64] As Frischmann and Lemley write, "[u]sing a work for educational purposes, for example, not only benefits the users themselves, but also, in a small way, benefits others in the users' community with whom

[62] William Fisher, "Theories of Intellectual Property," in *New Essays in the Legal and Political Theory of Property*, ed. Stephen R. Munzer (2001), 168, 193.

[63] See Arnold Plant, "The Economic Theory Concerning Patents for Inventions," *Economica* 1 (1934): 30, 40 ("The question which [supporters of strong patent rights] one and all failed to ask themselves, however, is what these people would otherwise be doing if the patent system were not diverting their attention by the offer of monopolistic profits to the task of inventing.").

[64] Brett M. Frischmann and Mark A. Lemley, "Spillovers," COLUM. L. REV. 107 (2007): 284–5, 288.

users have interdependent relations – reading and learning builds socially valuable human capital."[65]

From the Aristotelian perspective, then, intellectual property law should, among other things, aim to promote the development of human capabilities by creating incentives to produce the intellectual products without which we could scarcely develop into truly free moral agents and good neighbors.[66] But ensuring that people have adequate access to the goods protected by intellectual property law also contributes to the realization of the very same essential human capabilities. Thus, as with utilitarian intellectual property theory, the real question for Aristotelian intellectual property theory is not whether, but how much. Too little intellectual property protection will inhibit the creation of important intellectual innovations that contribute to human flourishing. Too much protection, however, risks undermining the contribution of these innovations to the promotion of the essential human capabilities by inhibiting access.

But while the general contours of the prescriptions of Aristotelian intellectual property theory bear a superficial resemblance to those generated by utilitarian intellectual property analysis, the two theories arrive at their conclusions through very different mechanisms. Utilitarian theory asks what structure of intellectual property law will generate the greatest supply of satisfied preferences (or wealth, or whatever definition of utility or welfare the theorist is employing). With its subjective accounts of human well-being, utilitarian theory does not provide the basis for criticizing a culture that, say, fails to give due weight to the distribution of access to intellectual property when providing such access would not necessarily happen to maximize utility (however defined). It takes human beings as it finds them and dissolves individuals within a sea of aggregate utility.

The only reason for limiting intellectual property that utilitarianism recognizes is the notion that, over the long run, overprotection will result in fewer satisfied preferences (or less wealth or less pleasure, etc.). Particularly as to theories that focus on aggregate wealth understood as "willingness to pay," Madhavi Sunder is correct when she observes that excessively narrow conceptions of value "fails to capture fully the struggles at the heart of local and global intellectual property conflicts."[67] Because Aristotelian theory employs an objective and pluralist conception of human well-being, it is capable of fostering more sophisticated deliberation about the proper boundaries of intellectual property protection as an instrument of human flourishing.

---

[65] Ibid., 289.
[66] See ibid., 284–5.
[67] See Madhavi Sunder, "IP$_3$," STAN. L. REV. 59 (2006): 257, 263.

Conclusion

POINTS OF CONVERGENCE

Throughout this book, we have tended to emphasize the differences among the competing theories of property we have explored. Although this focus has been useful in understanding what is distinctive about each theory, it risks leaving readers with a misimpression about the degree of disagreement among them. Of course, it is true that the theories diagnose many property problems differently and frequently generate conflicting normative prescriptions, but there are also important points of convergence. In this conclusion, we will discuss three of these areas of apparent agreement. The first is the overriding force of human necessity. The second is the importance of *things* in property law. And the third, which is related, is the value of so-called property rules.

While the different theories offer different explanations of these issues, there appears to be an overlapping consensus concerning their significance.[1] We cannot hope to provide a comprehensive discussion of these interesting topics, but their salience across numerous property theories suggest that they represent fruitful avenues for future property thinking.

Necessity

With the exception of the most doctrinaire contemporary libertarian theories, all the property theories we have discussed in this book have agreed in affirming the notion that private property rights must give way in the face of extreme human necessity. Although theorists disagree about what qualifies as the kind of necessity that will justify trumping rights of ownership, virtually all contemporary theorists

---

[1] We are using the term here as a loose analog of Rawls's sense of foundational principles that are appealing across a number of different competing theories. See John Rawls, *Political Liberalism* § 2.3 (1993).

make room for this accommodation of urgent human need. We have discussed the doctrine of necessity at various points in this book. As we saw in Chapter 2, John Locke affirmed it, making his "principle of charity" one of the central qualifications of the rights of private property that arise in the state of nature. And, as we observed in Chapter 5, the doctrine was central to Thomas Aquinas's theory of property. The doctrine is also easily accommodated within utilitarian and Hegelian property theories.

This is an important point of convergence for at least two reasons. First, it suggests that virtually all property theorists agree, at least in principle, with the notion that – to borrow the words of the New Jersey Supreme Court in *State v. Shack* – "property rights serve human values."[2] Second, since almost all property theories treat human necessity as generating an important (indeed, overriding) moral claim, the meaning and contours of *necessity* provide extremely fruitful avenues for further debate and reflection. A broad conception of human necessity rooted in Aristotelian conceptions of human capabilities, for example, might place the doctrine of necessity close to the center of a comprehensive account of the relationship among individual owners, nonowners, and the state. Amartya Sen has argued, for example, that the concept of necessity, though constant across contexts at the level of human capabilities, is extremely flexible at the level of the material resources that will be required in order to satisfy human need.[3] Thus, for example, the ability to participate in the social life of the community without shame is an invariable component of human flourishing and one that requires a certain amount of material resources to accomplish. But the material things needed to socialize without shame will vary dramatically from society to society and from one era to another in the same society. In contrast, extremely limited conceptions of necessity as concerned with brute physical survival could relegate the status of necessity to a narrow, though still significant, coda.

The Importance of Things in Property

In Chapter 7, we discussed the exclusion theorists' concern that the traditional law and economics account of property, with its focus on disaggregated use rights, has the tendency to dissolve the significance of things in property law. Their emphasis on the right to exclude is driven, at least in part, by the notion that property law should incorporate the informational efficiencies generated by the distinctiveness of things. The importance of this emphasis on things is magnified, in their view, by the fact that property rights are characteristically in rem rights, that is, rights good against the

---

[2]   58 N.J. 297, 303 (1971).
[3]   See Amartya Sen, *Resources, Values and Development* (1984), 324–45.

world. Tying those in rem rights to commonly accepted and recognizable objects
reduces the costs of figuring out who has rights to do what.

As we discussed in Chapter 7, we think exclusion theorists are mistaken when
they assert a strong conceptual connection between exclusion and thingness. Broadly
defined, spatial use rights are also consistent with the idea of property as concerned
with things. In addition, exclusion theorists fail to emphasize the degree to which
the concepts of the things that are the objects of property law – most significantly
land, but also intangible property (including intellectual property) – are themselves
the products of law and culture. As Bill Brown puts it, "however materially stable
objects may seem, they are, let us say, different things in different scenes."4 On the
other hand, as Brown seems to acknowledge, "there is *some* 'transcultural pole of the
institution of things,' one that 'leans on the natural stratum.'"5 Of course, this element
of naturalness for at least some things tells us very little about "what claims on your
attention and on your action are made on behalf of things."6 Despite this complexity, exclusion theorists sometimes make the mistake of treating thingness as if it were
exogenous to the law of property.

Even if the content of thingness is itself a cultural and legal artifact, exclusion theorists are right to insist that things often present themselves to us *as* discrete objects
and that property law (and theory) should be able to account for, and take advantage
of, this characteristically thing-centered way in which human beings experience the
world. Even when the content of the thing is almost wholly constructed by law and
culture, the possibility of that construction is facilitated by the stability of the legal
and cultural content of a standardized bundle of property entitlements. The most
obvious example in this regard is land, which the common law famously compre-
hends (and constructs) as everything within a column of space extending from the
heavens to the depths.7 But the same can be said of intangible property as well.8 This
stability, and the legal and cultural concept of a thing that grows out of it, generates
significant informational benefits for lawyers and lay people alike.

---

4   Bill Brown, "Thing Theory," *Critical Inquiry* 28 (2001): 1, 9.
5   Ibid., (quoting Cornelius Castoriadis, *The Imaginary Institution of Society*, trans. Kathleen Blamey
    [1987], 334) (emphasis added).
6   Ibid., 9–10.
7   Contrast this quintessentially Anglo American conception of land with the vastly different concep-
    tions held by Native Americans at the time of the European colonization of New England. See,
    for example, William Cronon, *Changes in the Land* (1983), 62–3 (arguing that, for Indians in New
    England, property rights in land "shifted with ecological use"). And, of course, the common law defin-
    ition of land has itself been subject to recalibration when necessary. See, for example, Stuart Banner,
    Who Owns the Sky? (2008) (discussing property law's struggle with, and eventual accommodation of,
    airplane overflights).
8   See, for example, Henry E. Smith, "Institutions and Indirectness in Intellectual Property," *U. PA. L.
    REV.* 157 (2009): 2083.

The exclusion theorists' emphasis on things as a unit of analysis in property law finds echoes in the other, nonutilitarian theories of property we have explored in this book, though the importance of things in those theories is often an unstated assumption rather than the object of extended reflection. For contemporary property rights libertarians, who trace their roots to Locke, the negative liberty that the law should protect is generated by legal recognition of a robust right to exclude nonowners from things whose boundaries Lockean theorists largely understand as given. There is a good fit between libertarian concerns with freedom conceived as protection from interference by other people and a property law whose primary objects of attention are things, whether the boundaries of those things are (as they tend to be with chattels) in some sense built into the physical structure of the world or (as they are with land and intangible property) largely constructed by law and culture.[9]

The more affirmative conceptions of autonomy at work in Hegelian and Aristotelian property theories likewise benefit from understanding property as concerned with discrete things. On the Hegelian view, human beings form their personal identities and communicate their status as persons to others through the manipulation of material objects. The communicative function of this manipulation is arguably enhanced when the object of the person's activities is discrete things, recognizable to others as such. Indeed, as Waldron has observed, the process of appropriation within Hegelian thought constitutes not only the appropriator as a bearer of rights, it also "constitutes nature as a realm of objects capable of embodying and sustaining his status as a rights-bearer."[10]

Finally, the capacious Aristotelian concept of human flourishing also recognizes the importance of treating discrete things as the primary object of property law.[11] As we discussed in Chapter 5, human beings require access to actual things – in order to flourish both physically and socially. Access to (merely) abstract conceptions of well-being, such as preference satisfaction or pleasure, is not enough.

It is worth noting that treating things as the basic unit of property analysis does not entail a commitment to any particular theory about how access to things should actually be allocated or shared, or what obligations are entailed by ownership of the thing. A concern with things is as consistent with robust Lockean libertarianism as it is with Aristotelian commitment to social obligation within property law. Nevertheless, the idea that property law is – or ought to be – concerned with things has broad theoretical appeal.

---

[9] This connection is brought out nicely in Laura Underkuffler's conceptualization of property as "protection." See Laura S. Underkuffler, *The Idea of Property* (2003), 38.

[10] Jeremy Waldron, *The Right to Private Property* (1988), 360.

[11] See, for example, David Lametti, "The Concept of Property: Relations through Objects of Social Wealth," *U. Toronto L. J.* 53 (2003): 325.

Property Rules

In Chapter 1, we introduced Guido Calabresi and A. Douglas Melamed's famous distinction between property rules and liability rules. Although those authors intended the category of *property rules* to apply significantly more broadly than the domain of property law, their use of the term *property* to refer to entitlements that, once allocated, cannot be transferred without the consent of its owner was no accident, since, as they observed, "much of what is generally called private property can be viewed as an entitlement which is protected by a property rule."[12] The qualified embrace of this predominance of property rules in property law constitutes another point of wide agreement among contemporary property theories.

Again, it is important to be clear about what we mean when we say that the various theories we have been discussing converge on the idea of the value of property rules in the law of property. We do not mean that they agree on particular distributive principles or in opposing involuntary redistribution of property. As we saw in Chapter 6, the theories disagree on both of these important points. Nevertheless, the property theories we have discussed largely support the idea that, however things are to be allocated (or even reallocated or shared), the law of property operates through the use of property rules far more frequently than does the law of contracts or torts. This reliance on property rules is not unrelated to the focus of property law on things, since the use of property rules arguably reinforces the bonds between persons and those things. The same normative considerations that lead different property theories to focus on things also lead them to favor property rules over liability rules.

The connection between property rules and property theory is most apparent for libertarian property theorists. Richard Epstein, for example, has forcefully argued for what he calls the "dominance" of property rules, by which he means both the use of property rules as a default within the legal architecture of property and a commitment to market transactions as the mechanism for allocating property entitlements.[13] (Obviously, our focus is on the first of these two meanings for the purposes of identifying this particular point of convergence.) We also find support for entitlements backed by property rules in Hegelian and Aristotelian property theory, albeit entitlements that are allocated according to different distributive principles than those Epstein favors. For the Hegelian, the creation of personal identity through the public manipulation of objects is facilitated by the legal recognition and stabilization of a person's control over and connection to an object, and property rules help

---

[12] See Guido Calabresi and A. Douglas Melamed, "Property Rules, Liability Rules, and Inalienability," HARV. L. REV. 85 (1972): 1089, 1105.

[13] See generally Richard A. Epstein, "A Clear View of the Cathedral: The Dominance of Property Rules," YALE L.J. 106 (1997): 2091.

to accomplish these goals. Similarly, human flourishing depends not just on access to the value of material resources, but requires stable and predictable access to (and control over) the resources themselves.

Since Calabresi and Melamed's groundbreaking article, the greatest support for the use of liability rules has come from within the utilitarian tradition.[14] More recently, however, exclusion theorists have provided credible utilitarian arguments defending the pervasiveness of property rules in the law of property.[15] Thus, as with the importance of things in property law, the main contemporary property theories appear to converge on the distinctive value of property rules in the law of property.

PLURAL VALUES AND THE VALUE OF PLURALISM
IN PROPERTY THEORY

Despite these important points of partial agreement, there remain significant differences among the property theories we have been discussing. These result primarily from the tendency of individual theories to give one value, such as utility or autonomy (variously understood), overriding importance. Such "value monism" can be found in various forms throughout property theory. The problem for monists is that a single fundamental value that supposedly grounds all of property law (or at least should do so, according to the theories' advocates) does a poor job of explaining property law's existing norms or recommends changes to those norms that seem objectionable because they give short shrift to other competing values.[16]

Probably the best example of value monism in the theories we have been exploring is utilitarianism. We have discussed at some length throughout this book some of the problems with treating utility – particularly when understood as preference satisfaction – as the sole normative foundation for a system of private ownership. But other theories that profess to be similarly single-minded in their reflection on property law's normative underpinnings suffer similar problems. In its most extreme form, libertarianism treats property rights as insuperable moral entitlements whose sole purpose is to protect individual freedom. As Ayn Rand put it, "[t]he right to life is the source of all rights – and the right to property is their only implementation."[17] And, of course, for Rand and other libertarians, rights are purely negative: "for every individual, a right is the moral sanction...of his freedom to act on his own judgment, for his own goals, by his own voluntary, uncoerced choice. As to his neighbors,

---

[14]   See Henry E. Smith, "Property and Property Rules," *N.Y.U. L. Rev.* 79 (2004): 1719, 1742–8 (describing the preference for liability rules within modern law and economics).

[15]   See ibid.; see also Stewart E. Sterk, "Property Rules, Liability Rules, and Uncertainty about Property Rights," *Mich. L. Rev.* 106 (2008): 1285.

[16]   See Gregory S. Alexander, "Property and Pluralism," *Fordham L. Rev* 80 (2001): 101.

[17]   Ayn Rand, "Man's Rights," in *Capitalism: The Unknown Ideal* (1966), 286, 288.

his rights impose no obligations on them except of a negative kind, to abstain from violating his rights."[18] And yet, when push comes to shove, the implications of following through with such a narrow moral vision are too stark for more thoughtful libertarians to swallow. To his credit, Epstein recognizes the deep problems with radically nonconsequentialist libertarianism, and so he blends his interest in liberty with more than a few doses of welfarism. Indeed, this move – attempting to marry individual liberty as the fundamental value with utilitarian or welfarist constraints – is characteristic of much of Epstein's property scholarship, and it reflects his discomfort with the attempt to build the structure of property law on a narrow foundation of either liberty or utility alone.[19]

Epstein is not the only libertarian who refuses to maintain an uncompromising commitment to individual liberty as the sole foundational value undergirding all of property law. Echoing themes in some of Epstein's own writings on Robert Nozick,[20] Barbara Fried has recently argued that the same mixture of utilitarianism and libertarianism lies hidden within Nozick's theory of property.[21] Fried contends that in *Anarchy, State, and Utopia*, Nozick actually puts forward three theories of property, which she considers mutually exclusive – Lockean libertarian, utilitarian, and "anything goes, provided that citizens have some unspecified level of choice among legal regimes."[22] To the extent that any one of them predominates, Fried suggests, it is utilitarianism.[23] Indeed, Fried goes on to suggest that most deontologists have not been able to provide detailed solutions to everyday moral problems on the basis of their deontological premises alone; rather, they have usually relied on assistance from utilitarianism.[24]

If utility and liberty have not fared well as the sole unitary foundation for property rights and property law, what about personhood? Hegelian personhood theory finds no more success than individual liberty. Margaret Jane Radin herself concedes that her neo-Hegelian theory is not a complete theory of property.[25] Even if it were, the theory implicitly acknowledges that not all values at work in property law can or should be reduced to self-development, or "personhood," as Radin calls it. The

---

[18]   Ibid.
[19]   See, for example, Margaret Jane Radin, "Time, Possession, and Alienation," WASH. U. L. REV. 64 (1986): 739; Robert C. Ellickson, "Adverse Possession and Perpetuities Law: Two Dents in the Libertarian Model of Property Rights," 64 WASH. U. L. REV. 739 (1986); Eduardo M. Peñalver, "Reconstructing Richard Epstein," WILLIAM & MARY BILL OF RIGHTS J. 15 (2006): 429.
[20]   See Richard Epstein, "One Step Beyond Nozick's Minimal State," SOC. & POL. PHIL. 22 (2005): 286.
[21]   Barbara H. Fried, "Does Nozick Have a Theory of Property Rights?" (Stanford Public Law Working Paper No. 1782031), available at http://ssrn.com/abstract=1782031.
[22]   Ibid., 4.
[23]   Ibid.
[24]   Ibid., 27–8.
[25]   See Margaret Jane Radin, "Property and Personhood," STAN. L. REV. 34 (1982): 958, 991, 1013.

dichotomy between personal and fungible assets recognizes that sometimes values other than self-development are the proper foundations of corners of property law.

Both Epstein's and Radin's efforts to reach beyond a single value underlying all of property law tell us something important about the moral foundations of property: It is simply too complex and heterogeneous to be explicable by reference to a single, all-encompassing moral value. Property law's heterogeneity has at least two dimensions. Radin's personal property–fungible property dichotomy points to one: the heterogeneity among types of assets (especially viewed in context). As Radin wonderfully shows, although people experience many assets as market commodities, viewing them for their capacity to create wealth, they value other types of assets for their contribution to and relationship with the construction of the owner's identity. And the same asset can affect different values differently depending on who is holding it. A home, for example, in the hands of a massive homebuilder like Toll Brothers embodies different values than the very same home several years later in the hands of its owner/occupant.

A second dimension of heterogeneity is the myriad forms and means of social interaction. For example, Epstein's refusal to give overriding importance to individual liberty makes room for him to take into account how the passage of time affects the relations between past and present possessors of land and also implicates other goods – including wealth-maximization, the self-identity that accompanies long-term possession, and so on.[26] More broadly, recent judicial applications of the public trust doctrine to encompass recreational uses illustrates how courts have recognized the importance of goods other than the negative liberty protected by the right to exclude.[27] These goods notably include friendship, sociality, and tolerance.[28] Nor can these goods simply be reduced to mere preferences. They are not merely objects of desire, the desire for which is a matter of indifference, something we arbitrarily either want or don't want ("I just do.").

Hanoch Dagan has argued that in property theory, pluralism takes a structural form.[29] By *structural pluralism* he means the multiplicity of realms of social activity and corresponding legal doctrines and institutions, each with its own attending value foundations. Thus, with respect to the family home, in relations between the owner and outsiders, the right to exclude is indeed paramount and appropriately so.

---

[26] See Richard A. Epstein, "Past and Future: The Temporal Dimension in the Law of Property," WASH. U. L. REV. 64 (1986): 667.

[27] See *Raleigh Avenue Beach Ass'n v. Atlantis Beach Club*, 879 A.2d 112 (N.J. 2005); *Glass v. Goeckel*, 703 N.W. 2d 58 (Mich. 2005).

[28] See Carol Rose, "The Comedy of the Commons: Custom, Commerce, and Inherently Public Property," U. CHI. L. REV. 53 (1986): 711, 779.

[29] Hanoch Dagan, "Pluralism and Perfectionism in Private Law," J. TORT L. (forthcoming 2011): [ms. 10].

In this realm, the law values individual autonomy and personal security. But in the context of marriage and marital property, a very different set of values prevails. Here, sharing, community, and cooperation are the values that are normative guideposts for the law. Individual autonomy and security are inappropriate as normative foundations for an intimate social relationship like marriage. This institutional multiplicity can be seen in further detail as we look at social organizations ranging from common interest communities to partnerships.

What needs emphasis is the fact that within this structural multiplicity lies value pluralism that is both foundational and normative.[30] The existence of multiple social spheres, each with attendant legal institutions and doctrines, reflects the pluralism of moral values. The various legal institutions and norms embody in different ways the basic moral values at work in the social spheres which the legal institutions regulate. Indeed, that the law creates multiple and diverse institutions is itself arguably prima facie evidence that the underlying values are genuinely diverse and plural. But, importantly, even within the same social sphere and the same attendant legal institution, there may well be multiple and diverse fundamental values that conflict with one another or at least are potentially in tension with one another.

Although we have not written this book primarily as a defense of our own preferred property theories, we believe that Aristotelian theory is unique among the approaches we have surveyed in its ability to embrace the pluralism of property. In addition to its compatibility with a range of realistic models of human behavior, Aristotelian property theory recognizes that human flourishing consists of a plurality of incommensurable goods, making it particularly well adapted to provide a means for acknowledging and balancing the full spectrum of the human goods implicated by property law.

Thus, unlike libertarian property theory, Aristotelian theory is able to give due weight to the consequences of particular property rules for human beings' material well-being. But it can do so without adopting the utilitarian position that those consequences are the only important moral considerations. Thus, in contrast to various utility- or welfare-maximizing normative theories, in which the idea of "maximum utility" stands, in Philippa Foot's words, "outside morality as its foundation and arbiter," within Aristotelian theory, utility exists "within morality as the end of one of its virtues."[31] Aristotelian property theory requires actors of various sorts – owners, nonowners, judges, and lawmakers – to weigh the consequences of their decisions for social wealth. But, as Foot points out, social wealth is just one value among many. The Aristotelian decision maker will also consider other factors, such as justice, fairness, or her proper role within a lawmaking structure, and will

---

[30] See ibid., 10–13.
[31] Philippa Foot, "Utilitarianism and the Virtues," *Mind* 94 (1985): 196, 206.

sometimes be justified in favoring a course of action that does not enhance aggregate wealth. From within an Aristotelian property theory, what we seek from owners and lawmakers alike is not simply cost-benefit precision, but also the capacity to appreciate and assign the proper weight to the many subtle and incommensurable values (including economic values) implicated by their decisions. Considered most broadly, Aristotelian property theory aims to encourage the development of decision makers who consistently exhibit the foundational virtue of practical wisdom.

Property institutions reflect the value of individual autonomy and interdependence, efficiency and fairness, and many others as well. It is property's location at the crossroads of these incommensurable values that generates its richness and (notorious) complexity. Ironically, it is also precisely this complexity that makes the competing monist theories superficially attractive. Each captures important aspects of property's pluralism. At the same time, each one promises to cut through the apparent disorder with elegant simplicity. Although it does not offer the false hope of diluting property's complexity, what Aristotelian theory provides is a comprehensive normative vision, one capacious enough to encompass (and even embrace) property's moral richness.

References

BOOKS AND ARTICLES

Acheson, James M. *The Lobster Gangs of Maine*. Hanover, NH: University Press of New England, 1988.

Ackerman, Bruce A. *Private Property and the Constitution*. New Haven, CT: Yale University Press, 1977.

"Regulating Slum Housing Markets on Behalf of the Poor: Of Housing Codes, Housing Subsidies and Income Redistribution Policy." *Yale L. J.* 80 (1971): 1093–197.

Ackerman, Frank, and Lisa Heinzerling. *Priceless: On Knowing the Price of Everything and the Value of Nothing*. New York: New Press, 2004.

Ackrill, J. L. "Aristotle on *Eudaimonia*." In *Essays on Aristotle's Ethics*, edited by Amélie Oksenberg Rorty. Berkeley: University of California Press, 1980.

Adler, Matthew D. "Future Generations: A Prioritarian View." *G.W. L. Rev.* 77 (2008–9): 1478–520.

Adler, Matthew D., and Eric A. Posner. *New Foundations of Cost-Benefit Analysis*. Cambridge, MA: Harvard Press, 2006.

Alexander, Gregory S. "The Concept of Property in Private and Constitutional Law: The Ideology of the Scientific Turn in Legal Analysis." *Colum. L. Rev.* 82 (1982): 1545–99.

"Pluralism and Property." *Fordham L. Rev.* 80 (2011): 1017–52.

"The Social-Obligation Norm in American Property Law." *Cornell L. Rev.* 94 (2009): 745–819.

Alexander, Gregory S., and Eduardo M. Peñalver. "Properties of Community." *Theoretical Inquiries in Law* 10 (2009): 127–60.

American Law Institute. *Restatement of the Law Second, Torts*. St. Paul: American Law Institute, 1965.

Anderson, Elizabeth. "Practical Reason and Incommensurable Goods." In *Incommensurability, Incomparability, and Practical Reason*, edited by Ruth Chang. Cambridge, MA: Harvard University Press, 1997.

Value in Ethics and Economics. Cambridge, MA: Harvard University Press, 1993.

Annas, Julia, and Robert H. Grimm, eds. *Oxford Studies in Ancient Philosophy*, supp. vol. New York: Oxford University Press, 1988.

Aquinas, Thomas. *Sententia Libri Ethicorum*. In *Santi Thomae Aquinatis Opera Omnia*, edited by Roberto Busa. Stuttgart-Bad Canstatt: Frommann-Holzboog, 1984.

Summa Theologica. Translated by Fathers of the English Dominican Province. 5 vols. Westminster, MD: Christian Classics, 1981.

Aristotle. *Nicomachean Ethics*. Translated by Martin Ostwald. Indianapolis: Bobbs-Merrill, 1962.

Politics. Translated by Ernest Barker. Oxford, UK: Oxford University Press, 1982.

Armitage, David. "John Locke, Carolina, and the *Two Treatises of Government*." *Pol. Theory* 32 (2004): 602–27.

Arneil, Barbara. *John Locke and America*. New York: Oxford University Press, 1996.

Ashcraft, Richard. *Revolutionary Politics and Locke's* Two Treatises of Government. Princeton, NJ: Princeton University Press, 1986.

Avineri, Shlomo. *Hegel's Theory of the Modern State*. Cambridge: Cambridge University Press, 1972.

Balganesh, Shyamkrishna. "'Hot News': The Enduring Myth of Property in News." *Colum. L. Rev.* 111 (2011): 419–97.

Banner, Stuart. *Who Owns the Sky?* Cambridge, MA: Harvard University Press, 2008.

Barlow, John Perry. "A Declaration of Independence of Cyberspace." EFF: Electronic Frontier Foundation website, February 8, 1996, available at https://projects.eff.org/~barlow/Declaration-Final.html.

"The Economy of Ideas." *Wired*, March 1994, available at http://www.wired.com/wired/archive/2.03/economy.ideas.html.

Barnett, Randy E. *Restoring the Lost Constitution*. Princeton, NJ: Princeton University Press, 2004.

Beck, Lewis W. "Five Concepts of Freedom in Kant." In *Stephan Körner, Philosophical Analysis and Reconstruction*, edited by Jan T. J. Srzednicki. Dordrecht: M. Nijhoff, 1987.

Becker, Gary S. *The Economic Approach to Human Behavior*. Chicago: University of Chicago Press, 1976.

Becker, Lawrence C. "Deserving to Own Intellectual Property." *Chi.-Kent L. Rev.* 68 (1993): 609–29.

Beebe, Barton. "An Empirical Study of U.S. Copyright Fair Use Opinions, 1978–2005." *U. Pa. L. Rev.* 156 (2008): 549–624.

Bell, Abraham, and Gideon Parchomovsky. "A Theory of Property." *Cornell L. Rev.* 90 (2005): 531–615.

Bell, Tom W. "Indelicate Imbalancing in Copyright and Patent Law." In *Copy Fights: The Future of Intellectual Property in the Information Age*, edited by Adam Thierer and Wayne Crews. Washington, DC: Cato Institute, 2002.

Benkler, Yochai. *The Wealth of Networks*. New Haven, CT: Yale University Press, 2006.

Bentham, Jeremy. *An Introduction to the Principles of Morals and Legislation*. London, 1789.

The Rationale of Reward. Bk. 3. London: John and H.L. Hunt, 1825.

Berger, Bethany R. "What Owners Want and Governments Do." *Fordham L. Rev.* 78 (2009): 1281–330.

Berlin, Isaiah. *Four Essays on Liberty*. London: Oxford University Press, 1969.

Beverton, RJH. "Some Observations on the Principles of Fisheries Regulation." *Journal du conseil permanent international pour l'exploration de la mer* 19 (1953): 56–68.

Blum, Walter J., and Harry Kalven, Jr. "The Uneasy Case for Progressive Taxation." *U. Chi. L. Rev.* 19 (1952): 417–520.

Blume, Lawrence, and Daniel L. Rubinfeld. "Compensation for Takings: An Economic Analysis." *Cal. L. Rev.* 72 (1984): 569–628.

Boyle, James. *Shamans, Software, and Spleens: Law and the Construction of the Information Society.* Cambridge: Harvard University Press, 1997.

Brown, Bill. "Thing Theory." *Critical Inquiry* 28 (2001): 1–22.

Brudner, Alan. *The Unity of the Common Law: Studies in Hegelian Jurisprudence.* Berkeley: University of California Press, 1995.

Buccafusco, Christopher, and Christopher Jon Sprigman. "The Creativity Effect." *U. Chi. L. Rev.* 78 (2011): 31–52.

Calabresi, Guido, and A. Douglas Melamed. "Property Rules, Liability Rules, and Inalienability: One View of the Cathedral." *Harv. L. Rev.* 85 (1972): 1089–128.

Camerer, Colin. "Individual Decision Making." In *The Handbook of Experimental Economics,* edited by John H. Kagel and Alvin E. Roth. Princeton, NJ: Princeton University Press, 1995.

Chang, Ruth, ed. *Incommensurability, Incomparability, and Practical Reason.* Cambridge, MA: Harvard University Press, 1997.

Chapman, John W., and J. Roland Pennock, eds. *Nomos XXXI: Markets and Justice.* New York: New York University Press, 1989.

Claeys, Eric R. "Exclusion and Exclusivity in Gridlock." *Ariz. L. Rev.* 53 (2011): 9–49.
  "Jefferson Meets Coase." *Notre Dame L. Rev.* 85 (2011): 1379–1446
  "Natural Property Rights and Privatization." *St. Louis L.J.* 50 (2006): 721–34.

Cohen, G. A. "Equality of What? On Welfare, Goods, and Capabilities." In *The Quality of Life,* edited by Martha Nussbaum and Amartya Sen. Oxford, UK: Clarendon Press, 1993.
  "Robert Nozick and Wilt Chamberlain: How Patterns Preserve Liberty." *Erkenntnis* 11 (1977): 5–23.

Coleman, Jules L., ed. *Readings in the Philosophy of Law.* New York: Garland Publishing, 1999.

Cronon, William. *Changes in the Land.* New York: Hill and Wang, 1983.

Dagan, Hanoch. "The Craft of Property." *Cal. L. Rev.* 91 (2003): 1517–71.
  "Pluralism and Perfectionism in Private Law." *J. Tort L.* (forthcoming).
  Property: Values and Institutions. New York: Oxford University Press, 2011.
  "Takings and Distributive Justice." *Va. L. Rev.* 85 (1999): 741–804.

Dahlman, Carl J. *The Open Field System and Beyond.* New York: Cambridge University Press, 1980.

Dan-Cohen, Meir. "The Value of Ownership." *J. Pol. Phil.* 9 (2001): 404–34.

Davidson, Nestor. "Standardization and Pluralism in Property." *V and. L. Rev.* 61 (2008): 1597–1663.

Demsetz, Harold. "Toward a Theory of Property Rights." *Am. Econ. Rev.* 57 (1967): 347–59.

Dittmar, Helga. *The Social Psychology of Material Possessions: To Have Is To Be.* New York: St. Martin's Press, 1992.

Donohue, John J., III, and James Heckman. "Continuous Versus Episodic Change: The Impact of Civil Rights Policy on the Economic Status of Blacks." *J. Econ. Lit.* 29 (1991): 1603–43.

Dorfman, Robert, and Nancy S. Dorfman, eds. *Economics of the Environment: Selected Readings.* New York: W.W. Norton, 1972.

Douglass, R. Bruce, Gerald M. Mara, and Henry S. Richardson, eds. *Liberalism and the Good.* New York: Routledge, 1990.

Dukeminier, Jesse, et al. *Property*. 7th ed. New York: Aspen Publishers, 2010.

Dworkin, Ronald. *Sovereign Virtue*. Cambridge, MA: Harvard University Press, 2000.

Easterlin, Richard E. "Diminishing Marginal Utility of Income? Caveat Emptor." *Soc. Indicators Research* 70 (2005): 243–55.

Eisenberg, Rebecca S. "Patents and the Progress of Science." *U. Chi. L. Rev.* 56 (1989): 1017–86.

Ellickson, Robert C. "Adverse Possession and Perpetuities Law: Two Dents in the Libertarian Model of Property Rights." *Wash. U. L. Rev.* 64 (1986): 723–38.

"Bringing Culture and Human Frailty to Rational Actors: A Critique of Classical Law and Economics." *Chi.-Kent L. Rev.* 65 (1989): 23–55.

Order without Law. Cambridge, MA: Harvard University Press, 1991.

"Property in Land." *Yale L. J.* 102 (1993): 1315–400.

Ellickson, Robert C., and Vicki L. Been. *Land Use Controls*. 3rd ed. New York: Aspen Publishers, 2005.

Ellis, Richard J. "Radical Lockeanism in American Political Culture." *Western Pol. Q.* 45 (1992): 825–49.

Emens, Elizabeth F. "Intimate Discrimination." *Harv. L. Rev.* 122 (2009): 1307–402.

Epstein, Richard A. "A Clear View of the Cathedral: The Dominance of Property Rules." *Yale L.J.* 106 (1997): 2091–120.

"*International News Service v. Associated Press*: Custom and Law as Sources of Property Rights in News." *Va. L. Rev.* 78 (1992): 85–128.

"Kelo: An American Original." *Green Bag* 8 (2005): 355–61.

"Liberty v. Property? Cracks in the Foundations of Copyright Law." *San Diego L. Rev.* 42 (2005): 1–28.

"One Step Beyond Nozick's Minimal State." *Soc. & Pol. Phil.* 22 (2005): 286–313.

"Past and Future: The Temporal Dimension in the Law of Property." *Wash. U. L. Rev.* 64 (1986): 667–722.

Skepticism and Freedom. Chicago: University of Chicago Press, 2003.

"Standing Firm, On Forbidden Grounds." *San Diego L. Rev.* 31 (1994): 1–56.

Takings. Cambridge, MA: Harvard University Press, 1985.

Farber, Daniel A., and Philip P. Frickey. *Law and Public Choice*. Chicago: University of Chicago Press, 1991.

Fehr, Ernst UrsFischbacher, and Simon Gächter. "Strong Reciprocity, Human Cooperation, and the Enforcement of Social Norms." 13 *Human Nature* (2002): 1–25.

Fennell, Lee Anne. "Efficient Trespass." *Nw. U. L. Rev.* 100 (2006): 1037–96.

"Revealing Options." *Harv. L. Rev.* 118 (2005): 1339–488.

"Taking Eminent Domain Apart." *Mich. St. L. Rev.* 4 (2004): 957–1004.

The Unbounded Home. New Haven, CT: Yale University Press, 2009.

Ferguson, Kirby. "Everything is a Remix, Part 3." Published June 20, 2011, http://vimeo.com/25380454.

Finnis, John. *Aquinas*. Oxford, UK: Oxford University Press, 1998.

Natural Law and Natural Rights. Oxford, UK: Clarendon Press, 1980.

Fisher, William. "Theories of Intellectual Property." In *New Essays in the Legal and Political Theory of Property*, edited by Stephen R. Munzer. New York: Cambridge University Press, 2001.

Foot, Philippa. "Utilitarianism and the Virtues." *Mind* 94 (1985): 169–209.

Fox, Lorna. *Conceptualising Home: Theories, Laws, and Policies*. Oxford, UK: Hart Publishing, 2007.

Fox, Lorna, and James A. Sweeny, eds. *The Idea of the Home in Law*. Farnham, Surrey: Ashgate Publishing, 2011.

Freyfogle, Eric T. "Land Use and the Study of Early American History." *Yale L. J.* 94 (1985): 717–42.

The Land We Share. Washington, DC: Island Press, 2003.

Fried, Barbara H. "Does Nozick Have a Theory of Property Rights?" Stanford Public Law Working Paper No. 1782031, available at http://ssrn.com/abstract=1782031.

"Wilt Chamberlain Revisited." *Phil. & Pub.Aff.*24 (1995): 226–45.

Friedman, Milton. *Capitalism and Freedom*. Chicago: University of Chicago Press, 1962.

Frischmann, Brett M., and Mark A. Lemley. "Spillovers." *Colum. L. Rev.* 107 (2007): 257–301.

George, Robert P. *Making Men Moral*. New York: Oxford University Press, 1993.

Gillette, Clayton P. "Local Redistribution, Living Wage Ordinances, and Judicial Intervention." *Nw. U. L. Rev.* 101 (2007): 1057–122.

Gintis, Herbert. "Strong Reciprocity and Human Sociality." *J. Theor. Biol.* 206 (2000): 169–79.

Gordon, H. Scott. "The Economic Theory of a Common-Property Resource: The Fishery." *Journal of Political Economy* 62 (1954): 124–42.

Gordon, Wendy J. "Fair Use as Market Failure." *Colum. L. Rev.* 82 (1982): 1600–57.

Gray, Kevin, and Susan Francis Gray. "Civil Rights, Civil Wrongs, and Quasi-Public Space." *Eur. Hum. Rts. L. Rev.* 4 (1999): 46–102.

Gregor, Mary. "Kant's Theory of Property." *Rev. of Metaphysics* 41 (1988): 757–87.

Grey, Thomas C. "The Disintegration of Property." In *Nomos XXII: Property*, edited by J. Roland Pennock and John W. Chapman. New York: New York University Press, 1980.

Guyer, Paul. "Kant's Deductions of the Principles of Right." In *Kant's Metaphysics of Morals: Interpretive Essays*, edited by Mark Timmons. Oxford, UK: Oxford University Press, 2002.

Hardin, Garrett. "Tragedy of the Commons." *Science* 162 (1968): 1243–8.

Hare, R. M. *Freedom and Reason*. Oxford, UK: Clarendon Press, 1963.

Harsanyi, John C. *Rational Behavior and Bargaining Equilibrium in Games and Social Sciences*. New York: Cambridge University Press, 1977.

Hayek, Friederich A. *The Fatal Conceit*. Chicago: The University of Chicago Press, 1988.

Hegel, Georg W. F. *Hegel's Philosophy of Right*. Translated by T. M. Knox. Oxford, UK: Clarendon Press, 1952.

Heller, Michael A. "The Boundaries of Private Property." *Yale L. J.* 108 (1999): 1163–223.

"The Dynamic Analytics of Property Law." *Theoretical Inquiries L.* 2 (2001): 79–95.

"The Tragedy of the Anticommons." *Harv. L. Rev.* 111 (1998): 621–88.

Heller, Michael A., and James E. Krier. "Deterrence and Distribution in the Law of Takings." *Harv. L. Rev.* 112 (1999): 997–1025.

Hemphill, C. Scott, and Jeannie Suk. "The Law, Culture, and Economics of Fashion." *Stan. L. Rev.* 61 (2009): 101–48.

Hobbes, Thomas. *Leviathan*. Edited by Richard Tuck. New York: Cambridge University Press, 1988.

Honoré, A. M. "Ownership." In *Readings in the Philosophy of Law*, edited by Jules L. Coleman. New York: Garland Publishing, 1999.

Hughes, Justin. "The Philosophy of Intellectual Property." *Geo. L. J.* 77 (1988): 287–97.

Hume, David. *A Treatise of Human Nature*. Bk. 3. Oxford, UK: Clarendon Press, 1967.

Jaszi, Peter. "Toward a Theory of Copyright." *Duke L. J.* (1991): 455–502.

Jolls, Christine, Cass Sunstein, and Richard Thaler. "A Behavioral Approach to Law and Economics." *Stan. L. Rev.* 50 (1998): 1471–550.

Kagel, John H., and Alvin E. Roth, eds. *The Handbook of Experimental Economics*. Princeton, NJ: Princeton University Press, 1995.

Kant, Immanuel. "The Doctrine of Right," Part 1 of the *Metaphysics of Morals*. In *Practical Philosophy*, translated and edited by Mary Gregor. Cambridge: Cambridge University Press, 1996.

Kaplow, Louis. "Primary Goods, Capabilities,... or Well-Being?" *Phil. Rev.* 116 (2007): 603–32.

Kaplow, Louis, and Steven Shavell. *Fairness versus Welfare*. Cambridge, MA: Harvard University Press, 2002.

  "Why the Legal System is Less Efficient than the Income Tax in Redistributing Income." *J. Legal. Stud.*23 (1994): 667–81.

Katz, Larissa. "Exclusion and Exclusivity in Property Law." *U. Toronto L. J.* 58 (2008): 275–315.

Kelly, Daniel B. "The Public Use Requirement in Eminent Domain Law." *Cornell L. Rev.* 92 (2006): 1–66.

Kendall, Willmoore. *John Locke and the Doctrine of Majority-Rule*. Urbana: University of Illinois Press, 1959.

Kennedy, Duncan. "The Effect of the Warranty of Habitability on Low Income Housing: 'Milking' and Class Violence." *Fla. St. U. L. Rev.* 15 (1987): 485–519.

Keys, Mary M. *Aquinas, Aristotle, and the Promise of the Common Good*. New York: Cambridge University Press, 2006.

Knetsch, Jack L. "The Endowment Effect and Evidence of Nonreversible Indifference Curves." *Am. Econ. Rev.* 79 (1989): 1277–84.

Knowles, Dudley. "Hegel on Property and Personality." *Phil. Q.* 33 (1983): 45–62.

Kramer, Matthew H. *John Locke and the Origins of Private Property*. New York, NY: Cambridge University Press (1997).

Kraut, Richard. *Aristotle*. Oxford, UK: Oxford University Press, 2002.

  Aristotle on the Human Good. Princeton, NJ: Princeton University Press, 1989.

Krier, James E. "Evolutionary Theory and the Origin of Property Rights." *Cornell Law Review* 95 (2009): 139–59.

Krier, James E., and Christopher Serkin. "Public Ruses." *Mich. St. L. Rev.* 4 (2004): 859–75.

Lametti, David. "The Concept of Property: Relations through Objects of Social Wealth." *U. Toronto L. J.* 53 (2003): 325–78.

Landes, William M., and Richard A. Posner. *The Economic Structure of Intellectual Property*. Cambridge, MA: Harvard University Press, 2003.

Laslett, Peter. Introduction to *John Locke, Two Treatises of Government*, edited by Peter Laslett. Cambridge: Cambridge University Press, 1960.

Lazarus, Richard J., and Oliver A. Houck, eds. *Environmental Law Stories*. New York: Foundation Press, 2005.

Ledyard, John O. "Public Goods." In *The Handbook of Experimental Economics*, edited by John H. Kagel and Alvin E. Roth. Princeton, NJ: Princeton University Press, 1995.

Leval, Pierre N. "Toward a Fair Use Standard." *Harv. L. Rev.* 103 (1990): 1105–36.

Levinson, Daryl J. "Making Government Pay." *U. Chi. L. Rev.* 67 (2000): 345–420.

Levmore, Saul. "Just Compensation and Just Politics." *Conn. L. Rev.* 22 (1990): 285–322.

Locke, John. *Two Treatises of Government*. Edited by Mark Goldie. Everyman's Library. London: J.M. Dent, 1993.

Lovett, John A. "Progressive Property in Action: The Land Reform (Scotland) Act 2003." *Neb. L. Rev.* 89 (2011): 739–818.

Lyons, David. *The Forms and Limits of Utilitarianism*. Oxford, UK: Clarendon Press, 1965.

MacIntyre, Alasdair. *Dependent Rational Animals*. Chicago: Open Court Press, 1999.

Macpherson, C. B. *The Political Theory of Possessive Individualism*. Oxford, UK: Clarendon Press, 1962.

Markovits, Daniel. "Legal Ethics from the Lawyer's Point of View." *Yale J. L. & Human.*15 (2003): 209–93.

Markovits, Richard. "The Distributive Impact, Allocative Efficiency, and Overall Desirability of Ideal Housing Codes: Some Theoretical Clarifications." *Harv. L. Rev.* 89 (1976): 1815–46.

Mayhew, Robert. "Aristotle on Property." *Rev. of Metaphysics* 46 (1993): 803–31.

Merges, Robert P., Peter Seth Menell, and Mark A. Lemley. *Intellectual Property in the New Technological Age*. 3rd ed. New York: Aspen Publishers, 2003.

Merrill, Thomas W. "The Economics of Public Use." *Cornell L. Rev.* 72 (1986): 61–116.

"Property and the Right to Exclude." *Neb. L. Rev.* 77 (1998): 730–55.

"Property Rules, Liability Rules, and Adverse Possession." *Nw. U. L. Rev.* 79 (1984): 1122–54.

Merrill, Thomas W., and Henry E. Smith. "What Happened to Property in Law and Economics?" *Yale L. J.* 111 (2001): 357–98.

Michelman, Frank I. "Property, Utility, and Fairness: Comments on the Ethical Foundations of 'Just Compensation' Law." *Harv. L. Rev.* 80 (1967): 1165–258.

Mill, John Stuart. *Principles of Political Economy*. Bk. 2. New York: Prometheus Books, 2004.

Utilitarianism. London: Parker, Son, and Bourn, 1863.

Monbiot, George. "Civilisation Ends with a Shutdown of Human Concern. Are We There Already?" *The Guardian*, 30 October 2007.

Mossoff, Adam. "What is Property? Putting the Pieces Back Together." *Ariz. L. Rev* 45 (2003): 371–437.

Mulgan, Richard. "Was Aristotle an 'Aristotelian Social Democrat'?" *Ethics* 111 (2000): 79–101.

Munzer, Stephen R., ed. *New Essays in the Legal and Political Theory of Property*. New York: Cambridge University Press, 2001.

A Theory of Property. New York: Cambridge University Press, 1990.

Murphy, Liam, and Thomas Nagel. *The Myth of Ownership: Taxes and Justice*. New York: Oxford University Press, 2002.

Murray, John Courtney. *We Hold These Truths*. New York: Sheed and Ward, 1960.

Nadler, Janice, and Shari Seidman Diamond. "Government Takings of Private Property: *Kelo* and the Perfect Storm." In *Public Opinion and Constitutional Controversy*, ed. Nathaniel Persily et al. New York: Oxford University Press, 2008.

Netanel, Neil Weinstock. "Making Sense of Fair Use." *Lewis & Clark L. Rev.* 15 (2011): 715–71.

Nobles, Gregory H. "Breaking into the Backcountry." *Wm. & Mary Quarterly* 46 (1989): 642–70.

Nozick, Robert. *Anarchy, State, and Utopia*. New York: Basic Books, 1974.

The Examined Life. New York: Simon and Schuster, 1989.

Nussbaum, Martha C. "Aristotelian Social Democracy." In *Liberalism and the Good*, edited by R. Bruce Douglass, Gerald M. Mara, and Henry S. Richardson. New York: Routledge, 1990.

"Capabilities and Human Rights." *Fordham L. Rev.* 66 (1997): 273–300.

"Human Rights and Human Capabilities." *Harv. Hum. Rts. J.* 20 (2007): 21–4.

Love's Knowledge. New York: Oxford University Press, 1990.

"Nature, Function, and Capability: Aristotle on Political Distribution." In *Oxford Studies in Ancient Philosophy,* supp. vol., edited by Julia Annas and Robert H. Grimm. New York: Oxford University Press, 1988.

"The Supreme Court 2006 Term, Foreword. Constitutions and Capabilities: 'Perception' Against Lofty Formalism." *Harv. L. Rev.* 121 (2007): 4–97.

Women and Human Development. New York: Cambridge University Press, 2000.

Nussbaum, Martha C. and Amartya Sen, eds. *The Quality of Life.* Oxford, NY: Clarendon Press, 1993.

Oates, Wallace E. *Fiscal Federalism.* New York: Harcourt Brace Jovanovich, 1972.

Oliveri, Rigel C. "Discriminatory Housing Advertisements Online." *Ind. L. Rev.*43 (2010): 1125–83.

O'Neill, John. *Ecology, Policy, and Politics.* New York: Routledge, 1993.

Ostrom, Elinor. "A Behavioral Approach to the Rational Choice Theory of Collective Action." *American Political Science Review* 92 (1998): 1–22.

Governing the Commons. New York: Cambridge University Press, 1990.

Ostrom, Elinor, James Walker, and Roy Gardner. "Covenants with and without a Sword: Self-Governance Is Possible." *Am. Pol. Sci. Rev.* 86 (1992): 404–17.

Peñalver, Eduardo M. "The Illusory Right to Abandon." *Mich. L. Rev.* 109 (2010): 191–219.

"Land Virtues." *Cornell L. Rev.* 94 (2009): 821–88.

"Property Metaphors and *Kelo v. New London*: Two Views of the Castle." *Fordham L. Rev.* 74 (2006): 2971–76.

"Reconstructing Richard Epstein." *William & Mary Bill of Rights J.* 15 (2006): 429–37.

Peñalver, Eduardo M., and Sonia K. Katyal. *Property Outlaws.* New Haven, CT: Yale University Press, 2010.

Penner, J. E. *The Idea of Property in Law.* Oxford, UK: Oxford University Press, 1997.

Pennock, J. Roland, and John W. Chapman, eds. *Nomos XXII: Property.* New York: New York University Press, 1980.

Persily, Nathaniel, Jack Citrin, and Patrick J. Egan, eds. *Public Opinion and Constitutional Controversy.* New York: Oxford University Press, 2008.

Peterson, Paul E. *City Limits.* Chicago: University of Chicago Press, 1981.

Polanyi, Karl. *The Great Transformation.* New York: Farrar and Rinehart, 1944.

Posner, Richard A. *Economic Analysis of Law.* 6th ed. New York: Aspen Publishers, 2003.

"The Ethical and Political Basis of the Efficiency Norm in Common Law Adjudication." *Hofstra L. Rev.* 8 (1980): 487–508.

"Utilitarianism, Economics, and Legal Theory." *J. Legal Stud.*8 (1979): 103–40.

Purdy, Jedediah. *The Meaning of Property.* New Haven, CT: Yale University Press, 2010.

Rabin, Edward H. "The Revolution in Residential Landlord-Tenant Law: Causes and Consequences." *Cornell L. Rev.* 69 (1984): 517–84.

Radin, Margaret Jane. *Contested Commodities.* Cambridge, MA: Harvard University Press, 1996.

"Justice and the Market Domain." In *Nomos XXXI: Markets and Justice,* edited by John W. Chapman and J. Roland Pennock. New York: New York University Press, 1989.

"Lacking a Transformative Social Theory: A Response." *Stan. L. Rev.* 45 (1993): 409–24.

"Market-Inalienability." *Harv. L. Rev.* 100 (1987): 1849–937.

"Property and Personhood." *Stan. L. Rev.* 34 (1982): 957–1015.

Reinterpreting Property. Chicago: University of Chicago Press, 1993.

"Time, Possession, and Alienation." *Wash. U. L. Rev.* 64 (1986): 739–58.

Rand, Ayn. *Capitalism: The Unknown Ideal*. New York: New American Library, 1966.

The Virtue of Selfishness. New York: New American Library, 1964.

Raustiala, Kal, and Christopher Sprigman. "The Piracy Paradox." *Va. L. Rev.* 92 (2006): 1687–777.

Rawls, John. *Political Liberalism*. New York: Columbia University Press, 1993.

A Theory of Justice. Cambridge, MA: Belknap Press, 1999.

Raz, Joseph. *The Morality of Freedom*. Oxford, UK: Clarendon Press, 1986.

Reynolds, Susan. *Before Eminent Domain: Toward a History of Expropriation of Land for the Common Good*. Chapel Hill: University of North Carolina Press, 2010.

Richardson, Henry S. *Practical Reasoning About Final Ends*. New York: Cambridge University Press, 1997.

Democratic Autonomy: Public Reasoning about the Ends of Policy. New York: Oxford University Press, 2002.

Ripstein, Arthur. *Force and Freedom: Kant's Legal and Political Philosophy*. Cambridge, MA: Harvard University Press, 2009.

Robinson, Russell K. "Casting and Caste-ing: Reconciling Artistic Freedom and Antidiscrimination Norms." *Cal. L. Rev.* 95 (2007): 1–73.

Rorty, Amélie Oksenberg, ed. *Essays on Aristotle's Ethics*. Berkeley: University of California Press, 1980.

Rose, Carol M. "The Comedy of the Commons." *U. Chi. L. Rev.* 53 (1986): 711–81.

"Property as Storytelling: Perspectives from Game Theory, Narrative Theory, and Feminist Theory." *Yale J. L. & Human.* 2 (1990): 37–57.

"The Story of Lucas: Environmental Land Use Regulation between Developers and the Deep Blue Sea." In *Environmental Law Stories*, edited by Richard J. Lazarus and Oliver A. Houck. New York: Foundation Press, 2005.

Rosenblum, Nancy L., ed. *Liberalism and the Moral Life*. Cambridge, MA: Harvard University Press, 1989.

Roth, Alvin E. "Bargaining Experiments." In *The Handbook of Experimental Economics*, edited by John H. Kagel and Alvin E. Roth. Princeton, NJ: Princeton University Press, 1995.

Ryan, Alan. *Property and Political Theory*. Oxford, UK: Basil Blackwell, 1984.

Sackman, Julius L. et al, eds. *Nichols on Eminent Domain*. Revised 3rd ed. New York: M. Bender, 1964.

Sagoff, Mark. *The Economy of the Earth*. New York: Cambridge University Press, 1988.

Sanchez, Julian. *An Interview with Robert Nozick*. Published July 26, 2001, http://www.trinity.edu/rjensen/NozickInterview.htm.

Schill, Michael H. "Intergovernmental Takings and Just Compensation: A Question of Federalism." *U. Pa. L. Rev.* 137 (1989): 829–901.

Schnably, Stephen J. "Property and Pragmatism: A Critique of Radin's Theory of Property and Personhood." *Stan. L. Rev.* 45 (1993): 347–407.

Schroeder, Jeanne L. "Unnatural Rights: Hegel and Intellectual Property." *U. Miami L. Rev.* 60 (2006): 453–503.

The Vestal and the Fasces: Hegel, Lacan, Property, and the Feminine. Berkeley: University of California Press, 1998.

Sen, Amartya. *Commodities and Capabilities*. Oxford, UK: Oxford University Press, 1985.

Development as Freedom. New York: Anchor Books, 1999.

Resources, Values, and Development. Cambridge, MA: Harvard University Press, 1984.

"Utilitarianism and Welfarism." *J. Phil.* 76 (1979): 463–89.

Sen, Amartya, and Bernard Williams, eds. *Utilitarianism and Beyond.* New York: Cambridge University Press, 1982.

Serkin, Christopher. "The Meaning of Value." *Nw. U. L. Rev.*99 (2005): 677–742.

Shiffrin, Seana Valentine. "Lockean Arguments for Private Intellectual Property." In *New Essays in the Legal and Political Theory of Property*, edited by Stephen R. Munzer. New York: Cambridge University Press, 2001.

Singer, Joseph William. "After the Flood: Equality and Humanity in Property Regimes." *Loy. L. Rev.* 52 (2006): 243–344.

"No Right to Exclude: Public Accommodations and Private Property." *Nw. U.L. Rev.* 90 (1996): 1283–497.

Singer, Peter. *One World.* New Haven, CT: Yale University Press, 2004.

Smart, J.J.C., and Bernard Williams. *Utilitarianism: For and Against.* Cambridge: Cambridge University Press, 1973.

Smith, Henry E. "Exclusion and Property Rules in the Law of Nuisance." *Va. L. Rev.* 90 (2004): 965–1049.

"Exclusion Versus Governance: Two Strategies for Delineating Property Rights." *J. of Legal Stud.* 31 (2002): S453–S487.

"Institutions and Indirectness in Intellectual Property." *U. Pa. L. Rev.* 157 (2009): 2083–133.

"Mind the Gap: The Indirect Relation between Ends and Means in American Property Law." *Cornell L. Rev.*94 (2009): 959–89.

"Property and Property Rules." *N.Y.U. L. Rev.* 79 (2004): 1719–98.

"Self-Help and the Nature of Property." *J. L. Econ. &Pol'y* 1 (2005): 69–107.

Sreenivasan, Gopal. *The Limits of Lockean Rights in Property.* Oxford, UK: Oxford University Press, 1995.

Srzednicki, Jan T.J., editor. *Stephan Körner, Philosophical Analysis and Reconstruction.* Dordrecht: M. Nijhoff, 1987.

Sterk, Stewart E. "Property Rules, Liability Rules, and Uncertainty about Property Rights." *Mich. L. Rev.* 106 (2008): 1285–1336.

Stern, Stephanie M. "Residential Protectionism and the Legal Mythology of Home." *Mich. L. Rev.* 107 (2009): 1093–144.

Stevens, Jacqueline. "The Reasonableness of John Locke's Majority." *Pol. Theory* 24 (1996): 423–63.

Stillman, Peter G. "Property, Freedom, and Individuality in Hegel's and Marx's Political Thought." In *Nomos XXII: Property*, edited by J. Roland Pennock and John W. Chapman. New York: New York University Press, 1980.

Stout, Lynn. *Cultivating Conscience.* Princeton, NJ: Princeton University Press, 2010.

Strahilevitz, Lior Jacob. *Information and Exclusion.* New Haven, CT: Yale University Press, 2011.

"Information Asymmetries and the Rights to Exclude." *Mich. L. Rev.* 104 (2006): 1835–98.

"The Right to Abandon." *U. Pa. L. Rev.* 158 (2010): 355–420.

"Social Norms from Close-Knit Groups to Loose-Knit Groups." *U. Chi. L. Rev.* 70 (2003): 359–72.

Strauss, Leo. *Natural Right and History.* Chicago: University of Chicago, 1950.

Suarez, Francisco. *Tractatus de legibus ac deo legislatore*, translated by Gwladys L. Williams and Henry Davis. Oxford, UK: Clarendon Press/London: H. Milford, 1944.

Sunder, Madhavi. "IP3" *Stan. L. Rev.* 59 (2006): 257–332.

Super, David. "The Rise and Fall of the Implied Warranty of Habitability." *Cal. L. Rev.* 99 (2011): 389–463.

Swanton, Christine. "Commentary on Michael Slote's *Virtue Ethics and Democratic Values.*" *J. of Social Phil.* 24 (1993): 38–49.

Taylor, Charles. "Atomism," in *Philosophy and the Human Sciences.* Vol. 2 of *Philosophical Papers.* Cambridge: Cambridge University Press, 1985.

"Cross-Purposes: The Liberal-Communitarian Debate." In *Liberalism and the Moral Life,* edited by Nancy L. Rosenblum. Cambridge, MA: Harvard University Press, 1989.

"Leading a Life." In *Incommensurability, Incomparability, and Practical Reason,* edited by Ruth Chang. Cambridge, MA: Harvard University Press, 1997.

Thierer, Adam, and Wayne Crews, eds. *Copy Fights: The Future of Intellectual Property in the Information Age.* Washington, DC: Cato Institute, 2002.

Timmons, Mark, ed. *Kant's Metaphysics of Morals: Interpretive Essays.* Oxford, UK: Oxford University Press, 2002.

Tomlins, Christopher. *Freedom Bound.* New York: Cambridge University Press, 2010.

Treanor, William Michael. "The Original Understanding of the Takings Clause and the Political Process." *Colum. L. Rev.* 95 (1995): 782–887.

Tullock, Gordon. "Smith v. Pareto." *Atlantic Econ. J.* 27 (1999): 254–59.

Tully, James. *A Discourse on Property.* New York: Cambridge University Press, 1980.

Underkuffler, Laura S. *The Idea of Property.* New York: Oxford University Press, 2003.

"*Kelo's* Moral Failure." *Wm. & Mary Bill Rts. J.* 15 (2004): 377–87.

van der Walt, Andre J. *Constitutional Property Law.* Cape Town: Juta, 2005.

"Housing Rights and the Intersection between Expropriation and Eviction Law." In *The Idea of the Home in Law,* edited by Lorna Fox and James A. Sweeny. Farnham, Surrey: Ashgate Publishing, 2011.

Waldron, Jeremy. *God, Locke, and Equality.* New York: Cambridge University Press, 2002.

"Homelessness and the Issue of Freedom." *UCLA L. Rev.* 39 (1991): 295–324.

"Nozick and Locke: Filling the Space of Rights." *Soc. Phil. &Pol'y* 22 (2005): 81–110.

The Right to Private Property. Oxford, UK: Clarendon Press, 1988.

Weinrib, Ernest. *The Idea of Private Law.* Cambridge, MA: Harvard University Press, 1995.

Williams, Howard. "Kant's Concept of Property," *Phil. Q.* 27 (1977): 32–40.

Wittgenstein, Ludwig. *Philosophical Investigations.* Translated by GEM Anscombe. New York: Macmillan, 1953.

Wood, Mary Christina. "Advancing the Sovereign Trust of Government to Safeguard the Environment for Present and Future Generations (Part 1)." *Envtl. L.* 39 (2009): 43–90.

Yntema, Hessel E. "Jurisprudence on Parade." *Mich. L. Rev.* 39 (1941): 1154–181.

CASES

Amalgamated Food Employees Union Local 590 v. Logan Valley Plaza, Inc., 391 U.S. 308 (1968).

Andrus v. Allard, 444 U.S. 51 (1979).

Appeal of City of Keene, 141 N.H. 797, 802 (1997).

Bell v. Town of Wells, 557 A.2d 168 (Me. 1989).

Berman v. Parker; 348 U.S. 26 (1954).

Borough of Neptune City v. Borough of Avon-by-the-Sea, 294 A.2d 47 (N.J. 1972).

Campbell v. Acuff-Rose Music, Inc., 510 U.S. 569, 579 (1994).

County of Wayne v. Hathcock, 471 Mich. 445 (2004).

Diamond v. Chakrabarty, 447 U.S. 303 (1980).

Glass v. Goeckel, 703 N.W. 2d 58 (Mich. 2005).

Hawaii Housing Authority v. Midkiff, 467 U.S. 229 (1984).

Hixon v. Public Service Comm'n, 146 N.W.2d 577 (Wis. 1966).

Holbrook v. Taylor, 532 S.W.2d 763 (Ky. 1976).

Hudgens v. National Labor Relations Board, 424 U.S. 507 (1976).

International News Service v. Associated Press, 248 U.S. 215 (1918).

Jacque v. Steenberg Homes, Inc., 563 N.W.2d 154 (Wis. 1997).

Javins v First Nat'l Realty Corp., 428 F.2d 1071 (D.C. Cir.), *cert. denied*, 400 U.S. 925 (1970).

Kelo v. City of New London, 545 U.S. 460, 469 (2005).

Loretto v. Teleprompter Manhattan CATV Corp., U.S. 419 (1982).

Lucas v. S.C. Coastal Council, 505 U.S. 1003 (1992).

Modderklip East Squatters v. ModderklipBoerdery (Pty) Ltd., 2004(8) BCLR 821 (SCA), aff'd on other grounds2005 (5) SA 3 (CC).

New Jersey Coalition Against War in the Middle East v. J.M.B. Realty Corp., 650 A.2d 757 (N.J. 1994).

Pallazzolo v. Rhode Island, 533 U.S. 606, 632–33, 636 (2001).

Penn Central Transp. Co. v.New York City, 438 U.S. 104 (1978).

Pennell v. City of San Jose, 485 U.S. 1, 21–22 (1988).

Pennsylvania Coal Co. v. Mahon, 260 U.S. 393 (1922).

Poletown Neighborhood Council v. City of Detroit, 410 Mich. 616 (1981).

PruneYard Shopping Center v. Robbins, 447 U.S. 74 (1980).

Raleigh Avenue Beach Association v. Atlantis Beach Club, 879 A.2d 112 (N.J. 2005).

Rase v. Castle Mountain Ranch, Inc., 631 P.2d 680 (Mont. 1981).

South Burlington County NAACP v. Township of Mt. Laurel, 67 N.J. 151 (1975).

State v. Shack, 277 A.2d 369 (N.J. 1971).

State ex rel. Thornton v. Hay, 462 P.2d 671 (Or. 1969).

United States v. Carmack, 329 U.S. 230, 241–42 (1946).

United States v. 50 Acres of Land, 469 U.S. 24, 25–26 (1984).

United States v. 564.54 Acres of Land, 441 U.S. 506, 511 (1979).

Uston v. Grand Resorts, Inc., 564 F.2d 1217, 1218 (9th Cir. 1977).

Uston v. Resorts Int'l Hotel, Inc., 445 A.2d 370 (N.J. 1982).

Wetherbee v. Green, 22 Mich. 311 (1871).

Whittemore v. Cutter, 29 F. Cas. 1120 (C.C.D. Mass. 1813).

Index